'BANGOR
PORT OF
BEAUMARIS'

*The Nineteenth Century Shipbuilders
and Shipowners of Bangor*

M. ELIS-WILLIAMS

GWYNEDD ARCHIVES

ISBN 0 901337 46 3

Cover design by Gwasg Dwyfor, Penygroes.

Cover Illustration

Port Penrhyn and Bangor, 1841: line engraving by J. C. Armitage after
W. H. Bartlett.

Published by:
GWYNEDD ARCHIVES AND MUSEUMS SERVICE, GWYNEDD COUNTY COUNCIL,
CAERNARFON

Printed by:
GEE & SON LTD., CHAPEL STREET, DENBIGH, CLWYD

Contents

LIST OF ILLUSTRATIONS

Introduction

The title of this book, 'Bangor Port of Beaumaris', comes from a memory from my childhood when I saw this inscription on the counter of a vessel after the vessel's name. I do not remember the vessel's name but I do remember that I was at the end of Bangor pier at the time. It was reinforced when I was writing the book when I received from the late Richard Dop of Felin Heli the photograph of *Pamela* (see *frontispiece*) which shows quite clearly on her counter —

PAMELA OF BANGOR

PORT OF

BEAUMARIS

Had I required further confirmation of my choice, it came from a most unexpected quarter. I attended a conference on the history of the Irish Sea at Belfast in the autumn of 1986 and among those who attended was Mr. Jack Tyrrell, the well known shipbuilder of Arklow. When I mentioned to him that I was working on the history of Bangor shipbuilders and shipowners he said that before the war he was intrigued by a shabby steam coaster, whose name he, too, had forgotten, which bore a similar inscription on her stern. It seems likely from the evidence provided by the Registers of Shipping that the vessel was either the *S.S. Bangor*, sold by Lord Penrhyn to a Belfast shipowner in 1933 or the *S.S. Penrhyn*, sold to a Lancaster shipowner in 1937.

The title bears witness to the fact that Beaumaris had been superseded as the premier port of Gwynedd by the effects of the industrial revolution —

the establishment of the copper mines of Amlwch and the slate quarries of the mainland. Up to 1840 the Beaumaris Registers covered the whole coast between the estuaries of the Clwyd in the north and the Dysynni in the south. For a period in the nineteenth century Caernarfon and Pwllheli were granted separate registers as sub-ports of Beaumaris. Bangor never achieved this distinctive status; but some Bangor shipowners, at least, felt sufficient pride in their home port to emblazon its name on the counters of their ships.

The Beaumaris Registers of Shipping form the backbone of this book. They are now at the Caernarfon Record Office of the Gwynedd Archives Service with the exception of the current ones which are at the Custom Houses at Holyhead and Caernarfon. I would like to have included in this book transcripts of the registrations of all the ships belonging to Bangor but as that would be obviously impossible I have been content to print a few representative registrations in the Appendix. As will be seen, they provide a record of a ship's identity, her age, her various dimensions, her original ownership and the successive changes thereof — all good raw material for the social and economic historian — until her de-registration. But this bare — one could almost describe it as legalistic — record tells us nothing about the history of the ship nor the men who sailed in her, what voyages she made, what cargoes she carried, what mishaps occurred, what lucky escapes she had, indeed, in many of the early entries, how she ultimately perished.

Fortunately there are other sources of information, random and fragmentary though they may be, which have enabled me to flesh out the bare bones provided by the registers. After 1863 we have the Crew Agreement Lists and the accompanying Logs for foreign going vessels, but before that date I have had to rely on the shipping intelligence in the local press, some of it of doubtful reliability, on press accounts of losses and launchings, and on items of record or of correspondence that random chance has preserved, such as the 1783 notebook of William Williams, the slate reeve of Llandegai and the papers of Robert Thomas, Abercegin and his family, which are in the Library of the University College of North Wales, or the case correspondence about the *Albion* and Benjamin Wyatt's involvement, which is to be found in the Poole Papers in the Caernarfon Record Office of the Gwynedd Archives Service. An unexpected bonus of this kind was the discovery by my good friend, His Honour Judge Michael O'Donoghue, in the drawer of a bureau in a second-hand shop of the rough log of the schooner *Cambria*, which he has generously allowed me to quote from and to reproduce (see between pages 104 and 105). The Penrhyn Quarry records of the loading of ships at Port Penrhyn are to be found at the Caernarfon Record Office and have also yielded much useful information.

Anyone interested in the maritime history of Gwynedd owes a deep debt of gratitude to Mr. Bryn R. Parry, at the time the County Archivist of Caernarfonshire, to Mr. Dewi O. Jones then County Librarian of Anglesey, and to Mr. Aled Eames of the U.C.N.W. for their vigilance in securing for their counties, now united in Gwynedd, the Crew Agreement Lists and Log Books of ships registered at Beaumaris or Caernarfon from 1863. The lists were stored in an aircraft hanger in the Home Counties and were destined for the University of Newfoundland (which is some indication of how highly that university in a maritime province prizes such primary historical sources) and were rescued, one is tempted to say, at the eleventh hour by the three above-mentioned gentlemen. With the exception of sample years extracted by the Public Record Office they are to be found at the Llangefni and the Caernarfon Record Offices for the Beaumaris and Caernarfon registrations respectively.

They have proved invaluable for clothing the skeleton of the shipping registrations with living flesh. There were two forms of agreement — for the Home Trade and the Foreign Trade. For the Home Trade a return had to be made every half year, on January 1st and July 1st. We thus know the full details of every member of the crew; his age, the county of his birth or his nationality, his last ship, the date of signing the agreement, the capacity in which he was employed, his monthly wage and the date and place of his discharge (or in some cases his desertion), and a report on his character, which was subdivided into his ability and his general conduct. Many of the seamen, and one or two who had signed as mate, particularly in the early years, signed with his mark. On another page are recorded the ship's movements from port to port, or whether she was at sea at the end of the half-year. It would have added immensely to our knowledge had the masters of vessels been required to state what cargoes they carried; in rare instances they did. I have perhaps lamented too much in the text the fact that this information was not required of them. The Board of Trade's main concern was with the numbers of seamen employed, and human nature being what it is, why should a captain with all his other preoccupations supply unnecessary detail on a form which was a bit of a nuisance anyway!

The Articles for a foreign-going ship differed only slightly. The scope of the intended voyage was defined in fairly broad terms, for example to Gibraltar and any port in the Mediterranean Sea or Morocco, with final discharge at any port in the United Kingdom. A limit was set on the time the voyage would last, six months, eighteen months or even longer for distant destinations. Foreign Articles contained a Log Book — not be confused with the Ship's Log — in which items relating to the crew's conduct, welfare, illness or death etc., were recorded. Frequently there were no items reported in this log. The details required about the crew were the same as those for the home trade agreements.

The Crew Agreement Lists are an embarassment of riches as far as source material is concerned and I have had to be strictly selective in quoting from them. There is, of course, the occasional gem, but many of them make somewhat unexciting reading with their repetitive return voyages from Bangor to Garston or Runcorn.

For the second half of the century the surviving annual reports of the Bangor Mutual Ship Insurance Society and its Rule Book are another source which was not available for the first half of the century. For the nineties and early years of the present century the Penrhyn Quarry records in the Caernarfon Record Office contain the ledgers of the schooner *Mary B. Mitchell* and the steam vessels of the Anglesey Shipping Company, which has made it possible to compare the relative economics of sail and steam but not, in view of the limited sample of evidence, to reach any firm conclusion.

The fact that we have a biography of Samuel Roberts ('*Bywyd y Parchedig Samuel Roberts, Bangor a Detholiad o'i Bregethau*' — 'The Life of the Revd. Samuel Roberts, Bangor and a Selection from his Sermons') has enabled me to enter into greater detail about his personal life than that of the other major characters; his reputation was not undeserved, because in his time he was a beneficial force among the shipowners of Bangor; nor have I been unduly influenced, I hope, by the fact that he was my remote kinsman, being my great-grandfather's brother. I inherited my great-grand-father's copy of 'The Life' and from this seed sprang the present enquiry into the shipbuilders and shipowners of Bangor.

What motivated them? Robert Thomas was a Merioneth man and came to seek work at Port Penrhyn as a wharfinger, John Parry was a Caernarfon born mariner, Richard Morris Griffith was a tallow chandler, Samuel Roberts was one of ten children born to far from affluent parents in Bangor — to give only a few examples. They were all self-made men. They went into an industry dominated by the arch-capitalists, the Pennant family and their agents, Worthington and the Wyatts. The indigenous local gentry and the professional middle class were more interested in mineral speculation on land than on maritime enterprise and gave them no support. By thrift, integrity, and hard work (Samuel Roberts, besides being an ordained minister, had at least three other occupations, as shipbuilder, as secretary of the Bangor insurance society and as a marine store dealer — he had been a grocer, too!) they rose by their own efforts to form a nascent mercantile and industrial middle class in Bangor which was oriented towards the sea.

Shipbuilding was the foundation; then there were the associated businesses — the timber yards, the foundries, the sailmakers, the blockmakers — most of them based on the Hirael and Garth areas, Bangor's maritime quarter. The industry was almost self-sustaining; apart from a few specialist items — the compasses for instance — nothing went into a Bangor ship that could not be produced locally. That this prosperity did not last very long is in no way to their discredit. They were overcome by economic forces beyond their control — by the railways, by iron and steel ships, by steamships — which eventually rendered the wooden sailing vessel obsolete. For the shipping industry of Bangor the final nail was driven in when Lord Penrhyn, who had effectively withdrawn from shipownership in 1868, purchased his first steamer, through the Anglesey Shipping Company, in 1894. The second world war brought that enterprise in its turn to an end.

This book has been written to commemorate the achievements of the ordinary folk of Bangor — as seamen they visited practically every port in Great Britain and Ireland and many on the continent of Europe, on shore they became skilled craftsmen and as shipbuilders and shipowners they not only provided employment locally but they also contributed to the general maritime and mercantile well-being of the nation. They formed in Hirael and Garth a distinctive and cohesive community which has now disappeared save for a few vestiges.

As one would expect, with a book so heavily reliant on primary sources, I have been glad of the help of a number of institutions and individuals. Chief among the institutions is the Gwynedd Archives Service; I am heavily indebted to Mr. Bryn R. Parry, M.A., D.A.A., the County Archivist, for his encouragement and support, and to his staff both at the Caernarfon and the Llangefni Record Offices for their ever ready assistance. I am also indebted to the successive Librarians of the University College of North Wales and particularly to the Archivist, Mr. Tomos Roberts, M.A.; to the Librarian of the National Library of Wales, Aberystwyth for some of the parish registers quoted, to the County Archivists of Dyfed and Clwyd for letting me consult the Shipping Registers of the ports of Aberystwyth and Chester respectively, to Mr. P. Harris of the Custom House, Caernarfon for granting me access to the recent Registers of Shipping. Mr. Peter Dickie, of A. M. Dickie and Sons, Bangor, gave me access to the title deeds of the firm which occupies the premises leased to Edward Ellis, Shipbuilder, in 1836.

Dr. Lewis Lloyd from his copious knowledge and familiarity with the local press of the last century has drawn my attention to several important extracts, and my other mentor, Mr. Aled Eames, read an early draft and made many valuable suggestions. I have already mentioned Judge Michael O'Donoghue's valuable contribution.

The Agent to the Penrhyn Estate, Mr. P. I. A. Collinson, gave permission for me to transcribe the 'Rules and Regulations to be observed by Masters of Vessels intending to load at Port Penrhyn.' Mr. Edmund Douglas-Pennant and Capt. Ian Metcalfe provided information about the past and present Port Penrhyn.

Mr. W. Richard Thomas and Mr. Eifion Buckland, both of Bangor, and the late Mr. Richard Dop of Felin Heli have generously allowed me to reproduce photographs in their possession and Mr. Denys Owen has permitted me to photograph his model of the schooner *Dorothea*. The other photographs in the book come from the Henry Parry Collection of the Gwynedd Archives Service. Compared with Caernarfon, there are very few contemporary photographs of Bangor ships; the reason is simple — no Victorian photographer could resist the magnificent back-drop of Caernarfon Castle.

My thanks are also due to two members of the Gwynedd Archives Service staff, Mr. Evan Hughes for preparing the prints for publication and for the photographs of *Dorothea* and Plas Llwyd, and Mr. Robert G. Williams who prepared the various plans and also for his accurate drawing of the John Wood map of 1834, which because of its delicate state could not have been otherwise reproduced.

Finally I have to thank my wife, Beti, and my daughter, Rhiannon, for their forbearance while this book was being written. To paraphrase a famous remark — it must have seemed to them at times that the River Cegin was flowing through our living-room.

Porthaethwy 1987

M. ELIS-WILLIAMS

CHAPTER I

The Background

It would be an exaggeration to say that for the greater part of the eighteenth century the little town of Bangor was a sleepy ecclesiastical hollow, situated as it was between Bangor 'Mountain' and the Aethwy Ridge, now crowned by the impressive buildings of the University college; an exaggeration perhaps, but only a slight one. The Cathedral and the Bishop's Palace and Park and other Church lands occupied much of the valley bottom. To the east, where the valley broadened out towards the sea, stood the Friars School estate whose boundaries still preserved the demense of the medieval Friary of the Dominican brotherhood. Indeed, the school still occupied, until it was rebuilt in 1789 by Bishop Warren, the much refurbished remains of the Friar House, dating back to the early years of the fourteenth century. The Dean and Chapter were the trustees of this estate also.

John Speed's map of Bangor in 1610 shows the long straggling main street, which is with us today. In the eighteenth century houses, shops and inns were clustered round the Cathedral, but were already spreading around the axis of the High Street — one is tempted to say — in an early form of ribbon development. Bangor had gained a little local importance in 1718 when it replaced Beaumaris as the post town of the area. But it was not a borough and the only local jurisdiction was the Bishop's court.

The outlying suburb or village of Hirael stood on the sea shore and was connected to the core of the town by that straggling main street. Here lived a few fishermen and others connected with maritime occupations. The late

11

David Thomas in his book, 'Hen Longau Sîr Gaernarfon', devoted a chapter to the slate trade of the eighteenth century. Slates had, indeed, been extracted from the hills of Gwynedd since early medieval times. The Dean of Bangor had been petitioned in a 'cywydd' by Sion Tudur to send a shipment from Aberogwen to Rhuddlan in 1570,[1] and there are a number of other references to the use of slate at this period. But it is to the eighteenth century that we must look for the first sign of expansion.

Hirael is close to Abercegin, as the place was called before the construction of Port Penrhyn on the site. From Abercegin it is recorded that as early as 1713 14 shipments amounting to 415,000 slates were sent to Dublin and in 1720 there were 8 shipments (155,000 slates) to Dublin, two to Drogheda (20,000) and one to Belfast (35,000). Two years later there was even a shipment of 80,000 slates to Dunkirk.[2] But according to the Port Books there were some years when no slates were sent overseas and only limited consignments coastwise.[3] The quarrying of slate had not yet been organised on an industrial scale. It was carried on in shallow pits and excavations by men who leased the sites from the Penrhyn Estate or other landowners and paid a royalty on the slates produced. Under these conditions there could be no regular production, very little mercantile organization and no real basis for a shipping enterprise. It is difficult to resist the conclusion that the Bangor trade in slates was on a casual basis and responded only to peak periods in the demand for the product. Lewis Morris, writing in 1747, remarks that Caernarfon exported annually 4,000,000 slates but makes no mention of Bangor. Of this period A. H. Dodd has written 'In the first six months of 1740 there are no recorded overseas exports, (from Bangor) and those carried coastwise amounted to less than a million slates. Caernarvon, as a long-established port with a harbour of sorts and a customs house, could command sea-going vessels on the spot; Bangor had nothing but fishing smacks, and masters of vessels from the outside were not disposed to go for slates to the creeks at Aberogwen or Abercegin when they could find both slates and loading facilities at Caernarvon.'[4] The development of Hirael would come at the close of the century.

The contrast between Bangor and Caernarfon is a telling one; Caernarfon was an ancient borough, Bangor a mere ecclesiastical adjunct, Caernarfon had a prosperous merchant class who dealt with all manner of 'shop goods' imported by sea in addition to the slate trade. There is also some evidence from a letter written in mid-century by John Paynter, the Penrhyn agent, that the Caernarfon slates (from the Cilgwyn quarry) were preferred because they were split more thinly.[5]

[1] D(avid) T(homas) 'Hen Longau Sir Gaernarfon', p. 16.
[2] D.T. p. 39.
[3] D.T. p. 44.
[4] A. H. Dodd, 'A History of Caernarvonshire' pp. 203-4.
[5] Jean Lindsay, 'A History of the N. Wales Slate Industry', pp. 30-1.

Another aspect of the contrast between the two places is their population. In the first official census of 1801 Caernarfon (the Parish of Llanbeblig) had over 3,600 inhabitants, the parish of Bangor, which then included what is now Pentir, only 1,770, and this is some years after the development of Port Penrhyn. In 1783 when there was an abortive scheme for building an embankment (a wooden bridge was later substituted) across the Menai Straits near Bangor, it was stated that the chief difficulty would be the removal of the fears of the Caernarfon merchants 'that the little town of Bangor may be so benefited by such a plan as to endanger a rivalship with the great city of Caernarvon.'[6] Indeed, it was a Caernarfon merchant, Edward Griffith, who formed a 'Committee of Navigation of the County of Carnarvon' and was largely instrumental in defeating the project. His committee developed into the Caernarfon Harbour Trust after the passing of the Act of Incorporation in 1793.

Two developments in the last thirty years of the eighteenth century were to bring Bangor into the main stream of the commercial and economic life of Gwynedd.

The first was the belated arrival of the turnpike road. The first Turnpike Trust Acts were passed in England in 1705-6, but the movement was slow to reach the remoter parts of the kingdom. The Denbighshire Trust was formed in 1759 and the Act covered a short stretch of road in Caernarfonshire from the Talycafn ferry to the town of Conwy. A trust was formed in 1765 for the road from the Porthaethwy ferry through Llangefni to Holyhead. It was not until 1769 that the Old Caernarvonshire Turnpike, as it was later called, took over responsibility for the road from Conwy, through Bangor and Caernarfon, to Pwllheli. Travelling became much easier; a daily coach service was started from the White Lion Inn at Chester to Holyhead in 1776, and three years later a rival service left the Raven and Bell at Shrewsbury for the same destination.[7]

The second, hardly less influential in its immediate effect and far more so ultimately, was the succession of Richard Pennant (1737-1808) to the control of the Penrhyn Estate in 1781.

For two generations after the death in 1678 of Sir Robert Williams the Penrhyn Estate had been divided between his two co-heiresses and their descendants, the Warburtons of Cheshire and the Yonges of Devon. Development of the estate had suffered by this dual control by largely absentee landlords. In 1765 Richard Pennant, the son of John Pennant, an immensely wealthy man who drew a considerable income from his estates in Jamaica and in this country, married the Warburton heiress, Susannah. Richard Pennant was from 1767 the M.P. for Liverpool, and from what transpired

[6] P. Stafford 'The First Menai Bridge Project etc' Welsh History Review, Vol. 9, No. 3.
[7] A. H. Dodd, 'The Industrial Revolution in North Wales', pp. 97-8.

later it is clear that he had close links with many influential merchants in that rapidly growing port.

There had been for many years protracted negotiations between the Warburtons and Yonges for the purchase of the moiety of the estate held by the Yonges. From about 1781 onwards 'Richard (Pennant) . . . secured at last control over the undivided Penrhyn inheritance. . . . In this way one of the historic estates of the shire fell into the hands of a man resident on the estate, amply provided with capital to develop it, and fortified by three generations of business experience on the grand scale. There could have been no more timely shot in the arm for Caernarvonshire's stagnant industries, communications and agriculture.'[8]

Practically his first act was to call in the fifty-four separate leases granted for the quarrying of slate on the estate and to concentrate them into his own hand on an industrial and commercial basis. Hardly of less significance for Bangor was his close association with the famous architectural dynasty of the Wyatts. Samuel Wyatt had been commissioned in 1781 to rebuild the ruinous medieval house at Penrhyn and his brother, Benjamin Wyatt, was appointed general agent to the Penrhyn Estate in 1786.[9] Energetic, enterprising and resourceful, Benjamin Wyatt played no small part in developing the three aspects of the area's economic life mentioned above, its industries, communications and agriculture.

Our concern, however, is with communication, both by land and sea. Wyatt's first task was to survey a new road from the quarry to Abercegin, capable of being traversed by horse-drawn vehicles rather than by pack horses. This having been accomplished, the road was extended through Nant Ffrancon to Capel Curig.

Having brought the slate with greater efficiency and in greater quantities from the quarry to Abercegin, Wyatt now addressed the problem of storing th slate and loading it on board the ships. Port Penrhyn came into being; a stone wharf was built at the mouth of the little River Cegin by 1790. This is shown on an estate map of 1803, drawn up by Robert Williams, together with new offices for the slate reeve.[10] The wharf extends seawards about a third of its present length. It was extended substantially in 1829-30, and a further extension took place in 1855 with the construction of a breakwater on the eastern side, forming an inner basin.

It has been stated that in the short period between 1790 and the outbreak of the wars with France a dozen ships left Port Penrhyn a month, mainly for Liverpool, but a few for Landon.[11] (This is a reflection of Lord Penrhyn's,

[8] A. H. Dodd, 'A History of Caernarvonshire', p. 232.
[9] See the article 'The Wyatts of Lime Grove, Llandygai' by P. E. Jones, in *Transactions of the Caernarvonshire Historical Society'*, Vol. 42, 1981.
[10] U.C.N.W. Penrhyn Papers (at the time of writing uncatalogued).
[11] A. H. Dodd, 'A History of Caernarvonshire', p. 246.

as Pennant now was, previous connections with Liverpool.) Most of the ships which called were, at this date necessarily, from other ports, such as Beaumaris, Caernarfon and Pwllheli, and, of course, Liverpool, though as early as 1787 Benjamin Wyatt and William Williams, his sub-agent, were registered among the owners of the 71 ton brigantine, *Albion* (Beaumaris Register 1787/90) and the 52 ton sloop, *Lord Bulkeley* (Beaumaris 1787/106).

The closing years of the eighteenth century were marked by a recession in the slate industry mainly because the distribution of slate in bulk by the only possible means in those days, by sea, was made hazardous, not only by the activities of the enemy but also of the pressgangs in their urgent need for experienced seamen.

So confident was Lord Penrhyn of the essential soundness of his enterprise that he employed the many hundreds of men who were laid off from the quarry in improving what we would now call the 'infrastructure' of his industry. Wyatt surveyed the route for an iron tramway from the quarry to the port and it was built at a cost of £5,000 in 1800. Traces of the original tramway of 1800 — when steam traction was introduced in 1876 it followed a different route down the Cegin Valley — may still be seen in the environs of Bangor. It crossed the present Bangor cricket field at Tŷ Newydd, went under Telford's road by a bridge, the parapets of which remain, skirted the wall of the Penrhyn Park (which had yet to be built) and descended Allt Marchogion by an inclined plane to the port. The old incline cottage still stands, its original stone archway through which 100,000 tons of slate passed each year, now adapted for residential purposes.

Wyatt claimed in 1803 that whereas it had taken 140 men and 400 horses to carry slate to the port before its construction, after that date a larger tonnage was carried by 12 men and 16 horses.[12] It was a long time before the other quarry concerns saw the advantages of iron tramways. Twenty years or more passed before Dinorwig was connected by tramway and inclined plane with its port at Felin Heli in 1824. In the Nantlle Valley there were several independently owned quarries and it was not until 1828 that they agreed to come together and construct the Nantlle tramway to the port at Caernarfon. Penrhyn was thus able to outsell its competitors for the best part of thirty years since the cost of cartage from mountain to coast represented a high proportion of the total cost of the final product.

This brief introduction must suffice; our enquiry does not purport to be the complete history of Port Penrhyn or of the many ships which sailed from there, only a small proportion of which had any other connection with Bangor. Our concern is with the development of mercantile enterprise in a city which had been until the last quarter of the eighteenth century a back-

[12] P. E. Jones, T.C.H.S. (ante) Vol. 42, 1981.

water in the economic life of the county. Bangor came late on the scene compared with the ports of Caernarfon, Nefyn and Pwllheli but its growing importance is shown by the fact that between the censuses of 1801 (pop. 1770) and 1821 (3579) its population doubled; it was to be redoubled by the census of 1841 when it stood at 7232, and was, with a slower rate of growth, to even out at about 10,000 in 1861 and thereafter. Until the development by Dean John Jones of Bangor from 1809 onwards of land held by him in the central area of Bangor (around Dean Street) this immigrant population was housed in the confined area of Hirael, between the High Street and the boundaries of the Friars Estate, which soon became Bangor's maritime quarter. John Wood's town map of Bangor of 1834 shows the development of Ambrose Street, Water Street and Foundry Street running towards the waterfront, and across them in grid iron pattern we see Ellen Street, Edmund Street, Mason Street, Fountain Street, Club Street and Lewis Street (now called William Street). Also in this area are a foundry, three slate yards, a wood yard and 'Mr. Parry's Ship Building Yard'. Succeeding censuses show that there was a concentration of seamen, ship-wrights, and slate loaders in this area of Bangor and in the adjoining suburb of Garth.

Surprisingly little documentary evidence has been found for the construction of Port Penrhyn and for the successive additions in the nineteenth century. The present Harbourmaster, Captain Ian Metcalfe, detects three distinct stages in its construction from the differences in the masonry and these are shown on the plan on page 18.

A lease of the necessary land at Tanybryn, and 'the shore and waste ground' to the west of the Cegin (i.e. the Hirael foreshore) was granted to Richard Pennant in 1786 by Bishop Warren for 20 shillings per annum; in 1801 Bishop Cleaver and Pennant made a straight exchange of a quillet of land adjoining the bishop's park in return for the lands covered by the lease. It was a shrewd move on Pennant's part; in view of the later development of Port Penrhyn there is no doubt as to which side obtained the better bargain.

The first stage was the building from 1790 onwards of a wharf and warehouse on the west bank of the mouth of the River Cegin and a short quay on the east bank on which were built the port office and other buildings, including a writing slate factory and a flint reducing kilns (for Worthington's trade, which will be considered in the next chapter) which were established around the turn of the century. Until the mouth of the Cegin was bridged about 1820 the smaller ships of the time could enter the Cegin Pool at high water to be loaded with slate stored on the bank. Precisely when the various installations were built is not known but a sluice gate was later built at the mouth of the river. When ships could no longer enter the pool because of the bridge, the lock still impounded the river water which when released served to scour the channel of the river as it made its way to the sea alongside

16

BANGOR.

(from the Ordnance Survey)

1831.

Map of Bangor (from the Ordnance Survey 1831) showing the boundary of the proposed Borough by Lieut. Robert R. Dawson. From the 'Report on Parliamentary Boundaries of Counties and Boroughs'.

the quay wall. An indenture of 1800 among the Penrhyn Papers refers to the 'new made wharf and quay with sheds and buildings thereon' and another agreement of 1801 refers to the 'new rooms at the Quay' (see page 30). John Wood's town map of 1834 shows that by this time the import warehouse (as it was then — later a writing slate factory and now the Toc H adventure centre) on the west side was as complete then as it is today and it also shows various buildings on the quay on the east side, only one of which is labelled as 'Office'.

The first quay, according to James I. C. Boyd in his book, published in 1985, *The Penrhyn Quarry Railways*,[13] extended only a little beyond the high water mark and ships could only berth on the west face of the quay. The completion of the tramway in 1801 meant that rubble from the quarry could easily be brought to Abercegin to form the core of the new works. The wharf was extended in 1803 far enough seawards to enable ships to berth on either side and this is shown on the estate map of 1803 by Robert Williams. In 1829-30 the wharf was further extended to a length of 1,000 feet. It was claimed that it could now accommodate 100 vessels.

Core samples were taken in 1976 at various points in the vicinity of the port and these showed that the port was built on boulder clay above peat with a layer of sandstone at some depth beneath. Capt. Metcalfe recalls that a vessel alongside once scoured silt away from the quay wall and that inspection revealed that the foundations of the quay were of wood — bundles of brushwood laid at right angles to the line of the quay so that only the tied ends were visible. They were hastily buried again. This method of securing a firm foundation on unstable ground was employed as a desperate measure by George Stevenson when faced with the necessity of crossing Chat Moss on the Liverpool to Manchester Railway.

In the mid-thirties the handsome Port House was built to the design of Benjamin Wyatt II and an ornamental iron bridge (since replaced by a modern concrete structure) connected both banks of the river, (the bridge is in the foreground of the illustration facing page 104).

The old quay (of 1829-30) received a further extension seawards in or about 1855 and a 'new quay and breakwater on the east side of the present quay' was built, according to a draft contract and specification, which is the only documentary evidence so far discovered.[14] The specification, which is dated 19th May 1855, states that the walls are to be built of 'good sound limestone from Penmon' faced with ashlar stonework. Captain Metcalfe confirms the soundness of the masonry which was further strengthened by iron dowels set in lead. The contractors were William Pritchard, Merchant,

---

[13] Narrow Gauge Railways in North Caernarvonshire Vol. 2 *The Penrhyn Railways*. James I. C. Boyd, The Oakdale press, 1985.
[14] U.C.N.W. Carter Vincent 1840.

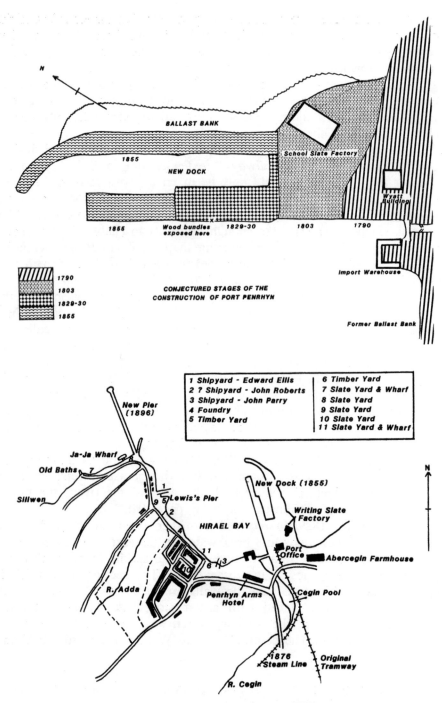

BALLAST BANK

School Slate Factory

1855

NEW DOCK

Wyatt
Building

1855   Wood bundles   1829-30   1803   1790
            exposed here

Import Warehouse

1790
1803
1829-30
1855

CONJECTURED STAGES OF THE
CONSTRUCTION OF PORT PENRHYN

Former Ballast Bank

1 Shipyard - Edward Ellis	6 Timber Yard
2 ? Shipyard - John Roberts	7 Slate Yard & Wharf
3 Shipyard - John Parry	8 Slate Yard
4 Foundry	9 Slate Yard
5 Timber Yard	10 Slate Yard
	11 Slate Yard & Wharf

New Pier
(1896)

Ja-Ja Wharf

Old Baths   7

Siliwen

New Dock (1855)

Lewis's Pier

Writing Slate
Factory

HIRAEL BAY

Port
Office

Abercegin Farmhouse

R. Adda

11

6   3

Cegin Pool

Penrhyn Arms
Hotel

1876
Steam Line

Original
Tramway

R. Cegin

SIMPLIFIED SKETCH MAP SHOWING VARIOUS INSTALLATIONS

18

of Tanycoed, Bangor who was also, in the sixties, a major Bangor shipowner, and William Griffith, Mason, of Dean Street, Bangor. Scouring of the new dock was effected by the partial diversion of the river but the culvert has long since collapsed. There is a strong local tradition that the dock was floored with slate slabs but Captain Metcalfe has failed to find any despite rodding in several places.

But the evidence is there — on the ground. The railway tracks may have been removed but many not-so-elderly Bangorians remember the brisk locomotives of the Penrhyn Railway *(Y Lein Bach)* with their shining brass domes, busily engaged in shunting the little slate wagons while in the background a main line locomotive of the L.M.S., puffing away more sedately, performed the same function with life sized trucks. Remembered also are the Penrhyn steamers, with their yellow funnels topped in black and the red dragon device on either side of the funnel. And imagination, assisted by a few old photographs, helps to recall the tapering masts and the yards, bare and dense as a spinney in winter, in the days of sail.

$$*\qquad*\qquad*\qquad*$$

In 1786 most conveniently (everything happens in the last quarter of the eighteenth century!) an Act (26 Geo. III cap. 60) was passed by Parliament requiring all owners of sea-going ships to obtain a certificate of registry. The Beaumaris Registers (apart from the current one) are now deposited at the Caernarfon Record Office of the Gwynedd Archives Service. They cover all ports from Conwy in the north to Barmouth in the south, though for a period in the last century Caernarfon and, briefly, Pwllheli vessels were registered at those ports. What follows is derived from a detailed study of these registers, and in particular the information they yield on ships built at Bangor and on the participation of the people of Bangor in the ownership of ships built elsewhere.

The early registers state where the ship was built but not always the name of the builder, the owners are named but not the amount of their share holdings. From 1824 onwards the registers show the shares held by the individual shareholders in 64th shares.[15] In practice holdings of 1/64ths were rare, 2/64ths were the usual minimum, while 4/64ths or an ounce were the most common. Some ships were wholly owned by one man, but William Shakespeare's adage about not putting your goods all in one bottom was heeded by many. In modern parlance, they spread the risk.

The registers also give the occupations of the shareholders, and thus give us valuable source of information about the social status of investors at

---

[15] Aled Eames, 'Ships and Seamen of Anglesey' pp. 545 has an Appendix on the Beaumaris Registry of Merchant Ships.

differing times. 'Gentleman', 'Esquire', 'Clerk' (in holy orders) and 'Merchant' share ownership in the early books with 'Mariner', 'Ship's Carpenter', 'Farmer', 'Victualler', 'Maltster', 'Stonemason' and 'Draper'. There are rarer occupations — a 'Spinner' from Boduan, a 'Papermaker' from Caernarfon and a 'Harper' from Bangor. Without anticipating too much the results of this enquiry, it can be said that in the nineteenth century as a general rule the ownership of ships in Bangor tended to move from the gentry to the people.

Very few ships on the Beaumaris Registers in the early years of the nineteenth century were owned by joint stock companies. There was in existence, it is true, the Amlwch Shipping Company whose ships were registered in the names of nominees who held the shares as trustees for other (unspecified) shareholders. Another, and equally rare, instance is 'The Cardigan Bay Steam Navigation Company' which ran the steamer *Vale of Clwyd* between Liverpool and Porthdinllaen, Pwllheli, Barmouth and Aberdyfi in the early 1830s. Her ownership, as far as the register was concerned, was vested in three trustees, 'duly appointed by Trust Deed'. Later in the century, when Gwynedd investors moved from locally built ships to ocean-going steel ships or to steam vessels (both of which demanded substantially more capital), hundreds of shares would be sold in what became known as 'Single Ship Companies' but the ships themselves would be registered in sixty four parts in the name of trustees. These large vessels were in the nature of things registered at ports such as Liverpool rather than at Beaumaris. Company registrations formed a miniscule proportion of Beaumaris registrations throughout the century and to all intents and purposes can be ignored, so that the registers are an unique source for the social and economic historian, particularly for the period when banks and building societies were in their infancy where Gwynedd was concerned.

Shares in ships frequently changed hands and this was recorded in the registers, though there was often a time lag of three or four years between the actual transaction and the recording of it. In the middle of the nineteenth century a separate Transactions Register was brought in to record these transactions rather than have them cluttering up the page of the original registration.

Finally ,what of the process of de-registering a ship? In the early registers a laconic entry of 'Lost' or 'Lost with Register' in faded red ink is more often than not the only indication we have of a tragedy which overcame hundreds of seamen and their families. In the majority of entries no date is given but it can be surmised that it was after the last recorded transaction or change in master. As the nineteenth century progressed the registers are more forthcoming and usually supply a date and a place or position where the vessel was wrecked or foundered.

Of the 62 ships built at Bangor between 1775 to 1879 no fewer than 39 were recorded as having been lost at sea, 12 of them with the ominous addition of 'Lost with Register', indicating that the catastrophe was probably total; 11 were broken up or used as hulks, 9 were sold and registered at other ports, one was de-registered as being under 15 tons and the fate of the other two is unknown. Grim though these statistics are, they must be seen in proportion; some of the ships were lost quite early, but some survived to sail the seas for fifty years or more. The average life span of the 59 Bangor built ships (i.e. 62 ships less two whose end is unknown and one taken off the register) is a surprising 35 years. It may be that many of the ships towards the end of their lives were laid up in idleness, but to offset that, the nine which were sold and registered at other ports have been regarded, for the purpose of this exercise, as having been lost from the date of the transfer. Little is known about the subsequent history of the majority of them, but the schooner, *Emma Laura,* built in 1843, was sold to Chester after one year, in 1844. She survived there for 21 years in the ownership of one family, before being sold and re-registered at Ramsay in 1865. And there we lose sight of her.

CHAPTER II

1781 - 1831

History, as it unfolds, is seldom obliging enough to divide itself into neat chapter lengths of half a century, but there is nothing arbitrary about the heading of this chapter. It begins with the accession of Richard Pennant to full control of the Penrhyn Estate and ends, fifty years later, with the lifting of the duty on slates conveyed by sea. As early as 1794 there had been protests from the quarry owners of Caernarfonshire about the unfairness of the duty; Samuel Holland (the younger) called several meetings at Caernarfon in the twenties and sent several petitions to Parliament. The grievance felt by the Welsh quarry owners was that the Cumberland and Westmoreland owners "got their slates into English Counties, *duty free"* by shipping them at Barrow and other places to Preston where there was a Custom House. They then went up the Ribble and by canal to their destinations, but, because they had originated within the Preston customs area, they paid no duty.[1] The lifting of the duty after a long period of agitation was a great stimulus to production.

Two years after Pennant took full control but before the construction of Port Penrhyn an account book of the "Slates delivered from the Bank of Abercegin from the 1st of January 1783 to the 1st November in the same year by William Williams" has been preserved among the Penrhyn records

---

[1] "The Memoirs of Samuel Holland", p. 13-14. Merioneth Historical and Record Society, Extra Publication, Series I, Number 1.

deposited in the library of the University College of North Wales at Bangor.[2] Apart from being a devoted and much valued servant of the Penrhyn Estate for many years, William Williams had a deep interest in antiquarian and literary pursuits. He published *Observations on the Snowdon Mountains* in 1802 and left in MS form (eventually to be published in the Transactions of the Caernarfonshire Historical Society[3]) *A Survey of the Ancient and Present State of the County of Caernarvon.*

The account book is a detailed record of the numbers and sizes of slates shipped from Abercegin in the ten months covered by the book, together with the sums charged for slates and the cartage. The account confirms what has already been said about the high cost of cartage in relation to production before the construction of the Penrhyn tramway. The first entry, for 20th January, reads

"Delivered on board the *Thomas and Jane,* Evan Thomas, consigned to Mr. William Dale, Liverpool by the order of Richard Pennant, Esq., 20,000 Countesses at 31p. per thousand.

Sum paid for Slates	Sum paid for Cartage
£31. 0. 0.	£12. 0. 0. "

In all there were 31 recorded shipments for the period covered by the account book, 6 for Liverpool, 2 for Belfast, 1 for Chester, 2 for Conwy or 'Eglwys Vach', and the remainder for destinations unknown, some of them local, such as the delivery "on board John Hughes' Boat for the use of John Hampton Jones, Esq. of 3,000 Doubles at 10/- Sum Paid for Slates £1.10. 0. Sum paid for Cartage 12s. 0d." This particular 'export' appears to have gone no further than Beaumaris and was possibly for the personal use of John Hampton Jones, a prominent merchant, for the repair or extension of his house at Henllys.

For all his meticulous accounting of the sizes and prices of the slate and of the amounts due for cartage, William Williams disappoints the maritime historian of two centuries later by his apparent neglect of accurate details of the ships concerned. Perhaps these were so familiar to him, and so irrelevant to his main purpose, as to seem unworthy of record. 'Delivered on a Vessel from S. Wales' or on 'a Vessel belonging to Mr. Lloyd, Havodunos, Owen Jones of Conwy, Master' or on 'Captain Tyrer's Vessel' are typical of many of the entries. Fortunately the Beaumaris Registers which were started three years later enable us to identify some of them and to say a little more about the type of vessel commonly used for the slate trade. A word of caution — Welsh shipmasters of this period tended to name their

[2] U.C.N.W. Penrhyn 1971.
[3] T.C.H.S., Vols. 33, 34 and 36.

vessels after their wives or girl friends, and the proliferation of Anns, Susans and Jennies often presents a problem; other popular names were Speedwell, Hope and Hopewell, with their placatory and optimistic overtones.

'Hopewell' is one of the names recorded by William Williams and there are no fewer than *five* possible candidates among vessels of this name which according to the register would have been extant at this time. All of them were sloops, with a single mast, bowsprit and possibly a square topsail, broad in the beam, varying in tonnage from 15 to 25 tons and in length overall between 30 and 38 feet. In order of seniority, they were built at Llanrwst in 1756 (as far as is known the only vessel built so far up the Conwy River), at Nefyn in 1760, at Pwllheli in 1761, at Aberystwyth in 1764 and at Conwy in 1775. They belonged in 1786, respectively, to the ports of Caernarfon, Caernarfon again, Amlwch, Nefyn and Beaumaris, and it is impossible to tell which of these *Hopewells* was at Abercegin in April 1783 and took a load of 8,000 doubles for Mr. Hugh Kyffin of Eglwys Vach.

The *Thomas and Jane* mentioned earlier can be identified with fair certainty as the vessel of that name (Beaumaris 1789/9) whose subscribing owner was Evan Thomas, Mariner of Beaumaris, which is also the name given to her Master in the account book. The other owners in 1789 are given as *Thomas* Roose, Merchant of Amlwch and *Jane* Roberts, Widow of Bangor. She was a 32 ton sloop, built in Barmouth in 1778 and in the period covered by the account book she made two voyages to Liverpool, one to Belfast, one to Chester and the destinations of the other two were not specified. The register states laconically 'Lost — Register cancelled 1802'.

Similarly the *William and Betty* (Beaumaris 1786/125) can be identified since the Master's name given in 1783 as Henry Williams is the same as one of owners noted in the register. There the owners are given as William Thomas and Henry Williams, Mariners of Llandegfan, and another Mariner, William Morgan, of Llandysilio was a non-subscribing owner. She took a cargo of slates 'for the use of the Lord Bulkeley' consisting of 1,500 ladies at 17/- and 20,000 doubles at 10/- at a cost of £15.15s 6d. plus £6.12s 6d. for cartage. The *William and Betty* was a 24 ton sloop built at Pwllheli in 1782 and she passed into Bangor ownership in 1800, when her owners were described as Richard Jones, Senior, Mariner, and Lewis Hughes, Maltster. Ten years later the grim entry 'Lost — Register not saved' was recorded.

The *Edward and Mary* which bears the distinction of being the very first ship to be registered under the 1786 Act at the Port of Beaumaris (Beaumaris 1786/1), made one voyage (destination unknown) in the period under review. Built as a 34 ton sloop in Barmouth in 1777 she was owned in 1786 by John Parry, Maltster and Margaret Evans, Victualler, both of Beaumaris. In her subsequent history she passed through the hands of many owners, almost exclusively from Beaumaris. She was altered in 1806 into a schooner, and among the many who had a share appear two Bangor names, Owen Williams,

Labourer and John Moses, Harper. She ended her life peacefully — "Vessel broken up and the Certificate of Registry taken away by the Master who has left the Country, see the Honble. Board's Order 30 April 1830, No. 89." A later note says "Register afterwards delivered up and cancelled." It seems that in the last century, too, men were sometimes a little remiss in sending official forms to the appropriate body.

There are three entries which record sloops belonging to Mr. John Griffith of Caernarfon, and in only one of them is the sloop named as the *John* (Beaumaris 1768/7). She was a fair size for this period, being over 47 feet long and registered as 38 tons, and was built in Chester in 1773. She sailed from Abercegin on June 12, and could have performed two other voyages on March 24 and May 5. Equally well, either or both these voyages could have been made by another sloop belonging to Mr. John Griffith, the *William*, (Beaumaris 1786/71), of 26 tons, built in Carmarthen in 1783. The *John* was lost in 1789 but the *William* was sold to Chester in 1820.

There is a fair certainty about the identification of the *Bridget* of Caernarvon, William Williams, Master, which was loaded with 7,700 countesses and 4,500 doubles on May 14 (Cost of slates £14. 0s. 6d., Cartage £5. 11s. 0d.) with the *Bridget* (Beaumaris 1796/131) a 50 ton sloop, built in Caernarfon in 1775, and owned in 1786 by David Evans, Mariner of the Parish of Llanbeblig (Caernarfon). The Register records that she was "taken by the French 1796".

Less certain in the absence of the vessel's name is the identification of "Captain David Lloyd's of Beaumaris vessel" with *Morning Star* (Beaumaris 1786/25). A 29 ton sloop, built at Aberystwyth in 1775, her owner and Master in 1786 was given in the Register as David Lloyd, Mariner of Beaumaris. A very faint entry in red ink on the Register can be deciphered as 'Lost. Register delivered up and cancelled.', which suggests that some at least of the crew were saved. No date is given.

Industry is probably the 50t. Brig of that name, (Beaumaris 1786/19), built in 1756, and owned in 1786 by Hugh Williams, Mariner and Robert Owen, Shipwright, both of Pwllheli, Owen Williams, Farmer of Llanbedrog, and Samuel Lloyd, Mariner of Nefyn. She made one voyage from Abercegin on May 28, bound for Liverpool. A less likely candidate would be the *Industry* of Barmouth (Beaumaris 1787/50), a big sloop of 82t. owned by six Barmouth people, and built in Aberdovey at some time in 1783. Whether she would have been ready to sail on 28th May is open to question.

Again we have two vessels on the Register called *Friendship*, both belonging to Caernarfon. One, a 26t. sloop (Beaumaris 1786/85) was rebuilt at Caernarfon in 1782 and she had a Bangor man among her owners, one Thomas Jones, a Merchant. After several changes of ownership she passed into the hands of John Owen, a Mariner of Dolgellau and she was registered *de novo* at Aberystwyth in 1805. The other *Friendship*, a 57t. sloop

(Beaumaris 1786/103) was built in Hull in 1768 and belonged to William Jones, Merchant of Caernarfon. The Register states that she was broken up in 1788. It is impossible to decide whether it was the one *Friendship* or the other which sailed from Abercegin on 3 October, 1783.

On June 7 there appears an entry in the Account Book "Delivered on the Flat *Charlotte* by the order of Mr. Fury" an amount of slates weighing almost 70 tons, considerably more than the cargo of any other vessel recorded. The *Charlotte* does not appear on the Beaumaris Registers and her likely port of registry was Liverpool. 'Mr. Fury' is possibly identifiable with John Fury who is named in Articles of Agreement made in 1801 between Richard, Lord Penrhyn and Samuel Holland, Michael Humble and Samuel Worthington, as an old customer.[4] This agreement, which will be dealt with more fully later, was, in effect, to appoint the three as sole agents for the supply of slate from the quarry, but exempted from its provisions certain old customers, among the John Fury who was to be supplied "for the trade on the River Weaver".

The *Charlotte* had already brought a cargo of coal to Abercegin on this trip as another entry in the Account Book shows, "June 7th Paid William Deakin Master of the *Charlotte* Flat towards paying duty for the coals." The coal, imported from Lancashire, was used for burning bricks at the Brick Bank at Abercegin. The name Abercegin was also applied to the farm holding which extended along the shoreline of the Penrhyn demesne from the mouth of the River Cegin eastwards to Bath Point, where later Wyatt built, in response to the popular fashion for sea bathing in the early years of the nineteenth century, an elegant sea water bath for Lord Penrhyn and his family. The Brick Bank was situated in a field inland of Bath Point. This brick making enterprise, combining the import of coal and the export of slates in the same vessel with the exploitation of raw materials available locally, is a typical example of the Wyatts' careful stewardship.

The *Charlotte* incident reminds us, too, of the ultimate destination of the Penrhyn slate. By 1790 canals and river navigations connected the Mersey with the Trent and the Severn estuary and opened up Manchester, Hull and the towns of the Midlands as potential markets for slate. Entry to this system was gained by Runcorn on the River Weaver and Runcorn was the destination of hundreds of shipments of Penrhyn slate in the nineteenth century.

The existence of William William's Account Book has given us a brief glimpse at the maritime scene at Abercegin before the construction of Port Penrhyn and some information about the vessels commonly employed. It will have been noted that none of them was built at Bangor and that Bangor interest in their ownership was marginal. The only Bangor names included

[4] U.C.N.W. Penrhyn 2034.

among the owners were Jane Roberts, Widow who was a non-subscribing owner of the *Thomas and Jane,* and Thomas Williams, Merchant who is listed among the predominantly Caernarfon owners of the *Friendship.* Also, among the vessels which have not been identified on the Beaumaris Register, presumably because she was under 15 tons, is 'John Hughes' Hirael, Boat' which made five trips to local destinations, among them Amlwch and Beaumaris, with small amounts of slate. The use of the term 'boat' suggests that she was an undecked vessel. For the next two decades, in the absence of similar evidence, we have to make do with what the Registers tell us.

The first vessel that is *recorded* with certainty as having been built at Bangor was *Fanny,* a 40 ton sloop, built in 1775. (Beaumaris 1786/189). Her owners in 1786 were given as William Edwards, Gentleman of Bangor, another William Edwards of Anglesey and John Thomas, of Llanbedr, both Farmers. She seems to have passed into mainly Beaumaris ownership in 1789 with Erasmus Griffith, a prominent Beaumaris merchant heading the list of the subscribers. After a long career she was finally broken up in 1830.

William Edwards, Merchant of Bangor, (possibly the same William Edwards described as Gentleman in the preceding paragraph) was the sole owner of *Lady Penrhyn,* (Beaumaris 1786/82) a 43 ton sloop built at Bangor in 1783. He was also the owner, with Thomas and Humphrey Tyrer, Mariners of Beaumaris, of *Jenny and Nancy,* (Beaumaris 1786/83) a 24 ton sloop, which was, according to the Register "condemned in His Majesty's Court of Exchequer Easter Term 1786 by the name of *Mayflower* for certain reasons therein produced and sold by the order of the Honble. Commissioner of Customs as forfeited." What lay behind this bald account is not known, but that smuggling was prevalent off the coast of North Wales with its easy access from Ireland and the Isle of Man is a well attested fact. He does not appear to have had much luck with *Jenny and Nancy* since she was wrecked soon after in 1789.

To return to the *Lady Penrhyn,* whose very name seems to have destined her for the slate trade, among her owners in 1789 we see the name of Benjamin Wyatt, Gentleman, of Llandegai. Among others we have the name of Jane Edwards, Widow, and it may fairly be assumed that she was the widow of William Edwards since his name now disappears from the Registers. Benjamin Wyatt's name from 1787 onwards appears with some frequency in the Registers, and with it is associated in some of his ventures the name of William Williams, who is described as a Merchant, of Llandegai.

Albion, newly built in 1787 at Kidwelly (Beaumaris 1787/90) was a brigantine of 71 tons, quite a different kind of vessel from the coasting sloops hitherto favoured by Bangor owners. She was regularly employed between Port Penrhyn and London carrying slate for Samuel Wyatt. Her naming is very probably derived from the Albion Steam Mills at Blackfriars, designed by Samuel Wyatt, the opening of which was said to have been attended by Lord Penrhyn.[5]

Benjamin Wyatt was joined in this venture by William Williams, the sub-agent and slate reeve, by John Cooper, Architect of Beaumaris, and later by William Jackson, Innkeeper of Bangor (of the Bangor Ferry Inn, known later as the George Hotel). We do not know the amount of individuals' shareholdings at this period since it is not until 1824 that the registers record them in sixty-fourth fractions. The *Albion* was sold to Richard Woosnam, Merchant of Pwllheli in 1793 and subsequently registered *de novo* in the Port of London, though it is possible that she continued trading between Port Penrhyn and London under her new ownership.

Among the Poole papers at the Caernarfon Record Office is a bundle of correspondence relating to the *Albion.*[6] Most of the letters are about a claim by the widow of a former master, Owen Williams, against one of the shareholders, John Lewis, Eglwysbach for money owed to her late husband, but among the papers there are the bill of sale for the *Albion* which shows that she cost £800, an account rendered by Benjamin Wyatt to the other shareholders which indicated a nett. profit of £73. 6s. 10d. to be divided into £18. 6s. 8½d. for each share, (which shows that at this time there were four shareholders), and an account of the freight carried by *Albion* in 1788 and 1789. It shows that under the system then operating half the earnings of the ship, after deducting port charges and other expenses, went as profit to the shareholders, the remaining half to the captain, out of which he paid the wages of the crew and the cost of victualling.

"25th October to 25th January	From Bangor to London	£58.10. 8.
To April 5th	From London to Carnarvon, Bangor and Liverpool	£45. 2. 3.
April 24th	From Liverpool Beaumaris and Bangor	£16.15. 6.
May 24th	From Bangor to London	£58. 8. 6.
September 20th	From London to Carnarvon and Chester	£70. 1. 0.
October 6th	From Chester to Bangor	£15.16. 0.

Amount of freights		£264.13.11.
Port Charges and other expenses	£52.17. 8.	
Profit	£211.16. 3.	
	£264.13.11.	
One half profit to the owners	£105.18. 1½.	
One half profit to the Captain for Wages and Victuals	£105.18. 1½."	

[5] P. E. Jones, T.C.H.S. Vol. 42, 1981 pp. 85-6 and footnotes.
[6] Gwynedd Archives Service C(aernarfon) R(ecord) O(ffice) Poole 5221-5236.

It was a system under which there was every encouragement to the Captain to economise both with wages and with victuals to his own advantage.

Wyatt and Williams were also shareholders in *Lord Bulkeley,* a 52 ton sloop built in Beaumaris in 1787 (Beaumaris 1787/106), together with John Hampton Jones, Esquire and John C. Jones Esquire and a nice mixture of more ordinary folk, Robert Williams, Mariner, Edward Edwards, Victualler, William Williams, Grocer and Ann Crow, Spinster, all of Beaumaris. She was sold in May 1793 to Ann Griffith, Widow and Sarah Lewis, Shopkeeper, both of Bangor, and John Oliver, Anglesey, but was reported lost in 1795.

Green Linnet (Beaumaris 1799/17), a large sloop of 76 tons, built at St. Helen's (Lancs) in 1786 and originally registered at the port of Liverpool in that year, is worth noting, since she passed from one of the only two major industrial enterprises in Gwynedd at this time to the other, from the copper trade of Amlwch to Penrhyn slate. She was owned originally by Michael Hughes, Merchant of Ravenhead, Thomas Williams, Esquire of Llanidan (The Copper King) and John Dawes, Merchant, City of London. She passed into the mainly 'gentry' ownership of Thomas Jones, Bryntirion, Esquire, the Revd. John Williams, Clerk, of Bangor, John Parry, Plas Newydd, Gentleman and Benjamin Wyatt, Esquire, now of Lime Grove, Bangor, his new house designed for him by his brother, Samuel. The other shareholder was Owen Griffith of Llanddaniel, Mariner and the vessel's master. Nothing further is known about the vessel save the fact that she was registered *de novo* at Limerick in July, 1810.

One vessel in her long life seems to encapsulate the Penrhyn interest in shipping. The 73 ton sloop, *Raven,* built at St. Helen's in 1788 had William Thomas, Cadnant, as Master holding an interest (as was usual) and among other shareholders we find Benjamin Wyatt, John Roberts, Gentleman and William Jackson of the Bangor Ferry Inn. She was sold in 1815 to Samuel Worthington, Merchant (of whom more later) and George Dale, Master Mariner of Bangor. She was altered from a sloop to a schooner in 1817, which strikes one as a sensible re-arrangement of the sail plan; the main boom of a single masted vessel measuring 63 feet overall must have itself been well over thirty feet long, and to have been taken unawares, on going about by a spar of those dimensions must have been, to say the least, a painful experience for the crew. Samuel Worthington sold all his shares to George Dale in 1821, who ten years later, in 1831, sold half the vessel, 32/64ths, to James Wyatt, Lime Grove, who had succeeded his father as the Penrhyn agent. After George Dale's death his widow, Mary, sold out her half, 8/64ths to James Wyatt, 16/64ths to William Baxter of Penrhyn Castle and 8/64ths to John Parry, described at this time as 'Shipwright' of Bangor. John Parry and later, his son, Thomas T. Parry were to be closely connected with the Penrhyn interests. After William Baxter's death James Wyatt acquired 56/64ths of the vessel. In 1854 he transferred 8/64ths to his younger son Arthur. Thus three generations of the Wyatt family, each of whom in turn served as agents to the Penrhyn Estate, had an interest in the vessel, and the *Raven* in her time carried not only slates for Penrhyn but flint stones for Worthington's enterprise at Llandegai.

Samuel Worthington's association with Lord Penrhyn began at least as far back as 1796 with an agreement which allowed him to search for minerals on the estate.[7] An Indenture Lease in 1800 was granted to Michael Humble, Samuel Holland (the elder), Nicholas Hurry and Samuel Worthington in respect of three water mills at Melin Isa, Melin Hen and Melin Ucha 'and all that new made wharf and quay with sheds and buildings thereon situated on the tenement now called the Penrhyn Arms lately called Penybryn in the Parish of Bangor'.[8] (This is probably the site of the old slate works now occupied by the Toc H Outdoor Activities Centre). The rental for the Flint Mill was £400, for the Corn Mills and Farm £250, for the Ochre Works £40 and for the Wharf and Quay £30. Flint stones were imported from the south of England to Port Penrhyn, ground in the mill and exported to Humble and Holland's Herculaneum Pottery Works at Toxteth Park, Liverpool. The ochre was sent to Liverpool or used on the spot to make paint.[9]

A further agreement was made between Lord Penrhyn and Humble, Holland and Worthington in August 1801 for them to be supplied 'with all the slates made and manufactured at Cae Braich y Cafn' (as the Penrhyn Quarry was known at this date).[10] This agreement allowed the three partners a virtual monopoly of the production of the quarry with the exception of certain old customers, as has already been remarked in the case of John Fury, the River Weaver trader. Other exceptions were the two Wyatts, Samuel and James, practising as architects in London, whose exploitation of slate as an ornamental as well as a roofing material was particularly valuable to the Penrhyn fortunes. William Hayes of Frodsham and Barker Chifney of London were similarly exempt.

The agreement is also interesting for the light it throws on the facilities existing at this stage in the development of Port Penrhyn. It agrees 'also to accommodate the said Samuel Worthington, Michael Humble and Samuel Holland, their administrators, agents and servants . . . (in) the new rooms at the Quay now occupied by William Williams and Robert Thomas.' One wonders what was the reaction of the two displaced persons — William Williams we have already encountered, and Robert Thomas plays no small part in later shipping developments. The agreement goes on to state that the

[7] UCNW Penrhyn 2033.
[8] UCNW Penrhyn 2302.
[9] See T. M. Bassett 'Diwydiant yn Nyffryn Ogwen', T.C.H.S., Vol. 35, 1974 for an account of Worthington's enterprises.
[10] UCNW Penrhyn 2034.

partners have rights to 'a proportion of the Wharf or Quay not exceeding a half as shall be necessary for the laying down and shipping of the said slate'.

Robin S. Craig and Rupert Jarvis have meticulously recorded and analysed the early Liverpool Registry of Merchant Ships (printed for the Chetham Society, Manchester). From their researches we can gain some idea of the relative standing of Michael Humble and Samuel Holland among the ship-owning merchants of the port of Liverpool. Sixty-seven names are listed by them as owners or part owners of over 40,000 tons of shipping between the years 1786 and 1804. Michael Humble occupies the second place among the merchants of the port with full or part ownership of 56 vessels with a total tonnage of 13,381 (clearly most of them were ocean going) and Samuel Holland was seventh with 40 vessels totalling 9,447 tons. It was a formidable partnership. In addition, Nicholas Hurry, a co-signatory of the lease of the watermills and the premises on the Abercegin wharf, was a shipowner on a more modest scale, being fifty-eighth on the list with 16 ships with a tonnage of 4,473. These men, besides having a virtual monopoly of the production of the quarry were also in a position to exercise their considerable influence on the ships used for carrying the slate away from 1801 until about 1810 when the agreement lapsed.

It has already been remarked that Welsh shipowners (and this may apply to the English also) were not remarkably innovative in the matter of ships' names and a glance at the Shipping Intelligence in the columns of the North Wales Gazette published weekly at Bangor from January 1808 makes this plain. For the first time we now have a source other than the Shipping Registers for the Port Penrhyn trade, but with the proliferation of Janes and Peggys etc., it is not possible with any certainty to identify positively more than a few of the vessels with those built in Bangor or owned or partially owned by Bangorians.

Another complication is that some of the arrivals and departures are duplicated in the Beaumaris returns. David Thomas in 'Hen Longau Sir Gaernarfon' meticulously analysed the shipping intelligence in the North Wales Gazette for the year 1808 and discovered that in the course of the year there were 268 sailings from Port Penrhyn and 106 shipments of slate from Hirael, most of them to Ireland (105) and the north-west of England (161) but including 31 for London or ports in the south-east of England. There was a small quay in Hirael which was used by independent small producers of slate, and by a growing number of manufacturers of specialist products such as slate slabs and school slates.

In these early years the vast majority of ships which sailed from Bangor were from other ports. From the surnames of their masters it can be deduced that most of them were Welsh and they probably came from Barmouth, Pwllheli, Nefyn, Caernarfon or Beaumaris, but there was a fair sprinkling of English names. Always with the proviso that there is still some uncertainty about vessels with the same name, it is tempting to identify *Fanny* with the vessel of that name which was the first to have been recorded as built in Bangor in 1775 (Beaumaris 1786/189), and was in 1808 in Beaumaris ownership. Unlike most of the ships which called at Bangor, she was not in ballast when she arrived on March 3rd but brought a load of coal from Liverpool. As a local vessel she may have been favoured with an inward cargo. She sailed from Port Penrhyn for Liverpool with slates on March 17th.

There is more certainty about the two names which follow because of their distinctiveness — *Lady Penrhyn* and *Penrhyn Castle. Lady Penrhyn* (Beaumaris 1803/33) was not the vessel mentioned on an earlier page (p. 27) in which Benjamin Wyatt had an interest — she was recorded as lost in 1799 — but another vessel of the same name, a 38t. sloop, built at Caernarfon in 1803 but owned originally by three Bangor men, Richard Thomas and John Thomas, Farmers, and Humphrey Williams, Quarryman. (Beaumaris. 1803/33). Her registered owners in 1808 were Edward Parry, Gentleman, Llandegai, Edward Thomas, Maltster, Bangor, William Hughes whose occupation is given as 'Penrhyn Arms waiter', William Jones, Gentleman, Talybont, Edward Thomas, Farmer, Llandegai and Thomas Jackson Peale, Gentleman, Winsford.

In the first six months of 1808 the North Wales Gazette records no fewer than five round voyages from Port Penrhyn, three to Liverpool and one each to Chester and Runcorn. On each occasion she carried an inward cargo of coals or coals and sundries. When most of the ships which called at the port for cargoes of slate arrived in ballast, the owners of *Lady Penrhyn* could congratulate themselves on earning freight income for both journeys. It seems likely that locally owned vessels were thus favoured and, of course, their owners would have been aware of local requirements. They also achieved a quick turn round if they had a cargo to discharge and this was to prove to be a source of bitter dispute later in the century.

It would clearly be an impossible task to record the comings and goings and the ultimate end of each and every ship with Bangor associations but a brief digression on *Lady Penrhyn* would not be out of place even if it means departing from the strict chronological order of the narrative. She was re-registered four times for changes of ownership, alterations and for the admeasurement of 1836,[11] so that she presents on interesting pattern of ownership. In the early years she was owned by a nice mixture of the gentry and working men, as the owners already quoted show. By 1823, when she was apparently lengthened, her owners were John Nanney, Mariner, John

[11] The successive registrations in the Beaumaris Register are 1803/33, 1808/2, 1823/21, 1825/144 and 1836/206.

Jones, Shipbuilder, and Evan Evans, Brazier, all of Bangor, together with two spinsters, Mary Peale, the surviving daughter of Thomas Peale of Winsford and Ann Thomas of Bangor. By various transactions by July 1833 ownership was in the hands of John Nanney (32/64), John Jones (16/64) and Robert Evans, Stonemason (16/64). Robert Evans' name occurs with increasing frequency in the registers from this time forward. *Lady Penrhyn* survived in the same hands, save that after John Jones death, his share was held in trust for his son, until the vessel was lost in 1851 — 'letter of Robert E. Evans 1851' is the only record in the register.

Penrhyn Castle (Beaumaris 1808/3) a 122t. snow, was built at Bangor in 1807 for James Greenfield, Esquire, Bryn Derwen, James Defferd, House Builder, Llandegai, Benjamin Wyatt, Esquire, Lime Grove, Revd. Samuel Rice, Bangor, John Mann, Butler, Llandegai, Daniel Vawdrey, Esquire, Middlewich and Robert Lovely, Merchant, Dublin. The pattern of share-holdings is predominantly what has been called for convenience 'gentry', and one suspects Penrhyn influence in the inclusion of James Defferd, the house builder of Llandegai and John Mann — was he the butler at Penrhyn Castle? More pertinently, James Greenfield of Bryn Derwen, near Bethesda, was the engineer of the Penrhyn Quarry and had married Benjamin Wyatt's daughter, and Daniel Vawdrey had married another daughter.[12] Another daughter is said to have married a Mr. Rice, and if this was the Revd. Samuel Rice, the major part of the shareholding was within the family.

Penrhyn Castle was by far the largest vessel built at Bangor to date, and very different from the 40-50t. sloops with their fore and aft rig. She had square sails on yards on both her masts, and a small mast erected immediately aft of the main-mast bore a trysail. Comparisons of tonnage can often be misleading because of the different ways of calculating register tonnage at different times but both in length (70' 10") and in register tonnage (122t.) *Penrhyn Castle* was not exceeded by the shipbuilders of Bangor until we come in 1855 to the 143t. brigantine *Glanogwen* built by John Parry which was 82' 6" overall.

According to the North Wales Gazette *Penrhyn Castle* made two voyages to Dublin during the first six months of 1808 which are under review, probably in the interest of Robert Lovely, the Dublin merchant, the one shareholder without a local connection or address. She was transferred to the Register of the Port of London in 1816.

Edward and Mary (Beaumaris 1786/1) was built in Barmouth in 1777 as a 34 ton sloop but by 1806 had been altered into a schooner. Among her eight owners were two Bangor men, Owen Williams, Labourer and John Moses, Harper whose names occur again in connection with *Margaret;* the other six owners were all from Beaumaris. In the first six months of 1808

[12] P. E. Jones, T.C.H.S. Vol. 42. 1981 pp. 95-6.

she sailed from Bangor for Liverpool with slates, and returned once with a cargo of coals and sundries and once in ballast. After a long life she was 'broken up and the Certificate of Registry taken away by the Master who has left the Country'. A later note on the register states that it was 'afterwards delivered up and cancelled.'

Margaret, (Beaumaris 1800/13) a 19t. sloop was built in Pwllheli in 1800 and the owner was a William Roberts, Mariner of Edern. A note on the register dated February 1806 states that William Jones, Brazier, John Roberts, Esquire, Owen Williams, Labourer and John Moses, Harper, all of Bangor are now the sole owners. She sailed from Bangor with a cargo of slates for Newry in January 1808 and returned with a somewhat strange cargo of flaxseeds in April. In May she took a cargo of slates for Bidston returning at the end of the month in ballast. There must be another unrecorded sailing in June because she was back again in Bangor with coal and sundries by the end of the month. She it yet another instance of knowledge of local requirements leading to an inward cargo, whereas the vast majority of ships from elsewhere came in ballast. The register records laconically 'Lost' Register cancelled.' No date is given but it must have been after November 1821 when the last change of master was recorded.

Another possible identification is the 42t. sloop, *Mary Catherine,* built in Caernarfon in 1805. (Beaumaris 1805/16). Her owners according to the register were John Jones, Beaumaris, Mariner, Owen Owen, Beaumaris, Shopkeeper, John Taylor, Bangor, Gentleman, Hugh Jones, Bangor, Doctor, John Jones, Bangor, Waiter, and Owen Jones, Amlwch, Farmer. The name of Dr. Hugh Jones occurs again in the registers as a Bangor shipowner. *Mary Catherine* is reported in the shipping intelligence as having arrived in ballast in the week ending 25th February and having sailed with slates for Liverpool in the week ending March 10th. By 1812 she had been sold to owners from Caernarfon and was lost in 1829.

The *Raven,* which was singled out for mention earlier, made one voyage during the period under review with slates for Runcorn. Another vessel in which Benjamin Wyatt had an interest, the 71t. flat *Olive* built in Frodsham in 1788, (altered to galliot in 1808) (Beaumaris 1805/30) made one voyage to Liverpool with slates. Hugh Jones, 'Surgeon' of Bangor, together with James Greenfield and James Defferd, who now qualifies for the title 'Gentleman', having previously been recorded as 'House Builder,' together with her master, Richard Hughes, Mariner, Bangor were the other shareholders.

One local vessel which was recorded both by William Williams in 1783 and in the North Wales Gazette for 1808 was the *William and Betty* (see page 24) which took a strange mixture of slates and 10 quarters of malt to Holyhead in May 1808. The explanation is simple — one of her owners was Lewis Hughes, Bangor, whose occupation is given as Maltster.

We now come to activity of a totally different order in the case of *Betties,*

(Beaumaris 1810/11) a 77t. galliot built at St. Helen's Lancs. in 1784 and owned outright in 1810 by Samuel Worthington, Merchant, of Llwynon, Llandegai. There is no reason to believe that she was not in Worthington's ownership prior to 1810 when the registration was transferred to Beaumaris from Liverpool, and one has only to look at the cargoes recorded in the North Wales Gazette to confirm this. She made in all no fewer than seven round trips from Bangor to Liverpool in the first six months of 1808. In the Gazette her first cargo inwards was 'sundries' and outwards '60t. ground flint in bulk, 25 live sheep, 4 live pigs and 5 tons slate'. In March she took '50 tons of ground flint, 20 boxes of writing slates and 8 tons slabs.' Her other cargoes inwards comprised coal, timber and 'sundries', and outwards slate and ground flint. One shipment of slates in June included an unspecified quantity of manganese. The Penrhyn Estate had been searched for minerals other than slate since the middle of the eighteenth century, mainly for copper and lead,[13] and it will be recalled that Samuel Worthington had received from Lord Penrhyn in 1796 articles permitting him to prospect for minerals on the estate. Another shipment recorded in the North Wales Gazette on board the *Success* (not registered in Beaumaris) obviously originated in 'Mr. Worthington's warehouse'; it consisted of 14 casks of manganese, 40 casks of yellow ochre, 5 casks of ground flint, 50 hogsheads of paint and 12 tons of slates. It seems pretty clear that the cargo of flaxseed imported in the *Margaret* from Newry was ground down in one of Worthington's mills to make linseed oil for the manufacture of paint.

To summarise; the Bangor built or Bangor owned or partially owned vessels recorded for the first six months of 1808 were the *Fanny, Lady Penrhyn, Penrhyn Castle, Edward and Mary, Margaret, Mary Catherine, Raven, Olive, William and Betty* and *Betties,* a grand total of ten. When this is set against a total of 95 or 96 separate vessels (there were probably two *Margarets* and two *Resolutions*) which are recorded in the North Wales Gazette, the native contribution at this time is proportionally small.

A brief postcript; vessels bound for the south coast ports could occasionally pick up flint stone as ballast and so make the return journey to Bangor a little more profitable than it would otherwise have been. The brig *Elizabeth* which sailed from Arundel was one of the lucky ones. There is no other record for the six months under review.

The ports to which these ninety odd vessels sailed were mainly in the Irish Sea and with a few exceptions, most of which have been noted, the cargoes consisted exclusively of slate. The list can be broken down as follows: —

North Western England: Liverpool 34, Runcorn 11, Chester 9, Preston 5, Carlisle 3, Bidston 1, Northwich 1.   Total 64.

---

[13] See T. M. Basset, T.C.H.S. Vol. 35, 1974.

Ireland:	Dublin 8, Newry 6, Cork 4, Drogheda 3, Waterford 2, Londonderry 2, West Port 2, Sligo 1, Galway 1, Dundalk 1, Ballyshannon 1. Total 32.
Isle of Man:	Douglas 8, Castleton 2. Total 10.
North Wales ports:	Amlwch 3, Holyhead 1, Pwllheli 1, Rhuddlan 1, Conwy 1. Total 7.
North of England and Scotland:	Dumfries 2, Berwick 1, Stockton 1, Langholm 1. Total 5.
Bristol Channel:	Bristol 5, Newport 1, Berkeley 1. Total 7.
London and South Coast:	London 10, Rochester 1, Southampton 1, Arundel 1, New Shoreham 1, Newhaven 1. Total 15.

With entry to the canal system at Runcorn, Chester, Preston and Bristol, to say nothing of London, it will be seen that most of industrial England lay open as early as this to penetration by Welsh slate.

Richard Pennant, Lord Penrhyn, died in January 1808 and was succeeded to the estate but not to the peerage by his nephew George Hay Dawkins who adopted the surname Pennant.

*   *   *   *

We now come to a remarkable character who was a servant of Lord Penrhyn and later a tenant of Dawkins Pennant, Robert Thomas, who was displaced from his room at Port Penrhyn when Humble, Holland and Worthington made the agreement with Lord Penrhyn in 1801. Robert Thomas appears to have been one of those who were attracted to the area by the increased employment prospects offered by Lord Penrhyn's enterprises for according to the 1851 census the place of his birth was given as Llanfair, Merioneth. He claimed to be 88 years of age at that census. Nothing has so far been discovered about the circumstances of his moving to Bangor and he first comes to light in November 1796, when he would have been between 30 and 33 years of age and wrote four love letters to his cousin, Susanna Davies, at Cefn Rhug, near Corwen which have been preserved among his papers at the University College of North Wales Library, Bangor.[14]

Even with this lapse of time one feels that it is almost an unpardonable invasion of privacy to plunge into another person's intimate correspondence. Sufficient to say that the letters display that the course of true love is never smooth — they vary in tone between the confident and anxious (at one time she was not answering his letters) but the final note is confident 'Don't be in any way afraid of coming with one that wish you all the happiness in this world and the next, dear cousin.'

[14] U.C.N.W. Robert Thomas 8594-8627.

Whatever qualms of conscience one experienced on first reading the letters disappeared with the realisation that Robert married his Susanna, and that both lived to a ripe old age. According to the Register of Burials for the Parish of Llandygai (in the National Library of Wales) Susanna Thomas of Penrhyn Port was buried on November 28th, 1854, aged 90 years. A fortnight later, on December 11th, Robert Thomas was buried in the same grave, aged 91 years.

One of the letters instructs Susanna to direct her reply to 'Robert Thomas, Wharfinger, Port Penrhyn'. In March 1797 Robert Thomas wrote 'Dear Love, . . . Last Friday I have paid £40 for a Quarter of a vessel which perhaps will be in (undecipherable) in a short time. She is called the *Jane* of Beaumaris 50 tons burthen. We may have £100 profit on her but think to get more. She may earn what she cost in a short time. Please keep it to yourself I have not sed one word to any one in this world about the Vessel but to the other owners You are the first that I mensioned about the matter. She is verry safe as presant. We mean to get her to be Irish Trader.' In his next letter of May 3rd, 1797 he inserts a P.S. 'The *Jane* has sailed for Dublin hope that she will be back in a short time for another cargo.'

The Beaumaris Register contains no fewer than six successive entries for *Jane* as she changed hands.[15] Built at Abererch in 1787 (Abererch has become Abersoch by the 1792 entry!) she was a sloop of 50 tons and her registered owners in 1797 were William Jones, Bangor, Mariner and Owen Williams, Llanallgo, Mariner. It has already been remarked that there was frequently a time lag between the actual transaction by way of bill of sale for the whole or part of a vessel and the recording of this in the Register, but there may be another explanation why Robert Thomas' name does not appear. He was obviously anxious to keep his part ownership secret in his letter to Susanna; this can be accounted for by the fact that in his capacity as wharfinger he was responsible for determining the order in which vessels were loaded and was anxious lest he be accused of giving *Jane* preferential treatment.

Sadly, Robert Thomas' first venture into shipowning did not last for a long time and we have no record of whether the anticipated profits were ever realised. The entry for *Jane* concludes 'Lost. Register not saved, 1800.'

After this brief glimpse into the world of shipping at the turn of the century the papers tell us little about the next twenty years. We do not know when he became the tenant of the farmhouse at Abercegin but in March 1817 a lease was granted (or renewed) by George Hay Dawkins Pennant, Esq., to Robert Thomas, Farmer, for the Old and New Weirs in the Parish of Llandegai for 7 years. The rental for the Old Weir was £90 and for the New Weir £60 per annum.[16] The lease refers to 'all those two

---

[15] Beaumaris Registers; 1787/21; 1787/113; 1790/39; 1791/48; 1792/21 and 1797/10.
[16] U.C.N.W. Penrhyn 1038.

several weirs or fisheries . . . the former lying along the shore of the sea below the lands of Tyddyn-canol . . . the latter situate below the lands of Abercegin . . . erected and built for the purpose of catching fish . . . in the tenure and occupation of the said Robert Thomas.' The last phrase suggests that this was a renewal of an earlier lease.

The rental suggests that the fishery was a profitable business; and, indeed, one can safely assume that this was so as the business was carried on at least until 1851 when Robert Thomas (at the age of 88!) gave his occupation and that of his son, another Robert Thomas as 'Fisherman'. In the earlier 1841 census Robert Thomas is described as 'Fishmonger' and Robert Thomas junior as 'Farmer'.

Robert Thomas' letters to Susanna show that he was articulate and fluent in English in spite of some misspellings, but he excelled in Welsh. He corresponded at various times with such literary figures as Dafydd Ddu Eryri (David Thomas), Gutyn Peris (Griffith Williams), Robert Davies (Bardd Nantglyn) and John Jones, Glanygors. He was generous with the fish he caught; there are several *englynion* from his literary friends thanking him for his gifts of *'pysgod cochion'*, i.e. salmon. Among the papers there is an *englyn* of his own composition in connection with the presentation of a cup to Captain Lewis of the *Susanna* for his service to the owners, and a draft (in English) of a similar presentation to the captain of the *Abel* for nine years service 'having within that space repaid the owners the prime cost of building.'

Which brings us naturally to a consideration of Robert Thomas' rôle as a shipowner; his years of experience as a wharfinger at Port Penrhyn and the fact that he lived at Abercegin in close touch with mariners lend credibility to the supposition that he may have been the prime mover in a loose consortium of local men which financed the building at Bangor of several ships, beginning with *Susanna* in 1817. It may be a coincidence that Susanna was also the name of Robert Thomas' wife (it was also the name of Lady Penrhyn but in this deferential age one would have expected the prefix 'Lady' to have been added). *Susanna,* a sloop of 80 tons, (Beaumaris 1817/15) was probably built by John Jones, since he figures among the shareholders, who were

> Thomas Lewis, Mariner, John Jones, Shipwright, both of Bangor; Robert Thomas, Farmer, Llandegai; Abel Davies, Merchant, Abergele; Lewis Hughes, Merchant, Robert Williams, Land Surveyor, Robert Jones, Smith, Robert Hughes, Grocer, Evan Evans, Brazier, Henry Morris, Mariner, William Price, Mariner, Richard Jones, Ferryman, all of Bangor; David Williams, Llandegai; Thomas Edwards, Merchant, London.

Robert Williams was the son of William Williams, Llandegai, the Penrhyn sub-agent. Abel Davies, the merchant from Abergele, who was also one of the owners of *Abel* of 1827 and held 20/64ths of *Susanna,* is an unexplained phenomenon. Was he, one wonders, a kinsman or even the father of Susanna Thomas (née Davies)? Such links in the chain are by no means impossible as the later connection with Captain John Parry shows.

Jane Ellin, (Beaumaris 1820/15) a 113 ton brig, built in Bangor in 1820, had three of *Susanna's* shareholders among her owners, Robert Thomas, Robert Williams, Land Surveyor, and Robert Jones, Smith, and possibly a fourth, Evan Evans, now described as 'Merchant'. Hugh Pugh, Mariner of Caernarfon was her first master and part-owner. By 1824, when *Jane Ellin* was re-registered, Hugh Pugh was no longer master nor shareholder; the reason will shortly become clear.

Ann, the daughter of Robert and Susanna Thomas, had married John Parry, a young sailor from Caernarfon, and was in Gravesend on July 20th 1821 when she wrote to her parents, from on board a ship, possibly the *Susanna.* John Parry's name does not occur in her list of masters on the register (this was before the days of Crew Agreement Lists) but he was certainly on board, possibly as mate. The letter by a happy chance has survived (and one wishes that many more of this nature had been preserved) and is worth reproducing in full not merely for the light it casts on Hugh Pugh's antics but also for its general interest.[17]

> "My dear Father and Mother,
>
> I wrote to you on Monday by Mr.(?) Lincoln and said that we should sail the next day but we did not until yesterday and we have got this far. We have been delayed here on acct. of carrying away the main topsail yard yesterday. John Parry was obliged to go back to London for another or we should be crossing the Channel by this. I have not heard anything of the *Jane Ellin* that can give you or Edward Thomas (Maltster, Bangor and a subscribing owner) any comfort. They informed me in London that she is about £100 in debt there already. He had 15 dozen of bottled porter at Evan Owen's before he went away and these are not paid for but he took care not to go there himself to order them but employed another person to do it for him and you may suppose that he would not do it for nothing, more likely that he will charge the Capt. 2s. or 3 a dozen for his trouble in ordering them but this we must keep to ourselves. The sooner Hugh Pugh goes the better it will be for Rbt. and Ed. Thomas o herwydd y nhw sydd yn gorfod diodde y pwys i gyd. (because it is they who must suffer the whole responsibility) Don't mention anything about the Porter story.
>
> The King was crowned yesterday but we came off too early to see anything but the Royal Standard of England hoisted on the Tower of London. We also saw a little of the fireworks at night. We have been told that the Queen tried to go in to see him crowned at three doors and was obliged to return as they would not admit her. If we are delayed any longer than he expects at Antwerp I will write to you from there and I hope that you will write to

---

[17] U.C.N.W. Robert Thomas 8601.

meet me in London if we go there which I will mention to you. Hoping that this will meet you both and all good friends in good health and begging to be remembered to all with love . . .

P.S. I saw Capt. Evans the *Louisa* the day before yesterday and he desired to be remembered to you when I write. I am obliged to eat dry bread, the butter here is so bad and all my mother's butter is gone.

John has written to Carnarvon so you need not send."

This letter speaks for itself; what is of additional interest is that the vessel was bound for Antwerp, which is an indication that as early as this Bangor slate was being exported to the Continent.

John Parry became the master of *Jane Ellin* on 4th September 1823 and the owners were rid of the troublesome Hugh Pugh. The re-registration of 1824 (when for the first time the amount of individuals' holdings were recorded) shows that between them John Parry with 22/64th and his father-in-law Robert Thomas with 12/64ths owned more than half the vessel. Edward Thomas, Maltster, Robert Jones, Smith and Robert Williams, Land Surveyor who were original shareholders still had shares when she was wrecked in February 1840 at St. Helen's, Scilly, in addition to John Parry and Robert Thomas.

Robert Thomas must have had a high opinion of his son-in-law since he concluded a lease in March 1822, with G. H. Dawkins Pennant, of Tyddyn Llwydyn with 42 acres, and it was here that John and Ann Parry settled. Tyddyn Llwydyn stood on the site of what is now the Maes Geirchen Housing Estate at Bangor, and was within easy distance of Port Penrhyn and Hirael.

Thomas and Anne, a 61t. sloop. built in Bangor in 1822 but not registered until two years later (Beaumaris 1824/13) had Robert Thomas with 24/64ths as the major shareholder. In 1828 John Parry, Master Mariner, Tyddyn Llwydyn, Bangor acquired 12/64th, and by further transactions in the forties had acquired 40/64ths. The vessel survived until December 1876 when she was wrecked on the North Bank near Liverpool.

Five members of the 'consortium' which financed the building of *Susanna* in 1817 were among the 11 original shareholders of *Abel,* a 113ton snow built at Bangor by the same builder, John Jones in 1827. (Beaumaris 1827/ 38). They were John Jones himself, Robert Thomas, Thomas Lewis (her master for nine years), Robert Williams and the mystery man, Abel Davies, Merchant, Abergele after whom she was named. John Parry with an ounce (4/64ths) held a share from the beginning. She was re-rigged twice, as a brig in 1836 and as a brigantine by 1854.

She was still usefully employed in the sixties. Her crew lists[18] at the

---

[18] Gwynedd Archives Service; L(langefni) R(ecord) O(ffice) W/DB/2.

Llangefni Record Office show that she was in the main a long range trader, making voyages to London, Hamburg or occasionally Dunkirk. In 1873 she sailed from Bangor to Hamburg in July, from Hamburg to Leith in August, from Leith to Plymouth in September, from Plymouth to Runcorn in October, and from Runcorn via Dublin to Bangor in December.

The first ship built by John Parry in his yard at Hirael was the *Bangor Packet,* (Beaumaris 1830/13) a 39ton sloop. Among the eleven original share-holders we find the names of John Parry himself with 8/64ths and Robert Thomas with 4/64ths, and an interesting first appearance of Richard Morris Griffith, Tallow Chandler of Bangor with 4/64ths. Most inconveniently there were two men of that name, father and son, and the registers do not always distinguish between them. The son was to grow into a very successful business man in Bangor, with his drapery and ironmonger's business; and his later career as a banker was very influential as far as Bangor shipping was concerned. Pigot's Business Directory for 1835 notes that he was the agent for the Northern and Central Bank of England and by 1844 he was described as the manager of the Bangor branch of the National Provincial Bank of England.

It is probably a reflection of John Parry's earlier career as a master mariner and his connections with other ports that among the eleven shareholders in *Bangor Packet* there are five names from Liverpool, most of them of obviously Welsh origin — John Price and Alexander Smith, Ropemakers and co-partners with 4/64ths, Richard Jones, Mariner, with 8/64ths, Peter Roberts, Mariner with 4/64ths and Hugh Pritchard, Baker, also with 4/64ths. John Price retained his shareholding at least until 1874; the vessel was hulked in 1887. Conversely, John Parry himself owned shares in vessels from other ports, notably Nefyn, with the 105 ton brig, *Antelope* (Beaumaris 1828/37) and the 98 ton brig, *Nevin* (Beaumaris 1827/25). These two ships are a good example of what can be called cross-fertilisation by transfer of capital, since, though mainly Nefyn owned, they also had in common holdings by two Bristol sailmakers, John Bennet and John Townley.

The shipbuilding industry at Bangor gradually gathered pace during the period between 1808 and 1831, where this chapter ends, and activity was by no means confined to Robert Thomas and his associates. But a due sense of proportion must be retained; during these years Bangor built thirteen or fourteen ships (the uncertainty will be cleared up later), but neighbouring Caernarfon produced 43 whilst Pwllheli built no fewer than 90.

The same alliance of men accustomed to put 'Esquire' behind their names that had financed the building of *Penrhyn Castle* in 1808 came together again in the same year to build the smaller *Bangor and Liverpool Packet* (Beaumaris 1808/25), a sloop of 25 tons — Benjamin Wyatt, Daniel Vawdrey, Revd. Samuel Rice and James Defferd, together with two 'Mariners', William Price of Bangor and Owen Griffith of Llanddaniel. The ship does not appear to have had a long life since she was lost with her register some time after 1816.

Nancy, an open boat decked over (Beaumaris 1821/30), a sloop of a mere 9 tons, was sold to James Wyatt, Esquire, of Lime Grove, Bangor in 1824, possibly for the delivery of slate locally, but the registration was deleted and cancelled as she was under 15 tons. *Louisa,* a 13 ton cutter, was built by John Jones in 1826 (Beaumaris 1826/118) for Stuart Majendie, 'Clerk' (in holy orders) who was also named as her master. The distinctiveness of the surname leads one to suppose that he was the son or a kinsman of Henry Majendie, the Bishop of Bangor, and so to the conclusion that she was a private yacht. She was registered *de novo* at Liverpool in 1827.

Penmon (Beaumaris 1828/1), on the other hand was a commercial proposition. She was a 26 ton sloop, built by John Jones who retained an 8/64ths share. The major shareholder was James Wyatt of Llandegai with 48/64ths, the other shareholder being Catherine Ainsworth, widow of Bangor. Her subsequent history is interesting for it is a symbolic demonstration of how ownership passed from the gentry to the people (if the use of those terms may be forgiven). In 1844, after the deaths of John Jones and Catherine Ainsworth, she passed into the ownership of James Wyatt, Lime Grove, his younger son, Arthur Wyatt who now lived at Tanybryn, a house which almost overlooks Port Penrhyn, and a close associate, John Lloyd, the Accountant at Port Penrhyn. In 1861 she was sold, 64/64ths, to Thomas Parry, Penmon, Quarryman, who promptly sold her to Hugh Jones, Beaumaris, Harbour Master, who two months later sold her to Henry Jones, Hatter and Owen Jones, Tanner, both of Beaumaris in equal shares. Henry Jones was for two months in 1869 her sole owner before he sold a half share (32/64ths) to John Williams, Mariner, of Beaumaris. She was broken up in 1885.

No 'Esquires' are to be found among the owners of the other three vessels built at Bangor during this period and no common pattern of ownership is discernible. *Speedwell* (Beaumaris 1811/28) was a small sloop of 14 tons and was registered in the names of Lewis Hughes, Merchant and William Hughes, Hostler, both of Bangor. *Jane and Alice* (Beaumaris 1822/5), a 45 ton sloop, though built in Bangor, was owned initially by Beaumaris owners; by 1825 two Bangor men, Robert Jones, Blacksmith and Robert Hughes, Grocer had each acquired a 4/64ths share. *Eliza Goddard* (Beaumaris 1824/53) a 57 ton smack was built in Bangor by John Jones. (From 1824 until 1855 the builder's name was recorded on the Register, though it must be borne in mind that the name is not necessarily the name of the shipwright but that of the person who organised the building.) All the original shareholders came from Holyhead or Amlwch, including the major shareholder, Thomas Phillips, Mariner of Holyhead who held 32/64ths. Among the other subsequent shareholders was a man who had swallowed the anchor, Hugh Jones of Beaumaris, 'formerly Mariner now Gaoler' whose name frequently appears in other registrations. By the forties and fifties *Eliza Goddard* had become a Bangor ship with John Williams, Master Mariner of Bangor holding the majority of shares, with Edward Ellis, Shipbuilder and Edward Owen, Mariner each holding one ounce (4/64ths). But this is to anticipate the narrative.

To recapitulate and summarise, the vessels known to have been built at Bangor from 1775 to 1829 are listed below.

Year	Name of Vessel	Tonnage	Rig	Builder	Ultimate End
1775	Fanny	40	Sloop	Unknown	Broken up in 1838
1783	Lady Penrhyn	43	Sloop	Unknown	Lost in 1799
1807	Penrhyn Castle	122	Snow	Unknown	Sold to London 1816
1808	Bangor and Liverpool Packet	34	Sloop	Unknown	Lost (after 1816)
1811	Speedwell	14	Sloop	Unknown	Lost (after 1818)
1817	Susanna	80	Sloop	?John Jones	Lost (after 1827)
1820	Jane Ellin	113	Brig	?John Jones	Wrecked St. Helen's, Scilly 1840
1821	Nancy	9	Sloop	Unknown	Del. under 15 tons
1821	Jane and Alice	45	Sloop	?John Jones	Lost in 1866
1824	Thomas & Anne	61	Sloop	Unknown	Wrecked 1877 Liverpool
1824	Eliza Goddard	57	Smack	John Jones	Wrecked, Deregis'd 1887
1826	Louisa*	13	Cutter	Unknown	Sold Liverpool 1827
1827	Abel	113	Snow	John Jones	Broken up 1879
1828	Penmon	26	Sloop	John Jones	Broken up 1885
1828	Pausillipo*	20	Cutter	John Jones	Sold Swansea 1841
1829	Margaret	90	Schooner	?Jas Harris	Lost 1885

* Private yachts

(The vessels built between 1830 and 1879 are listed on pp. 123-124)

*   *   *   *

Side by side with the growing shipbuilding industry there was an increasing interest in shipowning on the part of the people of Bangor. There is some overlap between the two activities, of course, and most of the builders had interests in ships built elsewhere as well as those built in Bangor; no firm line can be drawn between shipbuilding and ship ownership.

Since we last looked at the shipping intelligence in the North Wales Gazette of 1808 at least 42 ships on the Beaumaris Registers have at least one, in many cases several, Bangor names among their shareholders; in the period from 1803-1831 about 20 were owned exclusively by Bangor owners.

It would be tedious merely to list the names of ships and owners in chronological order; instead, let us consider a type of vessel, well adapted to the coasting trade, which was popular among Bangor owners, the Mersey flat. These were originally designed for inland navigations and estuary work where they were frequently employed in loading and discharging ocean-going vessels. In all but name they were barges, stoutly built, with flat bottoms and flush decks, a comparatively shallow draught for their carrying capacity and an efficient if simple rig, a fore and aft mainsail and a staysail. There was no bowsprit and no topsail yards, and they carried a large rudder mounted on the transom.

It was not long before owners of flats discovered that they were excellent for short coastal voyages — and economical, for they could be easily handled by a crew of only two. All that was required to adapt them was a low bulwark or even rails and some shelter below for the crew. They soon became the maids of all work as far as Port Penrhyn was concerned. The flat *Charlotte* which brought a load of coal to Abercegin and departed with slates for Mr. Fury, the River Weaver trader, in 1783 has been mentioned earlier and no doubt many Mersey flats were employed in a similar capacity during the intervening years. The first flat in Bangor ownership was *Olive* (Beaumaris (1805/30) with Hugh Jones, Surgeon, Benjamin Wyatt and James Greenfield among her owners. She was followed by *Grace* (Beaumaris 1810/12), built at Northwich and owned by Samuel Worthington. She was registered at 77 tons, was 65 feet in length and 16½ feet in the beam, but her depth of hold was only 6 foot 8 inches.

A smaller version, *Trefriw Trader* (Beaumaris 1811/33) was actually built in Conwy in 1809, one assumes for river navigation, but soon came into Bangor hands, a farmer, a yeoman, a mariner, two masons, a smith, a druggist and a spinster, and she remained mainly in the same hands until her sale in 1837 to Caernarfon owners. *Industry* (Beaumaris 1814/23) a 59 ton flat built at Runcorn in 1805 was owned from 1814 until 1825 by a Conwy merchant; he became bankrupt, and after three years in the owner-ship of a Caernarfon mariner, she was acquired 48/64 by the Bangor druggist, Thomas Rathbone and two John Roberts's with 8/64ths each, one a mariner and the other a sawyer.

The flat *Hope* of 58 tons was built at Runcorn in 1800 but was registered for the first time at Beaumaris (1821/19) having been 'hitherto employed in the river trade and inland navigation.' Her owners were James Wyatt and William Alexander Provis, Bangor, Civil Engineer, who was Telford's resident engineer for the Menai Suspension Bridge. Provis sold out to James Wyatt who became sole owner by 1825. The vessel was lost with her register in the following year. *Tabley* (Beaumaris 1823/19) built at Frodsham in 1787, but again with a note on the register that she had hitherto been employed on the river trade, had among her owners in 1825 William Baxter, Penrhyn Castle, Gentleman, who, one suspects was a high functionary of the Penrhyn Estate, since his name occurs in other registrations with that of the Wyatts.

John Wilson, Bangor Ferry acquired the 75 ton flat *Henry* (Beaumaris

1823/20), built at Northwich in 1803; she was sold to William John Lewis, a clerk in holy orders of Trosymarian, Anglesey, who seems to have had a liking for flats. In 1835 she was sold to John Parry, Tyddyn Llwydyn, Shipbuilder, converted into a schooner and sold to Beaumaris.

The Revd. Mr. Lewis is registered as the outright owner of the 72 ton flat, *William* (Beaumaris 1826/80) again a first registration since she was built seven years earlier in Northwich, of the 65 ton flat *Admiral Nelson* (Beaumaris 1827/39), built at Northwich in 1798 and of the *Peggy* (Beaumaris 1829/11) of 56 tons, also built at Northwich in 1798 and previously registered at Chester. All three were sold in 1832, together with another *Peggy* (Beaumaris 1828/34), a sloop this time, to Robert Williams, Farmer, of Tynyffridd, Bangor. It is intriguing to speculate why the reverend gentleman suddenly seems to have lost his enthusiasm for ship-owning — could it be that his bishop thought that his flock deserved more of his attention? The flat, *Peggy* later came into the ownership of John Parry, Shipbuilder until she was lost with all papers in the Mersey in October 1851.

Lastly, the flat *Hornet* (Beaumaris 1824/6) built at Frodsham in 1791 came into the ownership of Andrew Gibb, Mason, Penmon, and Hugh Hughes, Blacksmith, Bangor Ferry, about the year 1831. Subsequently William Baxter of Penrhyn Castle, whom we have already encountered, acquired half a share. She was reported lost in 1853.

To summarise; the major owners of Bangor in the nineteenth century up to 1831, where this chapter ends and where, coincidentally, Samuel Worthington's interests in the Ogwen Valley also came to an end with the ending of his leases (Dawkins Pennant took them over) can be broadly defined in the following way.

BENJAMIN WYATT, JAMES WYATT AND ASSOCIATES

Green Linnet (Beaumaris 1799/17) 76t. Sl. from 1799 to 1810 (sold to Limerick).

Raven (Beaumaris 1800/26) 73t. Sl. 1800-15 & Sr. 1831-65 (1815 sold to Worthington).

Olive (Beaumaris 1805/30) 71t. Flat from 1805 until sold locally in 1808.

Penrhyn Castle (Beaumaris 1808/3) 122t. Snow from 1808 to 1816 (sold to London).

Bangor & Liverpool Packet (Beaumaris 1808/25) 34t. Sl. from 1808 to 1816 (lost)

Friendship (Beaumaris 1809/28) 27t. Sl. from 1809 to 1826 (sold to Caernarfon).

Hope (Beaumaris 1821/19) 58t. Flat from 1821 to 1826 (lost).

Tabley (Beaumaris 1823/19) 56t. Flat from 1825 (acq. from Baxter) to 1832 (sold locally).

Penmon (Beaumaris 1828/1) 26t. Sl. from 1828 to 1861 (sold locally).

Talacre (Beaumaris 1829/31) 77t. Sr. from 1829 to 1867 (sold locally).

*indicates a vessel built at Bangor.

45

SAMUEL WORTHINGTON

Betties (Beaumaris 1810/11) 77t. Galliot from 1810 to 1830 (sold to Newry).

Grace (Beaumaris 1810/12) 77t. Flat from 1810 to 1830 (sold to Chester).

Nelson (Beaumaris 1811/2) 132t. Brigantine from 1811 to 1812 (sold to St. John's).

Raven (Beaumaris 1800/26) 73t. now Sr. from 1815 to 1831 (sold back to Wyatts).

Samuel (Beaumaris 1821/4) 105t. Brigantine from 1821 to ? (Lost — no date).

James (Beaumaris 1824/50) 124t. Galliot from 1824 to 1830 (sold to Newry).

LEWIS HUGHES, MERCHANT, BANGOR AND ASSOCIATES

William and Betty (Beaumaris 1800/21) 24t. Sl. from 1800 to 1810 (lost).

Hopewell (Beaumaris 1792/38) 23t. Sl. from about 1802 to 1812 (sold locally).

Indefatigable[20] (Beaumaris 1811/12) 65t. Galliot from 1811 to ? (lost after 1816).

Speedwell (Beaumaris 1811/28) 14t. Sl. from 1811 to ? (lost after 1818).

Venus (Beaumaris 1812/28) 157t. Snow from 1812 to c. 1821 (in association with Barmouth owners).

Hero (Beaumaris 1816/21) 21t. Sl. from 1816 to c. 1821 (sold to Caernarfon).

ROBERT THOMAS, ABERCEGIN AND ASSOCIATES

Susanna (Beaumaris 1817/15) 80t. Sl. from 1817 to ? (lost 1827-36).

Jane Ellin (Beaumaris 1820/15) 113t. Brig 1820 to 1840 (lost St. Helen's, Scilly).

Eagle (Beaumaris 1820/21) 15t. Cutter 1820 to ? (lost, no date).

Jenny (Beaumaris 1787/27) 20t. Sl. from 1821 to 1859 (sold to Caernarfon).

Thomas and Anne (Beaumaris 1824/38) 61t. Sl. from 1824 to 1878 (wrecked nr. Liverpool).

Abel (Beaumaris 1827/38) 113t. Snow/Brig/Brigantine from 1827 to 1879 (broken up).

Bangor Packet (Beaumaris 1830/13) 39t. Sl. from 1830 to 1887 (hulked).

*indicates a vessel built at Bangor.

---

[20] Register 'Prize taken from the enemies of Great Britain by the Private Ship (?) *Phaiant* and condemned by the High Court of Admiralty 26 June 1810.'

REVD. W. J. LEWIS, later mostly ROBERT WILLIAMS, TY'NYFFRIDD, BANGOR

Henry (Beaumaris 1823/20) 75t. Flat from 1826 to 1835 (sold locally).

William (Beaumaris 1826/80) 72t. Flat from 1826 to 1832 (sold to Robert Williams).

Admiral Nelson (Beaumaris 1827/39) 65t. Flat from 1826 to 1832 (sold to Rbt. Williams).

Peggy (Beaumaris 1828/34) 59t. Sl. from 1828 to 1832 (sold to Robert Williams).

Peggy (Beaumaris 1829/11) 56t. Flat from 1829 to 1832 (sold to Robert Williams).

Christy and Jean (Beaumaris 1830/25) 46t. Sl. from 1830 to 1832 (to Robert Williams).

THOMAS RATHBONE, DRUGGIST, BANGOR

Union (Beaumaris 1822/11) 70t. Sl. later Sr. from 1825 to ? (lost, no date but after 1840).

King William (Beaumaris 1825/14) 21t. Smack from 1825 to 1841 (lost).

Industry (Beaumaris 1814/23) from 1828 to ? (lost, no date).

Although the Registry entry gives no date for the loss of *Industry,* we know from the issue of the *North Wales Chronicle* of October 15th, 1829 that this occurred in the same month. The account states that "on Monday week about 11 a.m. during the prevalence of a heavy gale from the north west the flat *Industry* of this port, bound for Runcorn with a cargo of slates, sprang a leak about two miles off the Light Ship (in Liverpool Bay) and went down instantly. The crew got into the boat and were most providentially picked up by a Galliot from Dublin to Liverpool".

Rathbone's rather chequered ownership also provides an early example (the earliest as far as Bangor owners were concerned) of the later common practice of marine mortgage. It was not necessarily a desperate measure to stave off creditors; it later became a fairly common practice with the amount of the mortgage and rate of annual interest being recorded on the register. For most of the nineteenth century mortgages on ships stood at 5%, though exceptionally rates as low as 3% or as high as 7% were charged. Private mortgages from individuals or shipbuilders were the rule in the early days but later on professional bankers were the usual mortgagees. Shipbuilders sometimes were obliging enough to provide deferred terms of payment by way of mortgage for new construction, for lengthening, re-rigging or general repairs to a vessel. The practice eased what we would call the problems of cash flow and it provided new capital. Rathbone's mortgages of £700 each on *Union* and *King William* from Thomas Williams, Gentleman, Bangor (the rate of interest is not recorded) in 1828 could have provided capital for the purchase of *Industry* in that year.

Druggists in general figure largely among Gwynedd shipowners of the nineteenth century. In addition to Thomas Rathbone, another Bangor druggist of the same period, John Griffith, had a share from 1821 until 1823 in the Cardigan built *Friendship* (Beaumaris 1820/25), a 41 ton sloop together with George Francis Barlow, Gentleman of Treborth, Bangor. He was also a shareholder, with 8/64ths, in the Conwy built flat, *Trefriw Trader* (Beaumaris 1811/33) from the early twenties of the century up to her sale to a Caernarfon merchant in the forties, when the register records (Caernarfon 1843/12) that 8/64ths were held by 'John Griffith, Druggist, formerly of Bangor now residing in Van Diemen's land' (now Tasmania) — what fascinating story lay behind this bald entry in the register is not known.

Later in the century Rathbone and Griffith were succeeded both in their trade and as shipowners by Meshach Roberts of Bangor who played no small part in the civic business life of the city, as will appear in a later chapter. In the rest of Gwynedd the Pwllheli druggist, William Jones, was a major shipowner; and on a still larger scale a druggist from Llanberis, D. P. Williams, became the manager and secretary of the Eryri Shipping Co. Ltd. which owned several ocean going ships in the seventies; but this is to anticipate the course of the narrative.

The outstanding feature of the list of Bangor shipowners during this period is the fact that Robert Thomas and his associates were primarily responsible for establishing the shipbuilding industry in Bangor. The Wyatts and Worthingtons owned between them sixteen ships, but only three of them were Bangor built, whereas of the seven ships owned by Robert Thomas and his associates no fewer than five were the products of the local shipbuilding industry. The group included John Jones, Shipwright and, later, John Parry, Shipbuilder of Tyddyn Llwydyn. It is possible that John Parry took over the yard of John Jones since John Jones's name does not appear on the registers after 1830, the year in which John Parry built *Bangor Packet* and is named as her builder in the Register.

We last looked at the Shipping Intelligence in the North Wales Gazette for the first six months of 1808. Twenty years later the Gazette had become the North Wales Chronicle but it was still the only weekly newspaper in North Wales. Unfortunately only arrivals and sailings are recorded and there is no indication of where they came from nor whither bound, and no mention of their cargoes. There were 216 sailings in the first six months of 1828 (compared with 140 in the corresponding six months of 1808), and 98 vessels from other ports and 22 vessels associated in some way with Bangor performed these.

Samuel Worthington's galliot *Betties* made six round voyages (presumably to Liverpool) and she must have earned for her owner in the intervening years several times her initial outlay. Other ships which figured both in the 1808 and in the 1828 lists were *Raven* and *Lady Penrhyn*. The increase in the number of ships using the port was matched by an increase in the tonnage of the vessels — the ten Bangor ships in 1808 averaged 54 tons, while the 1828 average for 22 vessels was 69 tons. The Bangor built or owned vessels, in whole or part, are summarised below.

Name	Reg.	Tons	Rig	Ownership
*Abel	B.1827/38	113	Snow	Robert Thomas, John Parry etc.
Agnes	B.1817/10	84	Snow	Owen Owens, Mariner, Bangor 60/64
Betties	B.1810/11	77	Galliot	Samuel Worthington
Brothers	B.1825/56	38	Sl.	Robert Evans, Stonemason, Evan Evans, Mariner.
Friendship	B.1820/25	41	Sl.	George Francis Barlow, Esq. Treborth
Grace	B.1810/12	77	Flat	Samuel Worthington
Henry	B.1823/20	75	Flat	Revd. W. J. Lewis/Rbt. Williams
James	B.1824/50	124	Galliot	Samuel Worthington
*Jane Ellin	B.1820/15	113	Brig.	Robert Thomas, John Parry etc.
King William	B.1825/14	21	Smack	Thomas Rathbone, Druggist
Nevin	B.1827/25	98	Brig.	Mainly Nevin; John Parry, Mariner 4/64
Peggy	B.1829/11	56	Flat	Revd. W. J. Lewis/Robert Williams
Penrhyn Castle[21]	B.1828/4	41	Sl.	John Thomas, Mariner, Rbt. Jones, Grocer, Edwin Holford, Schoolmaster etc.
Lady Penrhyn	B.1803/33	42	Sl.	John Nanney, Mariner, John Jones, Shipbuilder, Evan Evans, Mariner, etc.
Raven	B.1800/26	73	Sr.	Samuel Worthington at this period.
*Speedwell	B.1811/28	14	Sl.	Lewis Hughes, Merchant, Wm. Hughes, Hostler
*Susanna	B.1817/15	80	Sl.	Robert Thomas, John Jones, Shipwright, Thomas Lewis, Mariner, etc.
*Thomas and Anne	B.1824/13	61	Sl.	Robert Thomas, John Parry etc.
Union	B.1822/11	70	Sr.	Thomas Rathbone, Druggist
Valiant	B.1826/64	122	Snow	Mainly Nevin. John Parry 16/64
Waterloo	B.1816/3	104	B'g'tine	Mainly Nevin. Edward Thomas, Land Surveyor 4/64
William	B.1826/80	72	Flat	Revd. W. J. Lewis/Rbt. Williams, Tynyffridd.

*indicates vessel built at Bangor

[21] Built at Runcorn by W. Evans, 1827; not to be confused with earlier *Penrhyn Castle* built Bangor 1807, and sold to London 1816.

The usual caveat must be entered about the certainty of identification of vessels of the same name, and this applies to *Peggy* and *Speedwell*, both popular names.

Another indication of the growing volume of maritime trade in Bangor is provided by an account in the North Wales Chronicle[22] of a public meeting 'of the Ship Owners and Masters and Tradesmen of the City of Bangor held at the Waterloo Tavern on Saturday 12th inst. (January) to take into consideration the propriety of petitioning the Honourable Board of Customs for facilities for entering and clearing Vessels in and out of this Port without the inconvenience and delay of going to Beaumaris'. The petition stated that in the year 1826 500 vessels, British and foreign were loaded, and 530 in 1827. Inconvenience and loss of time were experienced by masters of vessels who were obliged to report inwards and to clear outwards at the Beaumaris Custom House.

The petition pointed out that there were 'frequently five or six Masters of Coal Vessels wishing to discharge at the same time, but as there is but one Coastwaiter at this station whose duty occasionally calls him to Aber, more than five miles to the east of this port and sometimes to the Cadnant, on the other side of the Menai, the merchants and inhabitants are frequently inconvenienced in their supply.'

Among the Committee of thirteen appointed at the meeting there are some names of persons already encountered — Mr. Baxter (Penrhyn Castle), Mr. R. M. Griffith (Tallow chandler), Mr. J. Jones (Shipbuilder), Mr. R. Jones (Blacksmith), Mr. J. Nanney (Master Mariner), Mr. Parry (? John Parry, Master Mariner), Captain Dale (Master of the *Raven*) and Mr. D. Roberts (Ship Broker, the father of Samuel Roberts who appears on the scene a little later). The files of the newspaper over the next two years do not disclose whether or not the petition was succesful.

Unlike its modern counterpart the North Wales Chronicle of the early nineteenth century devoted considerable space to Parliamentary reports, 'foreign intelligence', and political matters (in 1828-29 it contained endless reports of meetings opposing Catholic Emancipation), and local maritime matters are on the whole given scant coverage. Occasionally there is an advertisement for a ship for sale by auction, such as the sale of the *Fanny*, built in Bangor in 1775 — 'For further particulars apply to Mr. Erasmus Griffith' (Beaumaris). She was eventually broken up in 1830, as has been stated previously. Similarly we can trace the sale of the sloop *Peggy* to the Revd. W. J. Lewis in 1828 to an advertisement of the sale by auction at the Point, Beaumaris on 26th May of that year.[23]

Of passing interest there is in 1828 an advertisement of 'that Fast sailing yacht called *King William* now lying in the Port of Carnarvon, lately the

[22] N.W.C. 17.1.1828.
[23] N.W.C. 22.5.1828.

property of Thomas Assheton Smith, Esquire, Lord Lieutenant of the County
of Carnarvon, of the burthen of 28 tons register or thereabouts . . . she has
seldom been surpassed in sailing by any Nobleman's or Gentleman's Yacht
on the River Menai. For further particulars — apply to Capt. William
Griffiths, Bangor'.[24] Built at Cowes in 1798 she was registered at Beaumaris
in 1826 in the sole ownership of Assheton Smith and her Master's name was
given as William Griffith. (Beaumaris 1826/127). In a subsequent registration
(Beaumaris 1829/5) her owner is given as 'William Griffith, Mariner, legatee
by the last will and testament of Thomas Assheton, Esquire', but, as has been
pointed out earlier, the registration date is frequently a year or two behind
the transaction it records.

What happened to the *King William* (which should not be confused with
another vessel of the same name in Thomas Rathbone's ownership) can only
be conjectured. It seems that William Griffith was unsuccesful in tempting a
nobleman or gentleman to buy the yacht which had been left to him; more
certain is the fact, attested by the Register, that he sold 16/64ths to William
Parry, Mariner, Carnarvon in February 1829, and that in February 1831
they both sold the vessel to Robert Thomas, Gentleman, Port Penrhyn and
to John Parry, Ship's Carpenter, Tyddyn Llwydyn, each holding 32/64ths.
It can be surmised that she was altered in John Parry's yard into a commercial vessel since she was sold Richard Owen, Nailer, Robert Thomas
junior, Mariner and William Jones, Mariner, all from the Port of Carnarvon
in 1833, and in her re-registration in 1836 she is shown to have increased
her draught from 5 foot 1 inch to 7.9 feet.

This is a reminder that the Menai Straits besides providing a livelihood
for seamen, fishermen and those in associated occupations offered a play-
ground for the rich and privileged in a uniquely beautiful setting of mountain
and sea. In July 1828 the North Wales Chronicle recorded that 'the cutter
launched from Mr. Jones' yard a few weeks ago was on Tuesday last taken
possession by the owner, Walter Davies Griffith, Esquire of Porthamel, who
steered her through the Straits to Moel y Don with a fine northerly breeze
about two o'clock the same afternoon in fine style and under a press of
canvas. She is likely to prove a good sea boat, and will no doubt afford as
much pleasure to the possessor as she has given satisfaction to the builder.'[25]
According to the Registers *Pausillipo* (Beaumaris 1828/31) remained in
Griffiths' ownership until she was sold to Swansea in 1841 so she must have
pleased him.

Occasionally shares in a vessel were advertised for sale by private contract,
such as the 'fifty two sixty fourth parts of the fast sailing sloop *Jane and Alice*
of the Port of Beaumaris, burthen per Register 45 tons' (Beaumaris 1822/5)

[24] N.W.C. 3.7.1828.
[25] N.W.C. 31.7.1828.

advertised in 1828.[26] *Jane and Alice* was built in Bangor in 1821 by John Jones, who is also one of the persons named in the advertisement as supplying further particulars of the vessel. When the vessel came up for re-registration by the admeasurement of 1836 there had been a complete change of ownership with the exception of 12/64ths held originally by John Bartley, Draper of Beaumaris, and held in 1836 by his executors.

Since the early 1820's steam packets had run between the Menai Straits ports and Liverpool and although they were neither owned nor, still less, built at Bangor, they reflect the growing importance of the port and its close connections with the mercantile and maritime life of Liverpool. By 1828 a regular service had been established with three sailings a week in each direction during the winter months and a daily service, apart from Sunday, during the summer. An advertisement in the North Wales Chronicle[27] states that the steam packet *Satellite* would be sailing from George's Dock, Pier Head Liverpool every Tuesday, Thursday and Saturday, and from Bangor Ferry (i.e. Menai Bridge) every Monday, Wednesday and Friday at 8 o'clock in the morning, but that from April 28th there would be a daily service with the packets *Ormerod* and *Prince Llewellyn* sailing on alternate days. Pigot's Directory for 1828 confirms these sailings and describes Bangor as 'a small episcopal city and seaport, pleasantly situated on the Menai Straits . . . It is one of the most flourishing and improving towns in North Wales. About 35 years ago there were only 93 houses, and within the last 15 years upwards of 800 have been built.'

The Directory notes among the tradesmen of the town two blockmakers from Hirael, two timber merchants from the same quarter, and John Jones, Ship and Boat Builder, Hirael, and the two undifferentiated Richard Morris Griffiths, who between them ran businesses as Grocers, Wholesale Ironmongers, and Linen and Woollen Drapers in Waterloo Place as well as a Tallow Chandlery. Among the Slate Merchants we find the names of Samuel Worthington and Son, Port Penrhyn, and William Baxter, described as Clerk of Works, Penrhyn Castle. (The present Penrhyn Castle, designed by Hopper was in course of construction from 1827 onwards.)

In addition to the Liverpool steam packets mentioned earlier there was another dimension, an American one, to Bangor shipping. A letter from a sailor on board the *Marquis of Anglesey* written from Port Penrhyn in 1822 records that their intended destination was in the United States — 'hefo slates i Washington yfory neu drennydd os bydd y tywydd fel ag y mae e yn awr, os yr Arglwydd a'i myn.' (*'with slates for Washington tomorrow or the day after if the weather remains as it is and the Lord so wills it.'*)[28]

[26] N.W.C. 28.8.1828.
[27] N.W.C. 27.3.28.
[28] See article by the late Frank Rhys Jones in *Maritime Wales/Cymru a'r Môr*, No. 10, (1986) pp. 121-130.

Although, strictly speaking, this is irrelevant to the main theme of this book since the vessel concerned was neither built at nor owned in Bangor, the general background to seaborne commerce in Gwynedd at this time cannot be totally ignored. *The North Wales Chronicle* in 1828 included the following item under the title 'The Slate Trade.'[29]

> "A fine American brig called the *Ventrosa* of Boston, commanded by Captain Abbot, is now lying in the Straits and loading with all expedition with the expectation of arriving at her destination before the provisions of the new American tariff come into operation. She is the first vessel we have had this summer for the United States, *though the Straits were formerly crowded with them from April to September,* (author's italics) and by the account she brings we learn that the slate trade in America is fast reviving and that we may shortly expect to witness the gratifying sight we have heretofore been accustomed to behold with such pleasure."

From as early as the end of the eighteenth century Gwynedd's slate trade with North America had been steadily increasing and this had included shipments from Port Penrhyn.[30]

In the following year *The North Wales Chronicle* briefly announced the sailing of the brig *Fame* Captain Barrow 'with a fair wind for America', and a later issue contained an advertisement —

> "To sail in about ten days for New York
> The Fine American Brig *Rising States,* Silvanus Snow, Master
> For passage (having good accommodations) apply to the Captain on board:
> or to Samuel Worthington and Sons, Port Penrhyn."[31]

We know that she never arrived at her destination. A report by Lloyd's Agent at Holyhead for 23rd May, 1829 states that "the *Rising States,* Snow, from Bangor to New York, drove upon the Platters Rocks, near the Skerries, yesterday afternoon, filled and went down; her sails and some stores have been taken to the Skerries." Nothing is said about the safety of the crew and passengers (if any there were) but under the circumstances of her striking, if the sails and some stores could be recovered, it is unlikely that the crew were imperilled. A later report in August stated that the hull of the vessel had been floated off and towed to Church Bay.

The part played by Port Penrhyn in Welsh emigration to America in the nineteenth century remains to be investigated.

The twenties also saw the firm establishment of the shipbuilding industry in Bangor. It was mentioned earlier that thirteen or fourteen ships were built between 1808 and 1831, thirteen according to the Beaumaris Register, fourteen according to David Thomas,[32] though he prints the fourteenth's name, *Margaret,* in italics to indicate that local registers are not the source.

[29] N.W.C. 24.7.1828.
[30] Lindsay op.cit., pp. 98-102.
[31] N.W.C. 23.4.1829 and 7.5.1829.
[32] D.T. op.cit. p. 197.

The explanation for this discrepancy lies in an advertisement in the North Wales Chronicle in 1828[33] which is worth reproducing in full for the light it throws on the materials and methods of construction of small sailing vessels of this period.

'Also (on sale) the whole or 2/3rds part of a round sterned vessel now on the stocks of the following dimensions, Length on decks 70 feet, ditto of keel 63 feet, breadth 19 feet, depth of hold 10 feet 6 inches, will register about 130 and expected to carry 160t. at light draught of water. This vessel will be ready to launch in June next and will be in every respect substantially and faithfully built; all her timbers are of well seasoned English and African oak, the planks of English oak, excepting the bottom and bend of amidships, the former of elm and the latter of Quebec oak. The shares will be sold with all materials found ready for sea or the hull alone, as may best suit the purchaser. Any person in want of a vessel of her description may now have an opportunity of examining her timbers before the ceilings are laid, on application to the Harris Yard, Hirael, Bangor.

James Harris, Beaumaris 7 April.'

In another advertisement for the sale of a ship James Harris is described as Lloyd's agent for Beaumaris.

Attempts to sell the ship were clearly unsuccessful. She stood on the stocks for almost another year as an advertisement in June of the following year makes clear.[34] 'A New Schooner launched in April last and now lying in the Port of Bangor'. The advertisement goes on to specify her dimensions and materials which are the same as those mentioned in the earlier advertisement and remarks —

'She is a very handsome model and expected to carry one-third more than the register tonnage, and having been built for and under the particular inspection of the present owners and no expenses spared to make her in every respect a strong substantial vessel, she is well worth the attention of those concerned with shipping of her description. etc'

The notice concludes that if the vessel is not disposed of by private contract in the meantime, she will be sold by public auction in the first or second week of July. It is signed 'Messrs. Harris and Co., Wine Merchants, Bangor.'

The auction was arranged for the '15th of July between 4 and 6 o'clock in the evening at the sign of the *Royal Oak*, High Street, Bangor'.[35] Whether it took place, or whether a satisfactory offer was received for the vessel, we do not know for she drops out of the written record until, twenty two years later, she reappears in North Wales, in the Registers of the Port of Caernarfon.[36]

[33] N.W.C. 17.4.1828.
[34] N.W.C. 11.6.1829.
[35] N.W.C. 9.7.1829.
[36] Caernarfon Registry 1850/6 and 1866/10.

There are several points of interest here; firstly, that David Thomas gives her builder as John Jones, a well-known Bangor shipbuilder of the twenties, but there is no mention of him in the advertisement. Secondly, that James Harris and Harris and Co. Wine Merchants seem to disappear from the face of the earth after this episode. It was remarked earlier that from 1824 until 1855, when the Registers gave the name of the builder, the person named was not necessarily the shipwright who was actually responsible for the construction of the vessel but the man who had arranged the finance. The location of the yards — or more properly, the sites because a ship could be built almost anywhere, on a river bank, on the foreshore, in a field where it would be launched with the aid of a team of horses — is not known with any degree of certainty as far as Bangor is concerned: the question will be examined in a later chapter but it is a fair inference that *Margaret* was the work of John Jones, Shipwright, possibly his last ship, that James Harris was financially interested, and that the Harris Yard which had an apparently evanescent existence was in fact John Jones's Yard in the short transitional period before it became John Parry's Yard.

Another point of interest is the relationship between a vessel's registered tonnage and the weight of cargo she could carry. There were several variations in the formulae used to determine a vessel's tonnage during the course of the last century; for instance the *Bangor Packet* built in 1830 was registered when she was built at 39 tons, as 30 tons when she was admeasured in 1836 and by 1867 as a mere 27 tons. The brig *Nancy,* advertised in the same advertisement in 1828 as the vessel that subsequently became the *Margaret,* is described as of register tonnage 57 tons 'and will carry 80 tons of slates'. Allowing for some exaggeration on the part of the vendor, this matches the statement made by the vendors of the *Margaret* that she is 'expected to carry one-third more than the register tonnage', which was given as about 130t. As the successive formulae tended to decrease a sailing vessel's register tonnage the amount she could carry would naturally increase as a proportion of her tonnage.

When the *Margaret* was re-registered at Caernarfon in 1850 (Carnarvon 1850/6) her tonnage was given as 90 which makes the 1828 estimate of 130 pretty near the mark. Her dimensions, too, approximate very closely with those in the advertisement (65'.2 x 17'.5 x 10'). Little is known about her history between her launch in 1829 and her re-appearance in North Wales except that she was re-registered in 1846 at Cardiff and received her Official Number (13882) at Southampton.

She remained in Portmadoc ownership until 1876, having been enlarged and altered at that port in 1866 and subsequently re-registered. She was sold to three Caernarfon men, a blockmaker and two slate loaders, in 1876. Her end came in 1885 when she was run into and sunk off Great Orme's Head, the certificate being lost with the vessel.

This digression has taken us fifty years or more beyond the intended scope of this chapter and its theme, the foundation laid down in the first third of the nineteenth century for the maritime and mercantile expansion of Bangor. It has often been mistakenly assumed that this began with the coming of the railway in 1848 but in fact it was communication by sea, at first with Chester and Liverpool and later more widely, that was the precipitating factor.

R. Merfyn Jones in *The North Wales Quarrymen* has stated in his introductory remarks that "today Gwynedd is considered a 'peripheral' region within Britain, but the remoteness of the area in the nineteenth century can too easily be exaggerated and thus the history of its people too conveniently interpreted as an example of 'backwardness'.."[37] He goes on to mention the dramatic economic changes in Lancashire and the part played by Richard Pennant and other Englishmen in providing capital for the development of the slate industry. The fact that the Pennants were also great landowners, besides being the masters of what was virtually the only great industrial enterprise in the district, accounted for the fact that there was no fully formed middle class. "The reason for the failure of a business, manufacturing middle class to emerge in Gwynedd is obvious; there was no real opportunity for it to do so." Nevertheless, in the shadow of the great Penrhyn enterprise, in the emergence of men like Robert Thomas, Lewis Hughes, Richard Morris Griffith and John Parry there are signs that an indigenous middle class of merchants, shipbuilders and shipowners was beginning to form.

[37] R. Merfyn Jones, op.cit University of Wales Press, 1982 pp. 1-6.

CHAPTER III

Mid-Century Expansion and Enterprise

The rapid growth of industrial towns in the Midlands and North of England and the vast expansion of London in the middle years of the nineteenth century were directly reflected in the growth of the North Wales slate quarrying industry. Roofs had to be provided for the hundreds of thousands of dwellings that had to be built to accommodate the ever expanding numbers of industrial workers, and also for the new civic buildings which pride demanded should adorn the new town centres.

There was also a corresponding expansion in the foreign trade, both to Europe and North America. The disastrous Hamburg fire in 1842 which had laid waste large areas of that city was a stimulus for the export trade, and for the remainder of the century Hamburg was the main *entrepôt* for Gwynedd slate destined for the continent. The trade between Port Penrhyn and New York and Boston began as early as the twenties, as has already been mentioned, and was sustained until well into the sixties.

Despite the competition from the railways — the Port Penrhyn branch line was opened in 1852 and the line to the Port Dinorwic dock in the same year, followed shortly by the line to Caernarfon — it was not until the late eighties that the total production sent by rail overtook the total sent by sea from Port Penrhyn. Porthmadog suffered less in this respect because the

Cambrian Railways line did not reach that port until 1867, and this partially accounts for the continued maritime prosperity of Porthmadog after the decline of Bangor, Port Dinorwic and Caernarfon as slate ports. The other reason for Porthmadog's survival was that she had developed her export trade to the continent far more than her rivals.

This brings us back to shipping. The ships of Bangor can be divided roughly into three categories, based on the range of their trading.

(i) The short range coasters traded mainly with the Mersey and Dee ports, sometimes with ports on the east coast of Ireland, the Isle of Man and Cumbria. They rarely left the Irish Sea. Most of the short range coasters were rigged as sloops, smacks or flats, and they averaged about 50 tons.

(ii) The medium range vessels traded in their time with practically every port in Great Britain and Ireland, but there are some curious gaps, particularly on the east coast of England where there does not seem to have been much trade for Bangor ships between Ipswich and Newcastle on Tyne. Both to the north, Aberdeen, Frazerburgh, Alnmouth etc. and to the south, London, Maldon etc., appear as frequent destinations, but Hull, one of the most important east coast ports, is scarcely mentioned in the returns. A possible explanation is that the industrial north of England even as far as the east coast was supplied through the river and canal system, whose port of entry as far as Bangor was concerned was Runcorn. Medium range traders made occasional voyages to the nearer continental ports, Dieppe, Antwerp or Hamburg. They were almost without exception schooners of between 70 and 80 tons.

(iii) The long range traders in the earlier part of the century were mainly brigs or snows; subsequently a number of brigantines were built and the earlier vessels were often re-rigged as brigantines. As the century advanced the schooner rig increased in popularity even for the long range traders. They were employed on the North Atlantic, the Baltic and occasionally the Mediterranean route as well as on the shorter journeys to the nearer continental ports, and when not required for this trade, they frequented almost all the ports of Great Britain and Ireland. Nevertheless it has to be admitted that Bangor's share of the export trade in slate is insignificant when compared with Porthmadog's and Bangor never seems to have been able to put together a package comparable with Porthmadog's famous triangular pattern of trade involving the continent of Europe, the Mediterranean and Newfoundland.

Meanwhile, what of Bangor and its people?

The population of Bangor began to level out at 9,564 in 1851 after increasing by almost 5,000 in twenty years. (1831 — 4,751, 1841 — 7,232).

The following twenty years saw a modest increase to 10,825. The Chester and Holyhead Railway had reached as far as Bangor by 1848 but old patterns of communication die hard. Throughout the fifties and sixties, as in the thirties and forties, there was a daily packet service between Liverpool and the Menai Straits during the summer months and a twice weekly one in winter. The following advertisement in a local paper as late as 1869 shows clearly that the service was not merely intended for tourists and holiday makers, but had a serious commercial intent[1]

"CITY OF DUBLIN STEAM PACKET COMPANY

Winter sailings between Carnarvon, Menai Bridge, Bangor, Beaumaris and Liverpool calling at Llandudno (weather permitting).

The 'Prince Arthur' (or other of the Company's steamers) is intended to leave Menai Bridge on Mondays and Fridays during the winter months and from Liverpool Wednesdays and Saturdays.

Goods for Carnarvon and the above places to be sent to the Clarence Dock on Tuesdays for the Wednesday sailings etc."

The City of Dublin Steam Packet Company at this time held the Royal Mail contract for the Holyhead — Kingstown service and the *Prince Arthur,* a paddle steamer of 427 tons, had been employed in that service from 1851 until 1860.

Slater's Trade Directory of 1850 after describing the city and its environs says that "the entrance to the port is perfectly accessible and presents a safe harbour of refuge, and vessels of fifteen hundred tons burden can enter without difficulty. A patent slip has been constructed at the yard of Messrs. Ellis, Jones and Co., Garth Point." Four Ship and Boat Builders were named, Ellis, Jones and Co., at Garth Point, John Parry at Hirael (he was also named as Surveyor of Shipping for Lloyds), John Roberts at Hirael and Rice Jones, a little further away at Port Dinorwic, which did not yet qualify for its own entry. Among slate merchants other than the Penrhyn Quarry we find that the Royal Bangor Slate Co., had a quay in Hirael and the Pant Dreiniog Slate Quarry Co., operated from a quay at Garth Point. This is a reminder that Penrhyn had competitors in the Ogwen Valley. A later edition of Slater's Directory gives the Royal Bangor Slate Company's quarry as 'Bryn Havad', otherwise Bryn Hafod y Wern at Llanllechid. The Pant Dreiniog Quarry was situated in Bethesda itself on the opposite side of the valley to the Penrhyn Quarry. As these quarries had to cart their production to the small quays at Hirael and Garth or to the railway station at Bangor, they existed only precariously.

There were two slate works at Garth Point; one of them was situated according to an 1854 map, in the form of a large wallchart, of the Bangor

[1] N.W.C. 5.1.1869.

Board of Health District[2] on the land now (1987) occupied by the engineers who are rebuilding Bangor Pier, the other on the shore near the Old Baths. From a newspaper account of 1863[3] the latter appears to have been the Pant Dreiniog Quay; recording a very violent storm in which the tide rose to an 'enormous height' flooding many houses in Hirael and covering the quay at Port Penrhyn to the depth of a foot, it goes on to say that the storm 'swept away a portion of the Baths pier at Garth belonging to the Pant Dreiniog Slate Company.'

The map shows two more slate yards on what is now Beach Road, several timber yards, a foundry and two shipbuilding yards, those of Edward Ellis at Garth and John Parry at the other end of the bay at Hirael. John Roberts and the other shipbuilders mentioned later must have built somewhere in the arc of the bay between these points but precisely where is not known. There have been considerable alterations in the shore line since the start of the nineteenth century and by progressive dumping, most of it in the present century, a substantial area of playing field and parking ground has been gained from the sea. An advertisement in the local paper in 1856[4] reads —

"By order of Mr. Nicholas Treweek, HIRAEL, BANGOR
Leasehold Warehouse, Yards and Dwelling Houses

All those capacious Yards, Warehouses and Premises, together with Nine commodious messuages or dwelling houses situated in Foundry Street and Water Street.

The Yards and Warehouse, *lying as they do, adjacent to the water's edge,* (author's italics) are well adapted for the Timber, Coal or Corn Trade. Further particulars etc./etc/"

This frontage is today about 100 yards from the water's edge.

Not only has there been a change in the shoreline but the existence of Port Penrhyn has also influenced the tidal flow so that over a period of nearly two hundred years this has resulted in progressive silting of Hirael Bay. The bay provided refuge and safe moorings while they awaited their turn for loading for scores of vessels, some of considerable size. According to Mr. W. R. Thomas of Garth (or Bo'sun as he is popularly known), whose grandfather was the master and owner from 1896 onwards of the 55 ton flat *Hector* (Beaumaris 1863/4), it was the custom on New Year's Day for every vessel in Port Penrhyn or Hirael to detail one crew member for the joint task of setting the 'Dead Men', posts at which vessels could moor fore and aft, both in Hirael Bay and round Garth Point, at the Old Baths. These 'Dead Men' are referred to in the 'Rules and Regulations for Vessels to be observed by Masters of Vessels intending to load at Port Penrhyn' (see page 132)

[2] C.R.O. XM/MAPS/2754.
[3] N.W.C. 24.1.1863.
[4] N.W.C. 6.9.1856.

and Appendix II) where Rule 6 states that "all vessels intending to load must be moored to West of the Buoys or Dead-man's Bank." Another interesting fact from the same source is that the small Look Out on Siliwen Road, much used by master mariners when they were anxiously looking out towards Beaumaris and the bay beyond for any sign of a breeze, was called 'Cangen y Cigfran', *Anglice* the 'Crow's Nest', literally 'Crow's Branch'.

Hirael in mid-nineteenth century was the focus not only of shipping and the industries associated with it, but of a burgeoning population explosion in its narrow streets, crammed between the High Street (Castle Bank) and the walls of the Friars Estate. The walls extended part of the way across the sea front so that until well into the nineteenth century there was no direct road connection between Hirael and Garth but a footpath only across the waste ground above the beach. The butt end of the wall can still be seen in Beach Road between the early nineteenth century pair of cottages and the obviously Edwardian villas on the north side, and it runs for some distance behind Water Street in the direction of St. Mary's churchyard. It, or parts of it, may well be the oldest structure in Bangor, apart from the cathedral since the Dominican friary dates from the late thirteenth century. Until the estate was sold in 1899 to a syndicate of developers it distorted the Bangor townscape and all but separated Hirael from Garth.

Such was the physical background in mid-century; it was also the period of expansion not only in the slate trade, but also of Bangor shipbuilding and its associated trades, and in ship-owning, as the chapters which follow will show. There was also expansion in financial businesses — locally based banks were beginning to give way to the great London institutions (as the business history of Richard Morris Griffith junior will show), the local insurance 'club' the Bangor Mutual Ship Insurance Society was established in 1853 and grew rapidly during the fifties and sixties, and two building societies were set up in Bangor during the sixties — the *City of Bangor Permanent Building Society* in 1863 and the *Bangor and Arfon Permanent Building Society* in 1867. There was a growing interest in, one might almost say a demand for more local government, exemplified in the establishment of the Bangor Board of Health in 1850 and culminating in 1883 with the granting of municipal borough status.

Along with this commercial expansion there is also a corresponding proliferation as the century progresses in the documentary sources available, and the narrative become more complex. Hitherto the main source of information has been the shipping registers, fleshed out from time to time by newspaper reports. For the period under review we also have at the Caernarfon and Llangefni Record Offices of the Gwynedd Archives Service a selection of Crew Agreement Lists commencing in 1863 and extending in some instances well into the present century. These are a valuable record of the manning of the ships and their voyages. Unfortunately perhaps for our purpose the masters of vessels were not obliged to give details of the freight they carried but they occasionally did so. Among the Penrhyn Quarry Papers at the Caernarfon Record Office there are the daily loading accounts showing in precise detail the amounts of slate — duchesses, countesses, doubles, slabs, etc. — loaded on board ship or despatched by rail, and they give some idea of the destinations and purchasers, either a Penrhyn agent or a direct customer, of each shipment. In addition to this kind of material, some of the Rule Books and some of the Annual Reports of the Bangor Mutual Ship Insurance Society have survived. They have been deposited variously at the Caernarfon Record Office or in the Library of the University College of North Wales at Bangor. And, as we approach the period covered by human memory there is more anecdotal evidence.

For these reasons, at the cost of some artificiality, it has been thought desirable to treat the shipbuilders separately from the shipowners even though most of the builders to a greater or lesser extent had an interest in the ships they built and in ships built elsewhere. Some of the shipbuilders were owners on a considerable scale, and where the functions overlap they have been treated in the chapters which follow in both functions. The reader must suffer indulgently any trespass from one category to another.

Each shipbuilding yard has been treated separately in the narrative at some cost to the chronological sequence, but this is rectified, at least partially, in the last chapter on the builders which contains a summary of the vessels built between 1831 and 1879 in the order in which they were built.

In the chapter on the shipowners, there has been inevitably a rigorous process of selection and only the more prominent owners have been dealt with in any detail. In addition to the sixty odd ships built at Bangor, there are well over two hundred registrations of ships built elsewhere in the hundred years from 1786 which have at least one Bangor shareholder. There are many Bangor names which occur once only in the registers, sometimes in registrations where all the shareholders came from elsewhere, and their connection with shipping must always remain a mystery. Others held their shares for so short a time as to be of insignificant importance.

The activities of the Bangor Mutual Ship Insurance Society form the basis of another chapter before we come to the inevitable account of the last days of Bangor sailing ships.

CHAPTER IV

THE BUILDERS i

John Parry

John Wood's Town Map of Bangor, published in 1834, shows the location of 'Mr. Parry's Ship Building Yard' to have been on Hirael beach at the bottom of what is now called Strand Street. There are extensive buildings shown on the map and what appears to be a slipway. Today nothing remains of the old site, since the area was radically altered in the thirties by the demolition of the Penrhyn Arms hotel and the construction of a new road from the entrance to Port Penrhyn to Beach Road through the site of the old hotel and its grounds.

It was postulated earlier that the yard belonged originally to John Jones who was responsible for the building of *Eliza Goddard* (Beaumaris 1824/53), *Louisa* (Beaumaris 1826/118), *Abel* (Beaumaris 1827/38), *Penmon* (Beaumaris 1828/1), *Pausillipo* (Beaumaris 1828/31) and possibly *Margaret* in 1829. Thereafter John Jones's name disappears and John Parry comes in. The reasoning behind this supposition is that the same group of supporting shareholders, whose names were associated respectively with Robert Thomas and the Wyatt family, continued to support John Parry's yard. John Jones had certainly died before 1836 since the re-registration of *Abel* in that year states that his share was held by trustees.

In the thirties the yard built five ships; the diversity of the shareholders in *Bangor Packet* (Beaumaris 1830/13) was mentioned earlier. The Liverpool

63

shareholders maintained their interest in her to the late sixties but she was mainly in the hands of Bangor men until her de-registration in 1887, when she became a coal hulk. In her sailing days she was mainly employed between Port Penrhyn and Liverpool or the Dee ports.

The next vessel built by John Parry was *Anne and Catherine* (Beaumaris 1832/17), a schooner of 84 tons. James Wyatt, the Penrhyn agent, held 44/64ths, William Baxter, the clerk of works at Penrhyn Castle, 8/64ths, Henry Benjamin Wyatt of Ryde in the Isle of Wight 8/64ths and her builder 4/64ths. She passed out of Wyatt ownership in the sixties and came into Nefyn hands. Her crew lists for the period from 1863 until her loss in 1881 are to be found at the Llangefni Record Office of the Gwynedd Archives Service.[1]

Her normal crew consisted of master, mate, two Able Seamen and a boy and from 1863 until 1873 she sailed regularly from Port Penrhyn though occasional voyages started at Llanaelhaiarn (variously spelt). Today Llanael-haiarn is the name given to a village with no apparent connections with the sea; the place she sailed from is more familiar to us today as Trefor, the quarry village nestling at the foot of Yr Eifl, where there was a jetty for loading granite. The quarry is now closed. The crew lists show during the course of the ten years that she visited ports in all parts of the United Kingdom as it then was — Cork, Dublin, Belfast and Galway in Ireland; Ayr and Leith in Scotland; inevitably Runcorn; Bristol, Cardiff and Briton Ferry among the Bristol Channel ports; London, Newhaven, Shoreham, Plymouth, Southampton and Portsmouth, and forays to the north-east which included the ports of Sunderland, Newcastle and Alnmouth.

One of the rare instances when the Master included details of his cargo occurs in the return for the first half of 1869. *Ann and Catherine* found herself in Garston on January 1st. The sailings for the next six months are as follows: —

Jan. 11	Garston to Holyhead	Coals	arr. Jan. 29
Feb. 11	Holyhead to Bangor	Ballast	arr. Feb. 12
April 10	Bangor to Alnmouth	Slate	arr. April 17
May 5	Alnmouth to Newcastle	Light	arr. May 5
May 17	Newcastle to St. Ives	Coals	arr. May 26
June 5	St. Ives to Llanelly	Ballast	arr. June 7
June 17	Llanelly to Dundalk	Coals	arr. June 28

This account shows clearly that besides their primary function of conveying slate from Port Penrhyn the little ships of Bangor played their part in the general maritime commerce of Great Britain.

In 1873 *Ann and Catherine* moved to Caernarfon ownership and ceased calling at Port Penrhyn for cargoes, loading instead at Caernarfon or

[1] Llangefni Record Office (L.R.O. henceforward) W/DB/40.

occasionally Port Dinorwic. The return for her last voyage in 1881 states — "Sailed from Carnarvon October 4th 1881 for Paisley, put in Beaumaris windbound same day. December 10 vessel sprang a leak and sank off Point Lynas. 11 December 5.30 a.m.. Crew saved and landed at Moelfre." The ship was in her forty-ninth year.

We have wandered some way both in time and space from Hirael and John Parry's yard in the thirties, and this will inevitably happen again if this book is to be more than a bald account of building, shareholding and ultimate disposal. *Ann and Susan* (Beaumaris 1835/3) was a 60 ton sloop with local men as shareholders. John Parry held a half-share (32/64ths), and the other shareholders were his father-in-law, Robert Thomas, Griffith Williams, mariner, and two Bangor inn-keepers, David Davies and Thomas Davies. It is a pity that Welshmen of this period had very few surnames and Christian names to share between them; Griffith Williams, mariner, may be the Griffith Williams, 45 Well Street, Bangor who was the master of *Penguin*, (one of the Wyatt vessels) from at least January 1863, when crew lists become available, until 1878 when he was aged 72. *Penguin* traded regularly, often making ten or a dozen round trips in each half year between Port Penrhyn and either Garston or Runcorn, so that the old man must have known the route like the back of his hand.[2]

Ann and Susan, named after John Parry's daughters, remained substantially in the same hands or in the case of Robert Thomas and John Parry, who each died between 1854 and 1855, in the hands of the 'firm' that succeeded them, until the vessel was lost off Amlwch in December 1865.

Harriet (Beaumaris 1837/33), a 26 ton smack, was built by John Parry for James Wyatt (32/64ths) and William Baxter (16/64ths), with the builder retaining 8/64ths, the other 8/64ths belonging to Catherine Ainsworth, widow of Bangor. On the death of William Baxter in 1844 his shareholding was bought by James Wyatt, bringing his own holding up to 48/64ths. The vessel was wrecked and subsequently broken up in 1853, before the days of the crew lists and we have to be satisfied with the bare account provided by the Shipping Register.

"On Monday forenoon the sight-loving population were gratified by the launch of an elegant schooner from the building yard of Mr. John Parry, Bangor," reports the *Carnarvon and Denbigh Herald* of 20th April, 1838. "At the appointed hour, eleven o'clock, the word was given and the *Anne* glided from the stocks into the waters of the bay with all possible *éclat* amidst the cheering spectators. The *Anne* is destined for the coasting trade and is a handsome looking craft of 140 tons burthen, of an improved construction having a round stern with the rudder's head on the inside, and is owned by Bangor tradesmen. The well wishers, workmen etc. to the number of 50 or 60 were entertained at the Waterloo Tavern in the forenoon".

[2] L.R.O. W/DB/309.

By contrast with the mainly Wyatt owned *Anne and Catherine* and the *Harriet,* the ownership of *Anne* presents a fair cross section of 'Bangor tradesmen' with a sprinkling of Liverpool maritime trades. The registry entry for *Anne* (Beaumaris 1839/22) records the following as shareholders —

John Roberts, Bangor, Mariner	4	
John Parry, Bangor, Shipbuilder	8	
Hugh Roberts, Bangor, Draper	4	(Subscribing Owners)
Rowland Parry, Corn Merchant	4	(Other owners)
John Davies, Victualler	4	
Richard Morris Griffith, Draper	4	
George Simpson, Gentleman	4	
John Pritchard, Corn Dealer	4	
Charles James, Gentleman	4	
Evan Evans, Victualler	4	all of Bangor
Robert Thomas, Port Penrhyn, Farmer	4	
Cornelius Roberts, Llandegai, Farmer	4	
John Bignall, Penrhyn Castle, Gentleman	4	
Hugh Pritchard, Liverpool, Baker	4	
John Price, Ropemaker and Alexander Smith, Ropemaker, Liverpool, co-partners	4	

John Parry by various bills of sale in 1841 and 1843 acquired a further 8/64ths which he held until the vessel was lost in 1853. His father-in-law, Robert Thomas was, almost inevitably at this period, among the shareholders and the name of Richard Morris Griffith, the future banker, will have been noted.

In the absence of any pictorial representations of early Bangor vessels the comments on the 'improved construction' of *Anne,* brief as they are, provide certain clues. They suggest that both the round stern and the internal rudder head were innovations as far as Bangor shipbuilders were concerned, and that previously the fashion had been for square transom sterns with rudder hung externally. The register entry gives *Anne* the following dimensions — 62'8" x 17'8" x 10'2" and her register tonnage was 88 tons, so that the newspaper's estimate of her carrying capacity as 140 tons erred only slightly on the optimistic side. Dr. Basil Greenhill has commented that by the end of the thirties of the nineteenth century the schooner rig was becoming established as the most popular rig for non-ocean going vessels from ports on the western side of Britain; Bangor shipbuilders were not slow in adopting the schooner rig for *Margaret* (1829), *Anne and Catherine* (1832), *Anne* (1839) and *Maria and Elizabeth* (1839 by Edward Ellis) before the end of the decade. Fore and aft sails were found to be more efficient when beating to windward than square sails and this was especially important on the west coast where the winds generally prevailing made it a particularly unattractive lee shore. The rig was also handier than the square rig in getting into or out of small harbours or tortuous channels or creeks, and there are many of these on the coasts of Gwynedd. The square rig came into its own on long runs off the wind on ocean passages, but even in these conditions it was less economical than the fore and aft rig which required less man power to handle it. The schooner rig, in the form of the three masted topsail schooners of Porthmadog — the so-called Western Ocean Yachts — reached its ultimate perfection in the closing years of the nineteenth century and the first decade of the twentieth.

The next vessel built by John Parry was the 49 ton smack, *Mary Grace*, first registered in 1841 (Beaumaris 1841/6). Tradesmen, mainly from Bangor, formed her original shareholders, among them Richard Morris Griffith, Draper, William Parry, Brazier and Thomas Davies, Painter, names which would recur with some regularity in future entries in the register; another name of interest, John Davies, Merchant, Menai Bridge shows the modest beginnings, with investment in local coastal shipping, of what was later to become the great Davies Brothers firm of shipowners of Menai Bridge which made the partners very rich men by the end of the century. John Davies owned a 16/64th share in *Eliza and Catherine* (b. Bangor by Edward Ellis in 1837) in which Richard Morris Griffith also had a 4/64ths share, in *Mona* (a 37 ton smack built by Edward Ellis, also in 1837), and 8/64ths in the Beaumaris built *Lady Bulkeley,* a 44 ton smack of 1837. John Parry held a 4/64ths share in her; as a shipowner he spread his investments widely between Caernarfon, Nefyn and Pwllheli ships, and it was good for business. Wooden sailing vessels were in constant need of repair and his yard in Bangor was at a convenient place for vessels calling for slate at Port Penrhyn.

To go back to *Mary Grace;* in 1856, after the death of John Davies his shares were inherited by his brother Robert who sold them to Richard Morris Griffiths, now described as a banker. In the same year *Mary Grace* was lengthened to 70 feet in John Parry's yard (owned since John Parry's death the previous year by his son, T. T. Parry and his partners) and became a 65 ton schooner. The vessel remained in Bangor hands to her very end, widows and other legatees inheriting shares from the original owners. The one surviving Crew Agreement List, for the second half of 1874,[3] gives T. T. Parry, Shipbuilder, Bangor as the Managing Owner and Robert Jones, Mount Street, Bangor as Master. It states that after leaving Bangor on August 20th she was run into on the 24th off Holy Island in the Clyde by the steamer *Glengarrock* and sunk. Of the crew of four, the master, mate and cook were saved but the young O.S. from Bangor, Edward Evans, was drowned.

Two years after the completion of *Mary Grace* a vessel of a very different kind emerged from John Parry's yard. She was the 118t. brig *Three Susans* (Beaumaris 1843/9), clearly intended as a long range trader of the type of

---

[3] L.R.O. W/DB/277.

Abel, the 113t. snow brig of 1827 or the earlier *Penrhyn Castle,* another snow of 1808, a reversion to the old tradition of brigs for longer voyages. However, she was re-registered at Beaumaris in 1848, her description being altered, as a brigantine, i.e. with square sails on the mainmast and fore and aft sails on the mizzen. (*Abel* was to be similarly rerigged by 1854).

Three Susans was exceptional for her period (it became more common towards the end of the century) in being owned by one man, her builder John Parry, and after his death jointly by his two sons. Thomas Thomas Parry and Robert Thomas Parry.

Her crew agreement lists for the ten months January to October 1863 at the Llangefni Record Office[4] are interesting for the light they cast on the qualifications of masters of vessels. Prior to the passing of the Merchant Shipping Acts of 1850 and 1854 there were no formal qualifications for master — experience and adequate seatime, the ability to command the confidence of owners and members of the crew together with in some cases the passing of the sometimes very searching questioning of the local Club, in other words, the Mutual Ship Insurance Society, were the nineteenth century equivalent to today's 'ticket'. For a period after the introduction of the Acts they applied only to foreign going ships; vessels in the home trade continued to be commanded by 'uncertificated' masters.

The Crew agreement lists for *Three Susans* nicely illustrate this; the list for the first half year ending June 30th 1863 shows that her master, John Pritchard, aged 30, of Nevin was not in possession of a certificate. With a crew consisting of mate, 3 A.B.'s and 1 O.S. she sailed from Bangor to London, thence to Maryport, thence to London again, thence to Newcastle before returning to Bangor via Cork, a voyage which shows yet again that Bangor ships were not merely slate carriers but played a part in the general mercantile trade of Great Britain.

The agreement for the second half is a different form — 'Agreement and Account of Crew — Foreign Going Vessel'. The master on this voyage is Ebenezer Roberts, aged 57, also of Nevin, Certificate Number 52384. The former master, John Pritchard, signs on as Boatswain, and the remainder of the complement is made up of two A.B.'s, one O.S. and one Boy. The destined voyage is 'to Gothenberg from thence to final port of discharge in the United Kingdom'. The voyage was duly performed and the list shows that the crew were discharged at Plymouth on November 2nd but that the master remained with the ship.

An entry on the register merely records 'Registry cancelled. Vessel lost in Porthdinllaen, 3rd December 1863. (Letter from R. & T. Parry, Executors late John Parry)'.

In the absence of a crew agreement list for the remainder of the year it is difficult to be precise about the circumstances of her end; the probability

[4] L.R.O. W/DB/383.

is that she was returning in ballast to Bangor when she put in to Porthdinllaen. A little light is thrown by a report in the *North Wales Chronicle* of Saturday, December 5th, 1863 which says that a 'gale of fearful severity seems to have swept over the entire country on Thursday last'. Elsewhere in the paper it says that Holyhead was struck by a N.W. wind — a hurricane. A more detailed report from Porthdinllaen states ". . . eight vessels were stranded in the course of Thursday, and one or two of them, it is apprehended, will become wrecks . . . Although most of the stranded vessels were so near the shore, the roar of the sea and wind made it impossible for the crews to hear those on the shore, and consequently they communicated with each other by writing on a board. Mr. Palmer, Assistant Lloyd's Agent and Mr. Hicks, the diver with his assistant, Mr. Shillito, were actively engaged. We understand that three of the vessels were immediately placed in Mr. Palmer's hands. The following are the vessels: — *Helen,* Carnarvon, on shore; *Bardsey,* ditto, a wreck, one man lost; *Nelson,* ditto, on shore; *Elizabeth & Margaret,* Pwllheli, on shore; *Three Susans* of Bangor, *Rebecca* of Shoreham, *Hephzibah,* Carnarvon and another vessel name unknown."

(A passing comment; in the long drawn out controversy between Holyhead and Porthdinllaen it was claimed that Porthdinllaen was superior as a harbour of refuge, not only for its better holding ground but also for its sloping shore on which waves were spent and for its sandy beach, off which it would be easier to float a grounded vessel than off a rocky shore). *Three Susans,* it will have been noted, is not recorded as having been beached and she may well have foundered.

A further report in the following week's issue of the *Chronicle* mentions that no lifeboat existed at Porthdinllaen, there was no life saving apparatus, only a small cranky boat "but it is impossible to pass without a special mention of the Revd. O. Ll. Williams, Bodfean, whose humane exertions in securing shipwrecked persons are already well known . . . He encouraged the men by words and his courageous example, and was at all times acknowledged as a leader whose knowledge and skill they could trust."

Owen Lloyd Williams was, of course, the son of the Revd. James Williams, Rector of Llanfair-yng-Nghornwy, and his wife Frances who between them pioneered the organization of the lifeboat service in Anglesey prior to the establishment of the national institution, as Aled Eames has written in *Ships and Seamen of Anglesey* (pp. 324 ff.). The son followed in his parents' footsteps; whether the old story that both father and son always had a lifejacket handy in the pulpit and would hastily bring the service to a close if the lifeboat maroon was heard is factually true or not, it certainly embodies a symbolic truth. In the ensuing weeks there was, according to the local press, much agitation for the establishment of a lifeboat station at Porthdinllaen, and in the following year, 1864, Porthdinllaen had its first lifeboat and has had one ever since.

Back, however, to Bangor and the year 1844.

The smack, *Port Penrhyn,* of 24 tons (Beaumaris 1844/15) was John Parry's next venture. *The Carnarvon and Denbigh Herald* on October 26th 1844 recorded her launching thus "A very beautiful modelled smack, the *Port Penrhyn,* was launched from the yard of Mr. John Parry at Hirael, Bangor, on Monday week. She glided into her briny element amidst the cheers of a multitude of spectators. The spirited owner, Mr. Parry, who may be said to be one of the *largest proprietors of floating capital in the principality* (author's italics) entertained his friends and about fifty of his workmen to a substantial dinner at the Waterloo Tavern, when that fine old veteran, Mr. R. Thomas, of the port, who is now in his 83rd year, presided." Allowing for some exaggeration on the part of the press, it seems that already in the mid-forties of the century John Parry was regarded as possessed of considerable capital; and it is interesting to note the benign father-in-law, Robert Thomas, in the background.

John Parry appears to have been her sole owner from 1844 until March 1847, when he sold 8/64ths to Evan Owen of Bangor, Master Mariner, who was her Master. It was wise policy on the part of the owner to have the master of the vessel as a shareholder since he would have an interest in speedy turn rounds, good freight terms and in generally running his ship as economically as possible. Evan Owen sold his share in April 1852 on relinquishing command to Griffith Williams, Mariner, Llanllechid who, in turn, sold it back to John Parry who was the sole owner until his death in April 1855.

After John Parry's death she continued to be run by Parry and Co. Her crew agreement lists have been preserved for most years between 1863 and 1877 but they do not make very exciting reading.[5] She was employed almost exclusively between Bangor and either Runcorn or Chester; in the returns for the first half year there are references to 'lying up at Bangor' until February or March, or in one instance until May. From 1872 onwards Amlwch appears in her ports of call and this was probably the result of the appointment of Richard Thomas, Upper Quay, Amlwch Port, as her master.

The last crew agreement list for the second half of 1877 says merely that she was 'employed in coasting trade between Bangor, Liverpool and Amlwch' but makes no mention of the number of voyages. The vessel was lost on December 7th 1877 off Hoylake whilst on a voyage from Liverpool to Amlwch.

The 73 ton schooner, *Lady Louisa Pennant* (Beaumaris 1847/8) was the next product of John Parry's yard. John Parry held a majority share (36/64th) up to his death in 1855. The other original shareholders were Griffith Williams, Mariner, William Evans, Draper, Hezekia Mather, Druggist

[5] L.R.O. W/DB/319.

(yet another!) and Samuel Roberts, Grocer, all from Bangor. As we shall see later, Samuel Roberts became a leading figure in the Bangor maritime community, and this was one of his earliest shareholdings. Designated by 1865 no longer as 'Grocer' but as 'Shipbuilder', Samuel Roberts acquired another 4/64ths share, and he held these shares until the end of his life.

Lady Louisa Pennant was 62.3 feet long, 16.5 in the beam and her depth of hold was 8.9 feet. Her effective draught would have been 10 feet or thereabouts. She had a female bust as figurehead. Her crew agreement lists are available at the Llangefni Record Office for most of the years between 1863 and 1902, when she met her end,[6] and for this reason and the fact that she encapsulates in her very naming the close and essential connection between the Pennant dynasty and Bangor shipping, her history in her life of fifty five years may be taken as typical of other medium range Bangor vessels.

In 1863, when the series of crew agreements begins, the Managing Owner of *Lady Louisa Pennant* was Griffith Williams, Master Mariner, Bangor, one of the original shareholders when she was built in 1847, and possibly the same Griffith Williams (see page 65) who was associated with Robert Thomas and John Parry in the building of *Ann and Susan* in 1835. After John Parry's death in 1855 his sons sold 24/64ths of his holding to Griffith Williams Gentleman, and of the remaining 12, 8 shares went to James Gregory, Garth, Bangor, Gentleman, and 4 to Elizabeth Griffith, also of Garth. Two months later James Gregory married Elizabeth Griffith and so acquired her shares; in fact James Gregory still owned 12/64ths when the last entry was made in the Transaction Register in 1896. Such was the situation in the last century before the passing of the Married Woman's Property Act.

Her master in 1863 was one William Griffith from Caernarfon and besides him she carried a Mate, an A.B. and an O.S.; a cook was occasionally carried but sometimes this duty was performed by a boy. On January 21st she left Bangor and arrived at Rochester on the 20th of February; she left Rochester on the 27th and arrived at London the next day. She left London on March 20th for Dundalk, arriving there on April 10th. She left Dundalk on the 17th for Belfast, arriving on the 19th. A week later she left Belfast and arrived at Bangor on May 1st. In her second voyage during the six months she sailed from Bangor to Shoreham. The return for the second half of the year shows that she returned to Bangor via Newhaven and Runcorn and made a second voyage to Ipswich and Maldon, returning to Bangor by December.

One of the few returns in which the cargoes were recorded was for the first six months of 1868. *Lady Louisa Pennant* took a cargo of slates to Dover, and from Dover she went to Par in ballast. From Par she took a load of clay to Runcorn and proceeded to Liverpool in ballast. At Liverpool she

[6] L.R.O. W/DB/235.

loaded wheat for Caernarfon, and then returned to Bangor in ballast. She took another cargo of slates to Dover and thence a cargo of oil cake to Poole. She was at Poole when the half year ended on June 30th. For the remainder of the year the cargoes are not recorded; she returned to Bangor via Runcorn in July. In September she went to Bristol and Cardiff and returned to Caernarfon in October. She sailed from Caernarfon for Liverpool and was back at Bangor before the end of the year. Once again this account bears out what has already been said about the part Bangor shipping played in the general mercantile carrying trade of Great Britain.

In the series of Crew Agreement Lists, which are not complete, there is only one account of a voyage to the continent — from Bangor via Frazerburgh to Harburg in September and October 1877, returning to Bangor via Runcorn in December, but for the thirty-nine years covered by the lists there is hardly a port in Great Britain which was not visited by her. The following is a brief summary: —

Ireland:	Dublin, Newry, Ardglass, Belfast, Drogheda, Londonderry, Galway, Sligo, Waterford, Wicklow, Cork.
Isle of Man:	Douglas, Ramsay.
N.W. England:	Liverpool, Garston, Runcorn, Barrow, Millom, Silloth, Whitehaven.
Scotland:	Glasgow, Greenock, Bowling, Stornoway, Montrose, Peterhead, Inverness, Frazerburgh, Aberdeen, Lossiemouth, Nairn, Thurso.
N.E. England:	Newcastle, Sunderland, Middlesborough, Berwick.
East Coast:	London, Maldon, Ipswich.
S. Coast:	Par, Fowey, Plymouth, Southampton, Poole, Shoreham.
W. Coast:	Bristol, Swansea, Cardiff, Briton Ferry, Port Talbot.

The only significant gap is between Middlesborough and Ipswich, and it is believed that this area was covered by the canal system from Runcorn in the west to Hull in the east.

The crews were drawn almost exclusively from Anglesey and Caernarfonshire. In a few cases the lists show the town or village of birth, rather than merely the county. In the return for the second half of 1868, when there were three separate voyages, nine different crew members were signed on in addition to the master, John Ellis, who was born in Nefyn. They all came from a very small area — three from Bangor, two each from Menai Bridge and Llandegfan, one from Pentraeth and one from Red Wharf. The same pattern repeats itself throughout the decade and the only crew members not born in either Anglesey or Caernarfonshire were Rees Thomas, an Ordinary Seaman from St. Dogmael's and an A.B. born in Liverpool — and his name was David Williams.

Captain John Ellis became the Master of *Lady Louisa Pennant* in June 1866, having purchased from Griffith Williams and the former master,

William Griffith, a 40/64ths interest. He was a comparative rarity among Bangor captains of this period since he held a certificate (No. 39045) and he also appointed himself as Managing Owner. He was master until 1871 when he was succeeded by Thomas Jones, but he remained the Managing Owner until her loss in October 1902.

In her fifty-five years afloat (thirty-nine of them covered by the Crew Agreement Lists) there is no recorded fatality, nor history of shipwreck or stranding except for one curious incident which occurred in September 1892. The Crew Agreement List for the latter half of that year merely records that on the 4th of September the master and crew were discharged at Burtonport (in Co. Donegal) and that on the 18th of September a new master and crew were signed. The Register of Shipping has a note "Vessel abandoned at Sea by Master and Crew on 4 September and picked up a derelict on 5.10.92 as per letter dated 29.10.92. Registry closed 29 Oct. 1892." There is clearly a mistake in the date on which she was picked up (probably in the vicinity of Burtonport), — and the date was the 5th of September, not October 5th, since according to the Crew Agreement List she left Burtonport on October 2nd with her new crew, arrived at Sligo on the 29th and was back at Bangor on December 3rd. The registry for *Lady Louisa Pennant* was reopened (the entry follows that for 1892/3 in the book).

The replacement master sent to Burtonport in 1892 was David Roberts of Bangor, son of Captain Elias Roberts of the *Bangor Packet* which was owned by his brother, Samuel Roberts. David Roberts in his old age wrote an interesting autobiography, the manuscript of which is in the University Library at Bangor.[7]

His memories of *Lady Louisa Pennant* and her crew — "the jolly lads that sailed her with me" — were sweet ones notwithstanding the terrifying gale they experienced in November 1893 when on a voyage from Falmouth to Runcorn with a cargo of china clay. They were within seven miles of the Smalls (off the coast of Pembrokeshire) when "the wind flew to the North-ward blowing a terrific gale with sleet." They hove to under a double reefed mainsail and were drifting towards Hayle Bay (St. Ives) when the wind changed to the N.E. enabling them to run for the Longships and eventually after an ordeal of four days to seek the shelter of Penzance. "The sea had carried away a lot of our bulwarks, several of our stanchions, our two gangways, our forehatch, skylight and several other things, in fact the vessel had been getting slowly broken up by the heavy seas that had broken on her." They were twelve weeks in Penzance repairing the damage.

David Roberts remained in command until 1896 when the first Penrhyn lock-out began and the ships left Port Penrhyn one by one to seek cargoes

<hr />

[7] U.C.N.W. 15085 (MS) and 11540 (Typescript).

elsewhere; David Roberts also left Bangor for Fleetwood where he was lucky enough to get another ship.[8]

The strike which followed in 1900 was a telling blow for Bangor shipping but it was not the only one. The general depression of trade which set in about 1880, though relieved by temporary and short-lived recoveries in 1883 and 1891, was making the small wooden sailing ship uneconomical because the freight rates were so low; added to this was the competition from the railways and the ever more efficient steamers. When David Roberts relieved the previous crew of *Lady Louisa Pennant* he took with him only a mate and an A.B./Cook. For some years the crews of schooners had been reduced in numbers and the vessels in their sail plans; the registers state that some were re-rigged as ketches but there is no evidence that this had been done with *Lady Louisa Pennant*. There are no Crew Agreement Lists extant from 1893 to 1901; this may be co-incidental, but equally it might suggest lengthy periods when the vessel was laid up. The final List for the second half of 1902 shows that she cleared Caernarfon on the 23rd of September with a full cargo of slates — her draft is recorded as 8'9" forrard and 9'9" aft — and that she left Bangor bound for Bowling on the Clyde on October 14th in company with the Bangor built schooner *Fomalhaut*. Neither vessel was heard of again. She had lasted for fifty-five years.

The next ship built by John Parry, also a schooner and named *John Parry*. (Beaumaris 1850/13) lasted almost as long. Slightly smaller than *Lady Louisa Pennant* and with a man's bust as figurehead her original shareholders were:

John Parry, Shipbuilder	16	
William Griffith, Master Mariner	4	
John Thomas, Slate Merchant	16	
William Pritchard, Slate Merchant	8	
William Parry, Brazier	4	all of Bangor, and
Henry Pace, Agent, Llandegai.	16	

In 1861 the vessel was sold to Arthur Wyatt, the Penrhyn Agent (48/64) and his close associate, John Lloyd, (16/64) Accountant, Port Penrhyn and became one of what the author of a letter to the *Carnarvon and Denbigh Herald* called in 1865 "Messrs. Wyatt and Lloyd's fine fleet" — a fleet which caused dissension among other owners because of the preferential treatment it received at Port Penrhyn. Like most other vessels in the fleet *John Parry* was disposed of in 1868 to certain nominees, some of them not so remotely connected with Penrhyn interests, as will be shown in greater detail later.

A medium range trader like *Lady Louisa Pennant* her pattern of voyages was very similar until 1885 when she was sold 64/64 to George Cuthbert of Bray, Co.Wicklow, Coal Dealer. One voyage in the second half year of 1880

[8] Aled Eames, *'Meistri'r Moroedd'*, (Gee, 1978) devotes a chapter to David Roberts's career.

74

is worthy of mention since the cargoes are specified; she took slate slabs from Bangor to Lossiemouth, sailed in ballast from Lossiemouth to Sunderland, took a cargo of coals from Sunderland to Thurso, stone slabs from Thurso to Liverpool, coals from Garston to Meath, and returned from Meath to Bangor in ballast.

She continued in Irish ownership until 1891 trading mainly between Bray and Troon and Bray and Garston. In that year she reverted to Bangor ownership with David Richards, of Robert Street, Hirael, Master Mariner and Dr. Richard Jones, Surgeon each owning half. She resumed her previous pattern of trading, mainly with ports in the Irish Sea. In the return for the first half of 1897 the master has specified the cargoes carried as well as the destinations; she left Caernarfon with slates for Irvine, and returned with coals, she left Caernarfon a second time with slates for Silloth, she took manure from Silloth to Dalbeattie, setts from Dalbeattie to Fleetwood, salt from Fleetwood to Liverpool, and coal from Garston to Bangor, a profitable half year, it would seem, for the owners since none of the voyages were in ballast. Dr. Richard Jones became the sole owner in 1900 after the deaths of his partner, Captain David Richards and his widow. Although in 1900 the vessel was still loading slate at Port Penrhyn, by the latter half of 1901 the lock out at the Penrhyn Quarry meant that there was little likelihood of a cargo from Port Penrhyn. It is not surprising, therefore, to find that the *John Parry* took slates from Port Dinorwic to Widnes returning to Bangor, and then went light to Caernarfon where she took a load of slates for Belfast. It was after leaving light that she was lost on December 9th, 1901.

John Parry's last ship — whether he saw her completed before his death in April 1855 is not known — was his biggest, the 143 ton brigantine *Glanogwen*, which exceeded in register tonnage and in length the previously biggest ship built in Bangor as long ago as 1808, the 122 ton snow *Penrhyn Castle*. *Glanogwen* measured 82.6 feet in length, 20 feet in beam and her depth of hold was 12.8 feet; she had a woman's bust as figurehead.

After John Parry's death his sons, Robert Thomas Parry, Abercegin, Gentleman and Thomas Thomas Parry, Bangor ,Shipbuilder inherited the vessel. They sold a 20/64ths share in 1856 to Richard Threlfall Power, T. T. Parry's partner in the shipyard and 4/64 to Owen Jones, Master of the *Glanogwen*. There are two reasons for devoting rather more space to *Glanogwen* than to other vessels; firstly she remained in the family of Robert Thomas and John Parry for three generations and suffered the same vicissitudes of fortune as the family, and secondly because she is a prime example of a long range trader, with frequent voyages to the continent of Europe.

Firstly, the history of the vessel as revealed by the Beaumaris Registers; R. T. Power mortgaged his 20/64ths portion for £500 with interest at 5% in 1867 to James Leach of Liverpool, Palm Oil Refiner, probably a business associate, and the mortgage was discharged a few years later. Owen Jones sold his 4/64ths share to Robert Thomas Parry on relinquishing his command.

The next entry in the register tells us that in 1883 R. T. Parry and T. T. Parry sold the remaining 40/64ths that they held jointly to R. T. Power, and that in June of the same year R. T. Power sold 40/64ths to Robert Thomas Parry. These complicated paper transactions, however, make sense, if one knows — and this fact is not revealed in this particular register entry — that Thomas T. Parry was adjudged bankrupt in 1882 and this particular transaction was intended to keep the vessel in the family. From June 1883 until his death in June 1890 Robert Thomas Parry was, on paper at least, the sole owner of *Glanogwen;* there are no means of telling whether there were any private arrangements between the two brothers.

Robert Parry's legatee was his sister, Anne, who had married William Thomas, Miller, Penylan, Llandegai[9] in 1841 and was now a widow. She in turn, by bills, of sale, disposed of the vessel to her two sons, 32/64ths each to Robert Parry Thomas, Talybont Isaf, Farmer and John Parry Thomas, Fisherman, Abercegin, i.e. the great-grandsons of Robert Thomas, Fisherman of Abercegin who first came to our notice as the lover of Susanna Davies in 1797. (It is no fault of the author that the males of four generations of this family had only two surnames, Thomas and Parry, and only three Christian names, Robert, John and Thomas, between them, but they did permute them skilfully.) Death struck once more and Robert Parry Thomas died in May 1893 and his widow, now living at Tŷ Mawr, Talybont sold her share of 32/64ths to John Parry Thomas, who now called himself 'Shipowner' of Abercegin.

He had little luck with his inheritance. He was obliged to mortgage the vessel to secure his account with James Tomkinson, Henry Platt and J. J. Alderson, Bankers of Chester in 1897 and the mortgage was later transferred to Lloyds Bank Ltd. The bank foreclosed the mortgage in September 1898 and sold the vessel outright to Evan Jones, Master Mariner, Porthmadog. On his death in 1913 his widow sold the vessel to the Falkland Islands Co., 61 Gracechurch Street, London and a year later the Company sold her to the Mayor, Alderman and Burgesses of the County Borough of Wallasey. Converted into a hulk, she was de-registered in 1915.

The first in the series of Crew Agreement Lists for *Glanogwen*[10] relates to the first six months of 1864 when her owner is given as T. Parry, Bangor and her Master as Owen Jones, 1 Erw Fair Terrace, Bangor (Certificate No. 42,165). In the half year she made one voyage to London and Newcastle, returning by way of Dublin to Bangor, and a second voyage which took her to Hamburg and Memel. The next year for which we have a crew list is 1867,

[9] N(ational) L(ibrary or) W(ales) Llandygai Parish Register No. 12.
[10] L.R.O. W/DB 173.

when she made two voyages to Aberdeen in the first six months, and voyages to Dieppe and London in the second half of the year.

The Agreement for a voyage (Foreign Going Ship) 'from Cardiff to Gibraltar and from there if required to any port or Ports in the Mediterranean, Spain, Portugal, Coast of Morocco or wherever the Master may direct and back to the United Kingdom — voyage not to exceed nine months' was entered into on 22nd June 1868. The voyage was duly performed, the vessel arriving at Gibraltar on 11 July and leaving on the 23rd, calling at Villa Real de Santo Antonio and returning to Glasgow on August 18. The log book attached to the crew list (this was not the official ship's log but was used to record items relevant to the crew — injuries, deaths or disciplinary matters etc.) shows that Captain Owen Jones had some trouble with the crew on this voyage. At the start of the voyage he records "went out of dock to the roads. 3 men drunk thought it provident to stop till they got sober" and this entry is signed, as was the usual practice by the Master and countersigned by the mate. At Gibraltar Bay the Master "gave liberty to the crew to (go) on shore They got drunk and verey Disorderly Two put in the Guard House (T. Williams and William Roberts) and I was obliged to go and liberate them by paying 4s. or one dollar expence or fine and 3s. I paid in addition to ease their going." It was little wonder that the Master declined to comment on their general conduct on their discharge though he stated that their seamanship was 'Good'.

In 1869 *Glanogwen* made two voyages to the continent, to Hamburg in May and to Toulon and 'Girgenty' (? Agrigentum in Sicily) in July. The first voyage started unpropitiously when they were at Carnarvon Bar "when in the act of hoisting on board the small boat the falls broke and the boat fell on the mate's foot and bruised it so that he insisted to be landed as he was near his house which was done with the pilot boat who was near." At Hamburg two crew members went ashore in the ship's boat which was then stolen. They commandeered someone else's boat but were caught by the River Police and put into custody "for which I was to pay for the fine of about 4 dollars and the same day being absent paid two substitutes to carry on the work . . ." After that there was no more trouble, at least nothing sufficiently serious as to merit an entry in the log.

Nothing so riles a sailor as unpalatable food presented by a lazy and inefficient seacook. On the second voyage (to Toulon) the Master's anger and frustration boils over in this breathless entry made when they had been at sea about a month "John Orr Cook first voyage No seasickness attacked him after all telling and putting him on the right way to do his work as cook, would not do, and what he could do but merely agrevating both myself and the mate found him in harbour concealed himself in the Head for a dodge and slept there. As for dates it is a Daily complaint Dirty and filthy and lazey" There was little improvement, if any, judged by this comment made

77

three days before the end of the voyage "Found a pound of tobacco concealed in the Cabin which he owned as his and more so Being short of oil found him using oil for kindling the fire. No doubt the same thing being done all the voyage useless to date because it was badly done and the mate oblidged to cook". In spite of it all the ship arrived safely in London on December 16th and the crew were discharged.

In the following January (1870) she sailed from London to Middlesborough, from there to Conway and from Conway to Bangor, arriving on March 20th. On May 6th she sailed for Harburg arriving on the 31st. She left Harburg on June 16th and arrived in Newcastle on July 1st. In March Richard Williams of Llanallgo took over as Master, and the rest of the crew consisted of

Mate	£3.10.0	David Williams	23	born at Nevin
A.B.	£3. 0.0	John Jones	24	Moelfre
A.B.	£3. 0.0	William Jones	27	Runcorn
O.S.	£2.15.0	John Lewis	23	Moelfre
O.S.	£1.15.0	Owen Lewis	18	Moelfre
Boy	£1. 0.0	Robert Lewis	15	Moelfre.

Were the three Lewises from Moelfre brothers? In the second half of the year *Glanogwen* sailed back to Bangor by way of Galway. Then in October she sailed for Hamburg, returning to Bangor by January 1st via Southampton and Dublin.

There is a three year gap in the series. Early 1873 finds *Glanogwen* at Briton Ferry, from where she sails to Dublin and on to Bangor. On the next voyage from Bangor to Harburg it is recorded that "Thomas Jones 29 neglected to join having signed articles. Owen Lewis joined at Beaumaris on 3rd April." From Harburg she sailed to Newcastle, from Newcastle to Penzance, from Penzance to Port Dinorwic. In the second half of the year she took a cargo of slate from Port Dinorwic to London and returned to Bangor with the almost inevitable call with a cargo for Dublin on the way.

Again there is a three year gap; in 1876 her owner is given as Robert Parry, Abercegin (she was still in the joint ownership of the brothers Parry (40/64ths) and R. T. Power (20/64ths) at this time) and her master was now Daniel Williams, a native of Nefyn. There may be a Foreign Going Vessel Agreement missing for the first months of 1876 since the first date on the Crew Agreement List is May 29th when she sailed from Bangor to London and returned via Amlwch. The second half of 1876 saw a voyage from Bangor to Montrose and back via Liverpool.

In 1879 she made two voyages to the continent, the first from Bangor to Hamburg and thence to Copenhagen, and the second from Port Dinorwic to Harburg. *Glanogwen* was by no means tied to Port Penrhyn and in each of the succeeding years she took a cargo of slate from Port Dinorwic to Harburg as well as carrying cargoes from Caernarfon to Dundee.

Throughout the eighties the same pattern is repeated; in most years she sails at least once, sometimes twice for Hamburg or Harburg, generally from Port Penrhyn but once, foreshadowing her future, from Porthmadog. Most of the cargoes went to Harburg, a small port up river from Hamburg, and on their discharge the vessel would move to Hamburg to seek a return cargo. Occasionally a cargo was found for a port on the west coast which was not too far from Bangor. In the ten years up to 1891 the return voyage from Hamburg was made to Runcorn (3 times), Garston (twice) once each to Stanraer and Irvine, and once to Cork. On the other hand return voyages to the east or south coast of Britain involved some delay. Newcastle was reached from Hamburg on May 14th, 1881, Bristol on 6th June, Swansea on the 12th, Dublin on the 25th, but it was not until 7th July that *Glanogwen* reached Caernarfon. In the following year she did no better reaching Newcastle on April 7th, London on 3rd May, Dublin on the 30th and Bangor on June 12th. Other return ports included Middlesborough, Invergordon and Portsmouth.

In 1891 when John Parry Thomas of Abercegin became the owner she made two trips to the continent. The first started at Bangor in December of the previous year; *Glanogwen* put into Weymouth on the 24th and there she remained until February 28th. No clue is given in the Crew Agreement List but such a long delay meant that she was probably undergoing extensive repairs. She arrived at Harburg on March 6th, left on 22nd March for Hamburg arriving on the 24th. From Hamburg she sailed for Rotterdam and then for London. From London she went to Whitehaven, thence to Castletown and finally to Porthmadog in June. In September she sailed from Porthmadog again for Harburg, and the return this time was made via Hayle, Liverpool and Runcorn to Bangor, which was reached on February 12th in the following year. In the absence of any accounts it must be said that the two voyages occupying more than a year cannot have been very profitable for the new owner. Five months were spent lying fallow — two at Weymouth for unexplained reasons and three at Porthmadog awaiting a cargo.

The following year saw two voyages to Stettin, the first in May and the second in September/October. For these voyages to the Baltic the master of the vessel, William T. Parry signed articles as Boatswain and a certificated master, George Davies, was employed. The foreign articles expired with the end of the second voyage at Tobermory in November 24th, and William Parry was re-instated and George Davies's employment terminated.

William Parry remained her master until the end of 1897. After the two voyages to Stettin William Parry took *Glanogwen* each year (apart from 1895, the record of which is missing) up to 1897 to Harburg or Hamburg (twice in 1896). One voyage deserves to be singled out for special mention as it shows once again the part Port Penrhyn ships played in the general carrying trade of Great Britain.

The voyage started from Bangor on July 29th 1893 for Harburg which was reached on August 23rd. From Harburg she sailed for Silloth on September 19th, arriving there on October 22nd. She left Silloth on November 8th and arrived at Bristol on the 21st. She sailed from Bristol for Swansea on December 2nd, arriving four days later. By now the crew could reasonably expect to return to their home port, having already by-passed it at least once (twice if they came south-about from Harburg to Silloth), but it was not to be; on December 29th they sailed for Plymouth which they reached on January 5th, 1894. The next stage of the voyage was to take them even further from home — to Guernsey, where they arrived on January 20th; leaving Guernsey on the 30th they reached Poole on February 4th. From Poole they sailed for London on the 24th, arriving on the 27th. On March 15th they sailed from London for Limerick and arrived there on the 26th. They sailed from Limerick on the 8th of April and arrived at Caernarfon on the 29th.

This coastal voyage had taken exactly nine months to perform, and the vessel had called at no fewer than nine intermediate ports between Bangor and Caernarfon — which were only 9 miles apart! (which is one way of looking at it). The longest period spent at sea was 33 days between Harburg and Silloth; in all 131 days were spent at sea and 144 in the nine ports of call, an average stay of just over 17 days with the longest stay at Harburg. This suggests a quick turn around in most of the ports, and a profitable voyage; once again one laments the fact that it was not obligatory for masters to give details of the freight carried on the crew agreement lists, but these were not intended for the benefit of maritime historians a hundred years later.

At some time prior to 1897 *Glanogwen* had been re-rigged as a schooner. In that year she made her last recorded voyages (as far as the Crew Agreement Lists are concerned) for John Parry Thomas; she was at Poole in January on her way to London. She left London on February 9th for Dundalk and arrived there on the 27th. She sailed in ballast from Dundalk to Porthmadog in March, and from there to Harburg in April and May. From Harburg in early June she sailed for Newcastle, thence to Rochester and Plymouth. From Plymouth she sailed again for Harburg at the end of August and returned via Silloth to Caernarfon in October. The private bankers who held the mortgage on the vessel transferred the mortgage to Lloyds Bank about this time, it will be recalled, and the bank foreclosed in the following year and sold *Glanogwen* to Evan Jones, Master Mariner of Porthmadog.

Managed by Prichard Bros., Cornhill, Porthmadog and sometimes under the command of Evan Jones himself, who was uncertificated, sometimes of various others who were, *Glanogwen* was active in the home trade and in the Baltic trade of Porthmadog which was now her home port, for a number of years.

On February 24th, 1913, at about 11 p.m., the Log records, the Mate was "called on Deck by Hugh Evans who informed (him) that the Master (Evan Jones) was overboard and had gone down. I kept the vessel hove to till midnight but no trace of the Master was seen or heard. I then made for St. Tudwals and anchored at midday the 25th. It would have been impossible to put the Boat out under the circumstances." The accident happened about 30 miles S.W. of St. Tudwals. The voyage was abandoned. The long series of Crew Agreement Lists dating back to 1864 ends here, and *Glanogwen's* days as a sailing ship probably ended at the same time as her Master's tragic death. The Register merely records that his widow sold the vessel in November 1913 to the Falkland Island Co., Gracechurch Street, London who, a year later, sold her to the Mayor, Aldermen and Burgesses of the County Borough of Wallasey. The Register was closed in February 1915 when the vessel was converted into a hulk. She had lasted sixty years.

We must go back sixty years to John Parry's death — it will be recalled that *Glanogwen* was his last ship and she was launched in the year of his death — and consider what part he played in developing the industrial and commercial life of Bangor. *The North Wales Chronicle*[11] in its account of his funeral says of him that he had been "an inhabitant of this city for many years past and one of its oldest tradesmen in the place and had obtained the universal respect of all classes." In addition to building 11 vessels beginning with the *Bangor Packet* in 1830 and ending with *Glanogwen* in 1855, John Parry had an interest in at least 20 other vessels between 1828 and his death in 1855. They are presented here in summary form:—

Jenny 20t. Sl.	B. 1787/27	48/64 from Robert Thomas, Abercegin from 1845 until 1855.
Raven 73t. Sr.	B. 1800/26	8/64 in 1834 with James Wyatt. Wyatt bought 8/64 after 1855.
King William 27t. Sma.	B. 1826/27	32/64 (Robert Thomas also 32/64) in 1829 until 1833.
Nevin 98t. Brig	B. 1827/25	4/64 from 1827 to 1855. Built at Nefyn for mainly Nefyn owners.
Antelope 105t. Brig	B. 1828/37	4/64 from 1828 to 1855. Built at Nefyn for mainly Nefyn owners.
Peggy 56t. Flat	B. 1829/11	64/64 from 1832 until 1855. (Lost in R. Mersey).
Penrhyn 42t. Sl.	B. 1831/10	8/64 from 1832 + 8/64 in 1847 = 16/64 in 1855.

[11] N.W.C. 25.4.1855.

81

Robert 43t. Flat	B. 1836/95	32/64 in 1836; 64/64 by February 1844, when he sold 56/64 to James Wyatt, retaining 8/64.
Stag 26t. Sl.	B. 1836/181	16/64 in 1842. James Wyatt bought the shareholding after John Parry's death.
Welcome 50t. Sr.	B. 1837/35	8/64 from 1837 until 1855. Vessel, built Pwllheli, lost in 1855.
Lady Bulkeley 44t. Sma.	B. 1837/69	4/64 from 1837 until 1855.
John and Eliza 105t. Sr.	B. 1838/3	4/64 from January to February 1838, when vessel lost near Youghal (16.2.38). Mainly Nefyn owners.
Vron 101t. Sr.	B. 1839/16	4/64 from 1839 until 1855. Built Nefyn 1839 for mainly Nefyn owners.
Eliza 107t. Sr.	B. 1839/27	4/64 from 1839 until 1855. Built at Pwllheli for mainly Nefyn owners.
Josephine 109t. Sr.	B. 1839/41	4/64 from 1839 to 1855. Built at Pwllheli for mainly Caernarfon/Llanddeiniolen owners.
Maria Catherine 88t. Sr.	Pwllheli 1842/7	4/64 from 1842 until 1855. Built Nefyn 1841 for Nefyn/Edern owners.
Maria 18t. Sma.	B. 1843/6	4/64 from 1843 until loss of vessel in 1852. Built at Beaumaris for mainly Beaumaris owners.
Dart 32t. Sl.	B. 1847/17	Mortgaged 42/64 to John Parry in 1847. Sold in 1848 to Thomas Williams, Painter, Bangor.
Samuel Dixon 53t. Flat alt. to Sr. 1854.	B. 1848/22	20/64 from 1848 until 1855.
Alice Anna 52t. Flat.	B. 1852/2	64/64 from 1852 until 1855.

The investment was not confined to Bangor but prudently spread between the ports of Caernarfon, Nefyn and Pwllheli. The association with the Wyatts, which was also noticed in connection with shipbuilding, is seen again in the shareholdings in *Raven*, *Robert* and *Stag*. (The association would continue after John Parry's death between the 'firm' that succeeded him and the Wyatts, both James and Arthur.) *The Carnarvon and Denbigh Herald's* reporter remarked of him in 1844 that he was "one of the largest proprietors of floating capital in the Principality" (see page 70); this remark may well be not very short of the mark in the mid-fifties when it is remembered that in addition to the vessels listed above he had very substantial holdings in vessels of his own construction, including out and out ownership of the two large brigantines, *Three Susans* and *Glanogwen*.

In the late forties he built for himself a handsome house halfway up Lôn Pobty, known then, and today, as Brynkinallt, and according to the 1851 census, his daughter Anne, married to William Thomas, the miller, lived at the old family home at Tyddyn Llwydyn. The same census return for Brynkinallt shows that resident there on the night in question were John Parry aged 55 whose 'Rank, Profession or Occupation' was entered as 'Shipbuilder employing 30 men.' His three sons were also at home, John Thomas Parry aged 27 years, Master Mariner, Robert Thomas Parry, 23 years, Farmer, and Thomas Thomas Parry, 19 years, Shipwright, and a second daughter, Susan, aged 21 and unmarried. (At the previous census in 1841 the two younger sons were staying with their grandparents, Robert and Susanna Thomas at Abercegin farmhouse — a schoolboys' delight with the two fishing weirs on the shore, the Cegin Pool (or as the family called it, 'Llŷn Wyatts') and the port, all close at hand. The two girls, Anne and Susan, were at Tyddyn Llwydyn with their parents. The eldest son, John, who would have been about 17 years old at the time, was presumably away at sea).

John Parry was a churchman and regularly attended services at the Cathedral; he was a Tory and for some years in the early fifties a member of the Bangor Board of Health.[12] The close association which existed between him and the Wyatts was an alliance of like with like. He died a wealthy man in 1855; he was already a widower, his father-in-law, Robert Thomas had died in the preceding year and at some time after 1851 his son, John, who was at sea had either been lost at sea or had died of natural causes. In his will, dated the 12th of October 1852, John Parry, who was born in Caernarfon, left to his sisters and brother certain leasehold properties in that the town. He then directed that the remainder of his property should be divided into five equal shares, one to be held in trust for any child or children of his son John, the remaining four to be divided equally between his surviving children, his sons, Robert Thomas Parry and Thomas Thomas Parry, and his daughters, Anne, who was married to William Thomas the miller from Llandegai, and Susan, who was at the date of the will still unmarried.[13] He appointed his sons, Robert and Thomas, as his executors.

It is necessary at this point to anticipate the narrative order and to consider what happened after John Parry's death. The elder son, Robert, took over the house and land at Abercegin together with his sister, Anne, and styled himself in subsequent entries in the Beaumaris Registers of Shipping as 'Gentleman'. His younger brother, Thomas, took over the shipbuilding yard with Captain Richard Threlfall Power of Liverpool, variously described in the shipping registers as Wine Merchant, Master Mariner or Shipowner.

[12] P. E. Jones, T.C.H.S. Vol. 37 'The Bangor Board of Health etc.,' and C.R.O. XM/2765.
[13] P.R.O. Rf. 1855 PROB. 11/2218.

Who was this Captain R. Threlfall Power? A clue to his early connection with Bangor lies in an entry in the marriage register of the Parish of Bangor where it is recorded that "David Power late of Liverpool . . but now of this Parish" married Margaret Maria Threlfall on June 21st, 1821. Another clue is that during his brief membership of the Bangor Board of Health in the fifties his address was given as Brynkinallt, the same as that of John Parry. The simple explanation is that Richard Threlfall Power, Bachelor, aged 24, Master Mariner, son of David Power, also a Master Mariner, married Susan Thomas Parry, Spinster, aged 24, daughter of John Parry, Shipbuilder on May 4th, 1854, in Bangor Cathedral according to the marriage register of the Parish of Bangor. In the last century a married woman's property passed to her husband so that when John Parry died in 1855 Susan's inheritance, her share in the shipyard, became Richard Threlfall Power's.

John Parry's house, Brynkinallt, was built half way up the steep Lôn Pobty on the south side of Bangor High street which led to Bangor Mountain. On the opposite side of the valley another new house had been built in the grounds of the old mansion, Penrallt (demolished long since to provide a site for the Arts Building of the U.C.N.W.) It belonged to another ship-builder, Edward Ellis. Both houses commanded views of the port and the sea beyond, and this their owners shared in common but little else.

CHAPTER V

THE BUILDERS ii

Edward Ellis

The only surviving shipyard in Bangor, the establishment of Messrs. A. M. Dickie and Son, incorporates the site of Edward Ellis's shipyard of 1836 which he held on lease from R. H. Dawkins Pennant. There he built in 1836 and registered in the following year the 54 ton smack, *Eliza Catherine* (Beaumaris 1837/16). If for no other reason, *Eliza Catherine* deserves to be remembered as being the first vessel in which 'John Davies, Merchant, Llandysilio' is recorded as having had the majority (16/64ths) interest. He also had an interest in another vessel built by Edward Ellis in the following year, *Mona,* a 37 ton smack (Beaumaris 1837/68). This time he appears in the Register as 'John Davies, Merchant, Bangor Ferry.' Associated with him in both ventures was Samuel Dew, Currier of Llangefni. From these small beginnings sprang the great shipping enterprise of Davies Bros., Menai Bridge which accumulated for the benefit of the brothers and their descendants up to the present century, great prosperity and untold wealth.

Both vessels lasted until the eighties under predominantly Bangor ownership. Crew Agreement Lists for the sixties and seventies[1] show that both vessels were employed in the Irish Sea, *Eliza and Catherine* being employed exclusively in trading between Bangor and either Runcorn or Garston under

[1] L.R.O. W/DB 127 *Eliza and Catherine* and W/DB 287 *Mona.*

the command of Thomas Williams of Garth, Bangor until 1876 when the series of lists ends. The vessel was totally lost in February 1881.

Mona was owned outright by 1865 by John Thomas, Master Mariner of Bangor and her crew lists show frequent voyages from Bangor to Liverpool or Chester but with occasional trips across the Irish Sea to Belfast, Drogheda, Dundalk or Portrush. She was wrecked on the West Hoyle Bank in December 1883.

Edward Ellis's next venture was the 77 ton schooner *Maria and Elizabeth* (Beaumaris 1839/62) built for a variety of shareholders who included Richard Morris Griffith, described at this period as 'shopkeeper' of Bangor, a mariner and a grocer from Liverpool, a ropemaker from Caernarfon and two spinsters from Beaumaris and Llangollen respectively. Edward Ellis himself held a 4/64ths share in her until 1850 when he relinquished his interest. Unlike John Parry he seldom held extensive holdings in the ships he built.

Edward Ellis was a Calvinistic Methodist by persuasion and he did not care who knew it. He published a letter in the *North Wales Chronicle* in February 1839 denying a charge made by a Wesleyan minister that a Calvinist preacher had said that hell was paved with the skulls of small children (i.e. those who had died unelect). That such recherché, indeed bizarre, aspects of theological dispute were matters of concern to laymen in the last century is perhaps a matter of surprise to us; the fact remains that the columns of the *North Wales Chronicle* were full of correspondents' letters for some weeks and the dispute spilled over to the correspondence columns of the *Carnarvon and Denbigh Herald* as well. The Methodist Revival which had begun almost a century earlier within the established church but which was now a separate denomination, had captured the hearts and minds of a wide section of the people of Wales.

The doctrine of laissez faire and the paramountcy of private enterprise in all commerce and business was unchallenged. How much the ethic of Protestantism contributed to this philosophy is best left to specialist scholars. But is is observable that in one small field, the development of shipbuilding and shipownership among Welsh people in the last century, members of the Calvinistic Methodist denomination were among the most prominent. Whether the theology of this latest Welsh denomination encouraged enterprise and capital formation is a question well beyond the scope of this book and its author's competence; it can be stated with some confidence that the virtues of self-denial and thrift, the conviction of belonging to an elect and the belief that wordly success was a sign of divine blessing or at the very least not inconsistent with the divine will — all these combined with powerful preaching formed a very potent mixture.

The Davies brothers of Menai Bridge who have already been mentioned as shareholders in some of Edward Ellis's ships were pillars of the Calvinistic Methodist cause and contributed between them over a period of half a century sums amounting to a good six figures for building and maintaining Methodist chapels. Edward Ellis was associated with another prominent Methodist in the shareholding of *Ellen,* a 20 ton sloop built in 1842. (Beaumaris 1842/10) Among the original shareholders we see the name of 'John Phillips, Preacher, Holywell' who owned a major shareholding of 16/64ths. John Phillips became in 1843 the paid agent of the British and Foreign Schools Society and helped to found many of the Society's 92 schools that existed in North Wales by 1850. He lived in Bangor and was a fellow member with Edward Ellis in the Tabernacle chapel. He became the founder principal of the Bangor Normal College in 1858.

In 1848 Edward Ellis and John Phillips were shareholders in the 377 ton ship rigged *Ann Grant,* built at Whitby in 1806 (Beaumaris 1848/13), each holding 28/64ths, the remaining 8/64ths being held by a John Scott, a merchant from Sligo. The vessel was engaged in the Menai Straits slate trade; according to the Register she was wrecked off Nova Scotia in 1851. The Register also states that Edward Ellis and John Phillips had mortgaged their shareholding with the Revd. John Parry, of St. David's, Merioneth as security for £350; there is no record that the mortgage was discharged before the loss of the ship.

John Phillips was a Cardiganshire man, having been born at Pontrhyd-fendigaid; his work in connection with schools took him to all parts of North and Mid Wales and this may partially account for the curious fact that Edward Ellis, alone among the shipbuilders of Bangor, built several ships for customers from other ports, as will appear later. Possibly his reputation as a shipbuilder was broadcast by his co-religionist and fellow investor, John Phillips. The most prominent of the New Quay consortium was called Evan Phillips but such is the paucity of Welsh surnames that too much should not be read into this coincidence.

Another prominent Methodist in the immediate vicinity of Bangor was the Revd. Rees Jones of Port Dinorwic who doubled as a shipbuilder — and a very good one. Between 1849 and 1894, latterly in association with his son, W. E. Jones, he built 28 ships at Port Dinorwic, among them the 887 ton *Ordovic,* the largest wooden sailing ship ever built in North Wales. Tradition has it that Rees Jones, a native of Barmouth, recognised the commercial possibilities of Port Dinorwic as a ship-building centre while on a preaching journey to Caernarfonshire. As we shall see later, he shared this capacity to attend to things spiritual as well as material with a fellow preacher and shipbuilder, Samuel Roberts of Bangor.

Edward Ellis built in 1841 the 100 ton schooner, *Douglas Pennant* (Beaumaris 1841/8), with a man's bust as figurehead. Besides himself, two Bangor men were the other subscribing owners, William Rowlands, Gentleman of Maesyporth and Richard Jones, Master Mariner. Of the other ten owners, two were farmers from Bangor, the remainder were from Liverpool.

Two years later, true to form, Edward Ellis relinquished his shareholding of 4/64ths to William Rowlands, who now appears in the Register as 'Master Pilot'. On Rowlands's death his executor, John Leace 'Pilots' Agent' took over his interest and acted for some years as Managing Owner.

The vessel was largely in the hands of Liverpool owners until she was sold, 64/64ths to William Evans, Master Mariner of Port Dinorwic in 1864. Her Crew Agreement Lists[2] from 1863 to 1868 show that she went foreign in 1863 to Gibraltar and Lisbon but that under William Evans's ownership she traded mainly between Port Dinorwic, Glasgow, Dublin and London until her loss in 1868. She struck the rocks at Dulas, off the coast of Anglesey, in January of that year, but the master and crew were saved.

Also in 1841 Edward Ellis built the 70 ton vessel *Benjamin Williams*. The late David Thomas in his splendid book '*Hen Longau Sir Gaernarfon*' (The Old Ships of Caernarfonshire') which was published in 1951 and is un-surpassed to this day for its meticulous research and fine scholarship besides being highly readable, listed all the vessels built in Caernarfonshire from 1786, the year which saw the introduction of the Registers of Shipping. His list for Bangor contains the name *Benjamin Williams* and her builder, Edward Ellis in italics to indicate that the source of his information is something other than the shipping register, and that the ship was not registered locally. A search of the local registers has confirmed this; the source is *The North Wales Chronicle* for April 28th 1841 which states:—

> "Launch: On Friday, a handsome craft, named *Benjamin Williams,* burden about 70 tons, was launched from the building yard of Mr. Edward Ellis, at Garth, in the presence of a large number of Spectators. In the afternoon the builders &c were entertained by the Owners at the Crown Tavern."

This was the first time that Edward Ellis built a vessel for owners from elsewhere. It is clear from the newspaper paragraph that she was not built as a speculation as the *Margaret* had been (see page 55), since the owners were sufficiently real to provide the traditional entertainment at the Crown Tavern. It was by no means the last occasion as the builder's later connection with Newquay was to prove. But nothing about the subsequent history of *Benjamin Williams* has so far been discovered.

The smack *Beatrice Catherine* of 34 tons (Beaumaris 1845/2) was named after and part owned by Mrs. Beatrice Catherine Mytton, of Beaumaris. The launch was recorded by the *Carnarvon and Denbigh Herald* in this report[3] "Mr. Ellis, of Garth, on Saturday, launched a very fine sloop from his yard. She was named the *Beatrice Catherine* by Mrs. Mytton, late of Pen y Lan in Montgomeryshire and glided off her cradle most majestically amidst the cheers of hundreds of spectators. The *Beatrice Catherine* is a

[2] L.R.O. W/DB 113.
[3] C.D.H. 1/2/1845.

88

round stern built sloop of 64 tons burden. Mr. Ellis with his customary liberality gave a dinner at the Vaynol Arms to fifty of his friends and workmen".

Edward Ellis himself held 48/64ths initially but by degrees reduced his holding to 16/64ths as the vessel was transferred piecemeal to Portmadoc ownership. A reflection of this was her to transfer to the port of Pwllheli for purposes of registration in 1848. Nothing is known of her trading and she was lost with her papers in October 1859.

Nine years later the yard launched the substantial schooner of 120 tons, *Ifor* (Aberystwyth 1854/8) for owners in Newquay. One has the impression that Newquay was exclusively populated by master mariners since no fewer than seven of the twelve original shareholders gave this as their occupation. There could hardly have been a greater compliment to the excellence of Edward Ellis's design and workmanship than that a group of experienced mariners should have chosen his yard in preference to ones closer at hand. It would happen again.

By 1857 the name of the builder of a vessel was no longer recorded on the Register entry but in most cases this can be deduced from the pattern of the shareholdings or by other evidence. In the case of *Idwal* (Beaumaris 1857/10) there is an account of her launching in the *Carnarvon and Denbigh Herald*[4] which states "On Saturday last, the 24th ult. a beautiful modelled schooner, the *Idwal* was launched from the building yard of Mr. Edward Ellis, Garth, Bangor, in the presence of a large concourse. The lines of this elegant vessel were drawn by Mr. Ellis's foreman, and reflect the highest credit on his taste and judgement. Great praise is also due to Mr. Ellis for the masterly manner in which he has completed it.

Length of keel	$64\frac{1}{2}$	feet
Extreme breadth	$19\frac{3}{4}$	feet
Depth of Hold	9	feet
Carries	125	tons

She is to be commanded by Captain Thomas Jones, of Ysgubor Fawr, Llanfairmathafarneithaf, who is the principal owner. The other shares are distributed amongst several tradesmen at Bangor. An excellent dinner was subsequently given by the owners at the Vaynol Arms Inn, to which upwards of a hundred persons partook."

Idwal was of register tonnage 69 which accords well with her expected carrying capacity of 125 tons and the dimensions given on the register are similar to the newspaper account. Her figurehead was a man's bust. She remained largely in the same hands until her loss in 1868. Her Crew Agreement Lists from 1863 onwards[5] show that Thomas Jones was still her

[4] C.D.H. 2/5/1857. I am indebted to Dr. Lewis Lloyd for drawing my attention to this and the other references from the C.D.H. which follow.
[5] L.R.O. W/DB 198.

managing owner and master, holding certificate no. 73520. They show that *Idwal* was fully employed in the general carrying trade as well as being a carrier of Penrhyn slate. Among her ports of call in one year, 1863, we find that after taking a load of slates to London, she called at Plymouth, Par, Liverpool, Dutton, Cardiff, Barrow and Larne.

The same pattern of voyaging persisted until her end in 1868 but the return for the second half of 1864 is worth quoting since it gives details of the cargoes carried. She left Garston on July 9th with a load of iron for Saundersfoot, a cargo of culm from Saundersfoot for Youghal, grain from Youghal to Briton Ferry, culm from Neath to Red Wharf and thence to Bangor. In October she took slates from Bangor to London, went from London to Newcastle in ballast and loaded coal for Milford where she arrived in January.

She was frequently at Sligo in 1866-67 so that Captain Thomas Jones was well acquainted with the perils of the west coast of Ireland, but after leaving Sligo in ballast on 20th January 1868 his vessel became a total wreck at Mallaghmore; Captain Thomas Jones was drowned, as were the mate, another Thomas Jones, aged 22, born at Llanwenllwyfo, and a seaman, William Rowlands aged 19 born at Penrhoslligwy. One was saved, Hugh Roberts, a seaman aged 24, born at Llanddona.

The same extract from the *Carnarvon and Denbigh Herald* which recorded the launch of *Idwal* also contained details of Edward Ellis's future plans. "We are glad" it says "to find that ship building is considerably on the increase at this port. Mr. Ellis has another new schooner building, which is rapidly advancing. She is the property of Jenkin Phillips, Esq., of Glyn, New Quay, Cardiganshire, together with several other gentlemen from the same county. The following are the dimensions of this vessel: —

Length of keel	76 feet
Depth of hold	12 feet
Extreme breadth	22 feet
To carry	220 tons

She is to be classed 12 years A1 at Lloyd's and is to be commanded by Captain O. Owens, brig *Betsy,* of Cardigan."

She proved to be the *Sarah Bridget,* (Aberystwyth 1858/22) a brigantine (not a schooner, as predicted by the newspaper) of 126 tons which somehow survived until she was broken up at Runcorn in 1936.

The same account continues "Another vessel, of the following dimensions, is to be immediately commenced by the same enterprising builder, for several respectable parties residing in New Quay: —

Length of keel	105 feet
Extreme breadth	23 feet
Depth of hold	13 feet
Tonnage	340 tons

to class 12 years at Lloyd's. The ship building yard has been considerably extended and improved, and with its patent slip steam machinery, and other appliances, stands unrivalled by any other than the Royal Docks in the Principality."

This second, and larger, vessel turned out to be the *Heather Bell,* (Aberystwyth 1860/3) a 257 ton barque, later re-rigged as a barquentine. She was, in fact, by far the largest ship built in Bangor. But more of the *Sarah Bridget* and the *Heather Bell* later.

This was the high-water mark of shipbuilding in Bangor; in the dozen years between 1854 and 1866 no fewer than 20 ships were built, ranging in size from the little 11 ton smack rigged *Victoria,* a 'Steam Vessel propelled by paddle wheels' built for the river trade of the Mawddach by John Roberts in 1854, to the *Heather Bell* of 257 tons. They were, in order of date of registration : —

Ifor (Aberystwyth 1854/28)	120t. Sr. by Edward Ellis
Victoria (Caernarfon 1854/35)	11t. Sma. by John Roberts
Glanogwen (Beaumaris 1855/26)	131t. Brigantine by John Parry
Idwal (Beaumaris 1857/10)	69t. Sr. by Edward Ellis
City of Bangor (Beaumaris 1857/17)	99t. Sr. by John Roberts
Arthur Wyatt (Beaumaris 1858/15)	96t. Sr. by T. T. Parry
Sarah Bridget (Aberystwyth 1858/22)	126t. Brigantine by Edward Ellis
Blue Jacket (Beaumaris 1859/9)	66t. Sr. by T. T. Parry
Jane and Elizabeth (Beaumaris (1859/13)	60t. Sr. builder unknown
Grampus (Beaumaris 1859/22)	132t. Brigantine by John Roberts
Cambria (Beaumaris 1860/18)	56t. Sr. by T. T. Parry
Pamela Pennant (Beaumaris 1860/21)	29t. Sma. by John Roberts
Heather Bell (Aberystwyth 1860/3)	257t. Barque by Edward Ellis
Sarah Jane (Beaumaris 1861/12)	73t. Sr. by Henry Owens
Dorothea (Beaumaris 1862/10)	74t. Sr. by T. T. Parry
Mary Edwards (Beaumaris 1863/5)	65t. Sr. by Edward Ellis
Charlotte Ann (Beaumaris 1864/5)	53t. Sr. by John Roberts
Eliza (Beaumaris 1866/10)	101t. Sr. by T. T. Parry
Eliza Jane (Beaumaris 1866/19)	38t. Sr. by John Jones
Petrel (Beaumaris 1866/22)	15t. Sl. builder unknown

In view of all this activity it is surprising to find that Edward Ellis's shipyard was offered for sale by private treaty in June 1856 and that an advertisement to this effect appeared in both local papers. The offer was not taken up and the yard continued to operate under Edward Ellis's direction at least until 1863 when *Mary Edwards* was built.

For the light it throws on the technological state of the shipbuilding industry (as far as small sailing ships were concerned) in mid-Victorian times it is worth reproducing the advertisement in full.

"BANGOR, NORTH WALES, IMPORTANT TO SHIP BUILDERS

To be disposed of by Private Treaty all that well-known and conveniently situated SHIP BUILDING YARD, held by Mr. Edward Ellis at GARTH POINT, BANGOR, under a Lease upon favourable terms from the Hon. E. G. D. Pennant, including the PATENT SLIP, SAW MILLS, SUITABLE BUILDINGS, CHANDLERY STORES, SAIL ROOMS, SMITHY etc.

The Mills are worked by a Steam Engine of 20 horse power, fitted up with Circular and Vertical Saws, all of which are perfectly new. The Slip is in good working order, and the Buildings in a most excellent state of repair.

These capacious premises (lying as they do so immediate in the Great Penrhyn Shipping Port) afford every facility and accommodation for carrying on a most extensive Ship Building, Repairing, Ship Smith's Works, Sail and Block Making business.

The arrangements are of a most complete and superior character, and combine all the necessary adjuncts for carrying on a most flourishing and lucrative trade, and at a comparatively small cost, beyond the first outlay.

May be viewed at any time and further particulars as to terms etc. can be had by applying to Mr. W. Dew, Auctioneer British Hotel, Bangor."

In the late sixties the yard was taken over by Parry and Co., the successors of John Parry.

But to return to Edward Ellis; whether it was his association with John Phillips or his prominence in his denomination or his activity as the secretary of the Auxilary Bible Society at Bangor which gained him greater than local acclaim among groups as diverse as New Quay master mariners and Bethesda quarrymen or whether it was purely his skill as a designer and craftsman is a matter of speculation. The three Aberystwyth registered ships, *Ifor*, *Sarah Bridget* and *Heather Bell* have one common shareholder, Evan Phillips Master Mariner of New Quay. Besides him three other master mariners from New Quay had holdings in common in the first two ships, Jenkin Phillips, Jenkin Owens and John Davies but with the exception of Evan Phillips a completely new consortium was formed to finance the *Heather Bell*. There were 18 mariners and farmers from New Quay and Llangrannog, 5 shipowners or brokers from Liverpool and 7 from the Bethesda area, 5 of whom were quarrymen and two widows, one from Gatehouse and one from Bangor. With a total of 30 shareholders it is not surprising that there were a dozen who held only 1/64th. In some ways the share pattern of *Heather Bell* foreshadows the 'Single Ship' Companies which would emerge on the Welsh scene later in the century.

It is interesting to see Bethesda quarrymen investing in shipping. At this period the quarries were flourishing but there were few banking facilities and in North Wales the building society movement was still in its infancy. What is more significant is that the investors were clearly satisfied with their

1860 investment in *Heather Bell* for in 1863 no fewer than 21 quarrymen came together with eight others to finance the *Mary Edwards*. Of the seven who had invested in *Heather Bell* six formed the nucleus of the consortium which owned the *Mary Edwards,* and one of them, John Hugh Jones Bethesda, Quarryman was for some years her Managing Owner.

In 1863 her Managing Owner (and major shareholder with 8/64ths) was Edward Ellis, junior, described in the register as a 'shipwright'. Incidentally, the vessel occupies more pages in the Register and Transaction Registers than any other vessel as some of the 29 shareholders sold their shares or died and bequeathed them to others. Nevertheless the vessel remained mainly in Bethesda hands until 1896 when 60 of the 64 shares were acquired by William Parry, a shipowner of Caernarfon, who sold her two years later to Alexander Grant of Port Dinorwic. Grant retained his ownership until 1913 when the series of Crew Agreement Lists ends and the vessel was sold to a fish merchant from Waterford. In 1918 she was sold to a Plymouth ship-owner and in 1928 to a barge owner of the same port. She was broken up at Plymouth in 1936 and her registry closed. Still on the register was the name of Mary Edwards Williams, Spinster of Gerlan, who in all probability gave her forenames to the vessel and could not bear to part with her 2/64ths share.

Her master from her launch in 1863 until 1876 was William Roberts (Certificate No. 74379) of Edmund Street, Bangor, and her crew in 1863 consisted of master mate, A.B., O.S. and boy. The lists over the years are typical of a medium range Port Penrhyn trader; no foreign articles are to be found but in her time there was hardly a British port which was not visited. The return for the second half of 1868, which is a rare instance of the cargoes being recorded, shows that in July *Mary Edwards* took a cargo of iron ore from Duddon to Cardiff; from Cardiff she went to Brading (Isle of Wight) with coals, and from Brading to Newquay (Cornwall) in ballast. In Newquay she loaded china clay for Runcorn, and went thence to Liverpool in ballast. From Liverpool she took a cargo of wheat to Larne, iron ore from Larne to Duddon, pig iron from Duddon to Cardiff. She then took a cargo of coals from Cardiff to Newry; the return trip from Newry to Porthmadog was made in ballast. Then in December she took a cargo of slates from Porthmadog to Ballina. With a few more returns with similar details it would be easy to construct an atlas of Britain's industrial, commercial and economic life.

Fortunately we have the Crew Agreement Lists of *Sarah Bridget,* too, for most of the years between 1866 and 1913.[6] In September 1866 she made a voyage from Cardiff to Naples, Gallipoli and Taranto which ended in January of the following year at Hull. Her managing owner at this time was

[6] C.R.O. 21672.

Jenkin Phillips a merchant of New Quay and her master was Joshua Griffiths, also of New Quay (Cert. No. 11,154). Among the other owners, mostly from New Quay and the surrounding district, we find the names of John Simon, Currier, and John Edmunds, Schoolmaster, both of Bangor, and Robert Roberts, Postmaster of Caernarfon. Both John Simon and Robert Roberts (who soon afterwards became Postmaster of Bangor) subsequently held shares in a number of Bangor ships.

There is a gap until 1873 and by then the Managing Owner is given as W. C. Dawber, a slate merchant of Hull and her master was John Jenkins, a native of Pwllheli but a resident at this time of Port Dinorwic .During the next few years until her sale in 1883 to John Richard Jones, Master Mariner of Caernarfon, her home port was Porthmadog and she took cargoes of slate to Newcastle, Sunderland and other ports in the north east of England.

She was re-registered at the port of Caernarfon 1883. Still rigged as a brigantine she was usually manned by six men, master, mate, 2 A.B.'s 1 O.S. and a boy or a cook. She made several trips to Hamburg in the eighties from Caernarfon or Port Dinorwic, but increasingly during the nineties she is to be found taking cargoes from Port Penrhyn to London or sometimes to Newcastle, returning by devious routes, wherever a cargo was available. She spent some time in the winter of 1896-7 being repaired at Bangor.

By that time she had passed into the ownership of a trio of Thomases — — Robert Thomas a master mariner of Liverpool and Tŷ Croes, later Llanrhyddlad, another Robert Thomas, a shipbroker and Hugh Thomas, a clerk, both also from Liverpool. After 1900 with the lock-out in Penrhyn, she ceased to call at Bangor, being employed, as far as one can judge from the ports of call recorded in the crew lists, in general trading anywhere in the British Isles.

She was sold to an Irish owner, Patrick Curran of Dungarvan, in December 1902 and thereafter sailed mainly, one would guess, with cargoes of coal from Cardiff or Newport for various ports in Ireland .Eventually, at the age of fifty-eight, she met a fate common enough to ladies of her age, conversion to a barge or lighter. She was sold in 1915 to Richard Abel & Son, Ltd., Steam Barge and Lighter Owners of Liverpool. She remained on the Caernarfon Register until 1936, when it was recorded that she was broken up at Runcorn.

Less is known about the *Heather Bell* in the absence of crew lists but it is certain that the five quarrymen from Bethesda and Catherine Evans, the widow from Gatehouse were still shareholders until at least 1870. *Heather Bell* was wrecked at Llangrannog in 1891.

There is an element of mystery about Edward Ellis's later career and that of his son, another Edward Ellis and almost inevitably some confusion in the references between father and son. The fact that the shipyard was offered for sale in 1856 and that by the time of the 1861 census the family was no longer living in the house they built at Penrallt, Brynhyfryd, but had reverted to living in Garth (possibly in their old home) suggests financial difficulties about this time.

It will be recalled that Edward Ellis did not usually have a substantial interest in the ships he built himself and in this respect he differed greatly from John Parry. On the other hand, between 1848 and 1851 he did make some investments in ships built elsewhere, and these investments seem to have been on the whole unproductive. *Ann and Sarah,* a 34 ton sloop built at Maryport in 1831 was registered (Beaumaris 1848/1) as being totally in the ownership of Edward Ellis. How she came into his hands is not known; she may have come into his yard for repairs and been sold to him or even been transferred in default of payment — which was by no means unknown. In 1855 she was mortgaged to John Williams, a banker from Chester for £200 at 5%. The mortgage was never discharged and 32/64ths of the vessel was sold to two Bangor men, one of whom was Robert Roberts, the postmaster, who eventually became a major shareholder.

Also in 1848 with John Phillips he took a large share (28/64ths) in *Ann Grant,* a fully rigged ship of 377 tons built at Whitby in 1806. Two years later both men mortgaged their shares for £350.

In 1849 Edward Ellis had a 4/64ths share in the 62 ton schooner *Holyhead Trader,* built at Frodsham in 1821. (Beaumaris 1849/4). The other shareholders were mainly from Holyhead, but among them was Meshach Roberts, the Bangor druggist (who had been born at Holyhead). Edward Ellis mortgaged these shares to John Williams and the mortgage was never discharged.

Similary the 52 ton schooner, *Speedwell,* built at New Quay in 1804 was registered (Beaumaris 1851/5) as being wholly owned by Edward Ellis who then sold 4/64ths to Hugh Edwards, shipwright, Bangor.

In 1852 he mortgaged the remaining 60/64ths to Thomas Peers Williams and John Williams, 'Bankers and co-partners', Bangor, and with his consent they sold the vessel to a Liverpool shipowner and she was re-registered at Liverpool. The likelihood is that she was bought and repaired or rebuilt by Edward Ellis as a commercial speculation and the mortgage loan from the bankers financed the operation. Perhaps, too, the fact that she was previously registered at Aberystwyth, having been built at New Quay, gave him an introduction to the mariners of that port which led to the building of *Ifor* in 1853.

Taken together, these mortgages, the apparent abandonment of the new house at Penrallt and the offering for sale of the shipyard in 1856, all suggest that the business was seriously under-capitalised. The advertisement of the sale in the newspapers suggests that much of the equipment was new and that the yard was more than adequately furnished. It is possible that Edward

Ellis was too competitive in his tendering for the large ships that he built for New Quay owners and did not allow himself an adequate profit margin.

The shipyard was sold at some date in the sixties since Pigot's Trade Directory for Bangor in 1868 makes no mention of Edward Ellis and gives Parry and Co. as being situated at Hirael and Garth Road. The Ellises, both father and son, disappear from view as far as Bangor was concerned. They became ship surveyors in Liverpool. A conveyance of land at Llanfairfechan to Edward Ellis[7] calls him a ship surveyor of Liverpool. Edward Ellis would have been about 68 years of age at the time of the conveyance (1878) and it is reasonable to suppose that he was seeking to build a house for his retirement. The Methodists refuse to be kept out of the story; the land concerned was surplus to their requirements for chapel-building. When it was bought by the Methodists in 1874 at least three of the seven trustees can be identified as shipowners — Samuel Roberts and Thomas Lewis of Bangor and Richard Davies formerly of Menai Bridge, now of Treborth Hall.

(There is no doubt that the purchaser was Edward Ellis senior, and not his son, since the signature on the conveyance is identical with that on another document at the Caernarfon Record Office[8] dating back to 1845, a contract by Edward Ellis, Shipbuilder to purchase some land from the proprietors of the Penrallt Estate, Bangor).

[7] C.R.O. XM 3018/5.
[8] C.R.O. XM/55/10.

CHAPTER VI

THE BUILDERS iii

T. T. Parry & Co.

After the death of John Parry in 1855, it will be recalled, his property was divided into five equal shares between his children or their heirs and his sons, Robert and Thomas, were appointed executors. The exact details of how the assets were divided are not known, but the upshot was that Thomas, together with his sister Susan, took over the ship-building yard and Robert, with his sister Ann, succeeded to the salmon weirs and the farm at Abercegin. From this time forth Robert seems to have felt entitled to style himself as Gentleman.

Thomas would have been 23 years of age and his sister Susan 25 at the time of their father's death and it is little wonder that they turned to a man who had some experience of the business, Samuel Roberts.

We know rather more about Samuel Roberts than about other characters in this book because Samuel Roberts after his death had a book written about him in his other capacity, that of a Methodist minister — *Bywyd y Parch. Samuel Roberts, Bangor a Detholiad o'i Bregethau*, ('The Life of the Revd. Samuel Roberts, Bangor and a Selection of his Sermons') which will be referred to from now on simply as 'The Life'.[1] According to this Samuel

[1] See 'Maritime Wales', No. 9 by the present author for a fuller account of Samuel Roberts.

Roberts was apprenticed to Captain John Parry as a shipwright but his employer soon saw that he had more useful talents than 'the mere use of the mallet and adze' and took him into his office as a clerk. At the time of John Parry's death Samuel would have been about 36 years of age.

According to 'The Life' the 'sons felt that it was to their advantage to give a share of the firm to Mr. Roberts. And so instead of being a servant he became one of the masters.' Whether it was simply thus, an act of benevolence on the part of the sons, or the result of some more complex negotiation it is impossible to say. Henceforward it was no longer 'Samuel Roberts, Bangor, Grocer' on the Shipping Registers but 'Samuel Roberts, Shipbuilder'. He was a man of many parts; besides the grocer's shop in High Street which he appears to have given up about 1854 he was the secretary of the Bangor Mutual Ship Insurance Society from 1854 until his death in 1875, and in the Census return for 1861 he was described as 'Welsh Calvinistic Methodist Minister Bangor Chapel'.

(A word of explanation for those who are perhaps wondering why with his convictions he did not devote all his time to the ministry. The answer is given in the 'Life' — 'every candidate for the ministry was expected to have at hand some means of livelihood so as to be largely independent of the Connection for his support'. In the first half of the last century the Welsh Methodist ministry was founded on itinerant preachers and the pastoral work was largely in the hands of the deacons. We do not have to go far to look for another example of a man who combined shipbuilding with his ministry in the Revd. Rees Jones of Port Dinorwic. He was a native of Barmouth and as has already been said he first noticed the commercial possibilities of Port Dinorwic as a ship-building centre when he was on a preaching journey in Caernarfonshire.

The first ship to be built by the firm of T. T. Parry and Co. was the 96 ton schooner *Arthur Wyatt* (Beaumaris 15 of 1858). The following were the original shareholders —

> Joseph Brindley, Bermondsey, Slate Merchant, 8; John Williams, London, Ship Agent, 4; John Richards, Bangor, Surgeon, 8; Peter Williams, Bangor, Merchant, 8; Robert Thomas Parry, Bangor, Gentleman, 4; William Edwards, Bangor, Master Mariner, 16; Thomas Thomas Parry, Bangor, Shipbuilder, 6; Richard Threlfall Power, Bangor, Shipbuilder, 6; Samuel Roberts, Bangor, Shipbuilder, 4.

The shareholdings are well spread between London slate and shipping interests, local persons of substance including Robert Thomas Parry, the shipbuilders themselves and the master of the vessel.

She presents at her registration a good example of the way marine mortgages were used to offer deferred terms of payment to customers. Joseph Brindley mortgaged his 8 shares to T. T. Parry, Power and Roberts for £272 at 5% in September 1858 and the mortgage was discharged by May 1860.

Her master, William Edwards, was assisted by a mortgage of £160 on the same terms by the same three and it was discharged by 1866.

London was her usual destination after leaving Port Penrhyn and she would return wherever there was a cargo to be had, typically, in 1867 by way of Newcastle, Poole and Ellesmere Port or in 1868 by way of Ardrossan and Runcorn. She rarely went to the continent; Oporto is seen as her destination in 1869, Danzig in 1870 and Harburg in 1877 and 1890. Her owners during the sixties and seventies are given variously as Parry and Co., Samuel Roberts or John Ellis as Managing Owners. In the mid-nineties she passed into Amlwch ownership. Her Crew Agreement Lists[2] record that she entered practically every port in Britain in her forty-five years; the only mishaps recorded occurred towards the end of her life. In March 1903 on her way from Boulogne to Hull she grounded on Groby Sands, Yarmouth but got off with the assistance of a tug, the only damage being that a new rail was needed on the starboard bow. In June of the same year she collided in the River Mersey with a lighter 'doing damage to the headgear figurehead etc.' She was lost later in that year on a voyage from Runcorn to Charlestown in unknown circumstances.

The compliment paid by the naming of the *Arthur Wyatt* was handsomely rewarded in the following year by an order from the Wyatts for a new ship, the 66 ton schooner *Blue Jacket* (Beaumaris 1859/9). The shareholders were James Wyatt, Gentleman, Lime Grove, Bangor (16/64ths), Arthur Wyatt, Gentleman of the same address (40/64ths) and John Lloyd, Accountant, of Port Penrhyn. (8/64ths) We shall meet this team of shareholders again; suffice it to say that they owned and controlled the vessel until January 1868, when they felt obliged to relinquish their interest — but more about this later. She was transferred to the outright ownership of William Dawbarn, a Liverpool merchant and a customer of the Penrhyn Quarries.

She seems from the Crew Agreement Lists[3] to have been employed for the first twenty years of her life solely between Port Penrhyn and the ports of the Mersey, Liverpool, Garston or Runcorn with the exception of an occasional foray during the seventies across the Irish Sea to Cork, Waterford or Dundalk. During 1880 she appears to have made a trip to Harburg and generally to have widened the scope of her voyage making.

In 1881 the vessel returned to local ownership briefly when she was bought, with the aid of a mortgage, by Thomas Jones, a Master Mariner from Caernarfon. She sailed from Swansea to a place given as Pontardmer (so obscure that it did not boast a British consul and the master had to have the ship's papers examined and stamped in Honfleur) and Le Havre, returning by way of Goole, Plymouth, Falmouth, Saltney and Abersoch to Portmadoc. Thomas Jones died early in the following year and the vessel

[2] L.R.O. W/DB 50.
[3] L.R.O. W/DB 61.

was sold to W. H. Hills of Herne Bay. She was no longer seen on the west coast, except that she called twice in Portmadoc in 1884, and her registration was transferred to Ramsgate in 1893.

Cambria a schooner of 56 tons (Beaumaris 1860/18) was the yard's next product for a rather different group of indigenous shareholders in the builders themselves (T. T. Parry 30/64ths and Samuel Roberts 10/64ths), John Jones, Innkeeper and William Parry, Brazier, both of Bangor. Her Crew Agreement Lists show a varied pattern of trading, mostly in the Irish Sea, but with occasional calls to places as far afield as Southampton and Aberdeen.

We have another, and a very rare source of information about *Cambria* in an exercise book which seems to have been used at different times by her different masters as a rough book for the official log. There are entries for most of 1872, February and March 1874, parts of March, May, June and July 1875, and for three days in November 1884. There is a Crew Agreement List for only one of these periods, for the latter part of 1872.[4] Rather surprisingly, while all the ports of call are given in their correct order on the Crew Agreement List, the dates of arrival and departure do not tally with those given in the log. But the essential part of the form was the crew agreement, which was accurately made out (if not the Custom House wanted to know why) and some masters got away with listing their voyages as, for example, 'six voyages between Bangor and Liverpool'.

The Crew Agreement List gives the owner as Samuel Roberts, Plas Llwyd, Bangor, and the Master as William Roberts, 'Anglesey'. (We know from another entry that he came from Moelfre). In addition to William Roberts who was aged 31, we have another William Roberts, aged 24, as Mate, Owen Roberts aged 28 as A.B. and the county of birth of all three is given as Anglesey. They had all served on the same ship for the previous six months. The mate and A.B. were discharged in September and William Owen, aged 55, born in Anglesey, previous ship *Betsy* of Beaumaris, was signed as mate and, Robert Williams, aged 17, born in Anglesey, pervious ship *Secretary* of Truro, was signed as O.S. for the next voyage. The vessel was about to be slipped for repairs and the wages of the crew could be saved.

The log starts in March 1872 with the *Cambria* sailing from Cork to Liverpool; in April she sails from Liverpool to Wicklow and it is mentioned incidentally that her cargo was corn. In May she sailed in ballast for Bangor and at the end of the month sailed for Sandwich, arriving on the 20th of June. On the 29th she sailed in ballast for Rye where she arrived on July 1st, and it is at this point that we have the confirmatory evidence of the Crew Agreement List.

Each page in the log is headed "Remarks of the Schooner *Cambria*"

⁴ L.R.O. W/DB 68 for Crew Agreement Lists of *Cambria*. I am grateful to His Honour Judge Michael O'Donoghue for lending me the MSS of her log and allowing the reproduction of parts of it here.

and, in this case, "from Rye towards Runcorn." The entry for each day begins with an account of the weather and ends invariably with a remark about pumping the ship — "Pumps (carefully, duly) attended", or "Pumps free". At sea the bearing and distance off of landmarks and lights are carefully noted, and one realises how *coastal* were the majority of these voyages recorded, how rarely was the ship out of sight of land, and how often the vessel had to anchor not only to seek refuge in high winds but also to defeat adverse tides when the wind was light. In the excerpts which follow only the punctuation has been added.

On Wednesday July 3rd the weather was fine and the "men employed washing the hold. At 10 a.m. commenced to take in cargo — took in about 42 tons of boulders. So ended this day. Pumps Free". The boulders were certainly not ballast as the ballast taken on at Rye had been cleared out. It is possible that they were flint stones of the kind that Samuel Worthington's vessels used to pick up at Arundel and elsewhere on the south coast in the early years of the century for grinding down for use in the manufacture of porcelain.

On the 5th "at 9 p.m. the Pilot came aboard; unmoored the ship. Towed out by the steam tug *Dragon Fly*. At 11 p.m. they let go; Pilot went ashore. Dungeness Light bearing East distance about 7 miles, winds — light airs from the Eastward. At 2 a.m. light breeze from N.E., set the square sail and trimmed the sails to the best advantage. At 4 a.m. do. wind, Beachy Head bearing W.N.W. distance 8 miles. So ended these 24 hours. Pumps carefully attended."

Two more days of light breezes followed and *Cambria* passed Beachy Head, the Owers Light Ship, St. Catherine's Light and the Needles, but with strengthening winds on the evening of the second day she "came to an anchor in Portland Harbour with 30 fathoms chain. Furled the sails, set anchor watch. Pumps free." She remained in Portland Harbour for two days; on the third day she sailed with a fresh breeze from the S.S.W. but that night in misty weather and a falling breeze she anchored in Saltcombe (sic) Bay. She got under way next day and passed Eddystone Light. The following day "the Lizard bore by compass W.$\frac{1}{2}$S. distance 8 miles" in a fresh S.W. breeze "with heavy head sea, ship plunging heavily." In the afternoon with the wind drawing to the Southward she got round the Longships and entered the Bristol Channel. The following night, in strengthening winds, she put in to Milford Haven and came to anchor at Hakin where she remained for the next 24 hours.

On Monday 15th July, in pleasant weather and a moderate N.E. breeze she got under way and was off St. Ann's Head by noon. Most shipwrecks are caused by either high wind and big seas or foggy weather; in the case of *Cambria's* lucky escape neither of these factors operated. In clear weather and light airs at 6 p.m. the South Bishop Light was bearing North, distance

3 miles. "At 8 p.m. . . . tacked ship. At mid-night calm and hazy weather. South Bishop Light bearing N.N.W. distance $1\frac{1}{2}$ miles. Put out the boat to pull her ahead but nothing available. Ship setting fast on the rocks; hauled up 90 fathoms of chain and let go the anchor. At 1.15 do. calm and hazy, ship still drifting on the rocks; paid out chain nearly an end, then the anchor held. Then the ship took a broad sheer towards the rock, then we were forced to slip the anchor to save the ship and cargo and clear the rock.

"At 2 a.m. a light breeze sprang up from N.N.W., got all clear inside South Bishops Rock. At 3 clear of all; wind drawed to S.E. pleasant breeze. Set the square sail and trimmed the sails as requisite. At 4 a.m. do. wind and cloudy weather. South Bishop Light bearing S.S.W. distance about 8 miles. So ended these 24 hours." After such a night William Roberts could have been forgiven had he forgotten the pumps, but they were "duly attended."

Two nights later they were off Caernarfon Bar which they crossed at 4 p.m. on the following afternoon "with the intention to go to the river for Supplies." They picked up the Pilot at 6 p.m. and anchored off Port Dinorwic to await the tide. They got under way at 3 a.m. and anchored at Bangor at 6.

The vessel, though bound for Runcorn, remained at Bangor (her home port) for a week for repairs. Her foremast was stripped down and new fore rigging fitted. A new anchor and cable was taken on board to replace the one that had been slipped at the South Bishop Rock. At noon on Wednesday 24th July, they were under way once more. After anchoring for the tide at Rhyl and Formby, they reached the Mersey and were taken in tow to Runcorn. They stayed exactly a week at Runcorn, from July 31st to August 7th, discharging and taking on board cargoes. The log mentions the amount of cargo carried from Rye which was 90 tons ,which bears out what was said previously about a ship's registered tonnage and the amount she could carry. (*Cambria* was of 56 tons register). The cargo which was taken on board at Runcorn was 82 tons of salt for Howth.

The vessel was then towed by the steam tug *Helen* from Runcorn to New Ferry where they anchored, before getting under way at 4 a.m. Two days later when the South Stack Light bore E. by $S.\frac{1}{2}$ S., distance 12 miles they encountered a strong breeze from the S.S.W. and a heavy sea; they took in all light sails and double reefed the mainsail, and bore away for Holyhead. They sheltered in Holyhead New Harbour for four days, the crew being employed on painting the ship inside and setting the fore rigging. On Wednesday, 14th August in fine pleasant weather, and with all sails set they crossed the Irish Sea and arrived at Howth the following morning. The cargo was unloaded and ballast taken in for the return voyage to Liverpool a week later.

The crossing was uneventful with a moderate northerly breeze and at 1 p.m. the following day in calm conditions and light variable airs they anchored in Cemlyn Bay in 8 fathoms of water. With a light breeze from the S.W. they reached Red Wharf Bay on the following day and put in to Red Wharf, where they stayed for the next three days with winds from the N.N.W. When the wind turned to S.W. with a moderate breeze they got under way and the following evening came to anchor "in Magazine, furled the sails all ready for going up to Garston".

At Garston, after discharging the ballast, the vessel "was hauled under the Drop to take in Cargo . . . took in 63 tons" and later was "hauled under to take the remainder of Cargo". The cargo is not specified but it was clearly coal, and destined for Kingstown, which is now called Dun Laoghaire.

Cambria got under way at noon on Friday, September 6th and came to anchor at 8 p.m. on the following evening in Moelfre Roads. At mid-night on Sunday in a light southerly breeze she got under way and at 3.30 a.m. "got round Carmel Head, turned into Holyhead Bay. At 4.30 a.m. wind S.W. and drizzly rain. Ship took the ground. Rocks. Skerries Lighthouse bearing N. by E.¾ E.; east end of the breakwater bearing N.W. nearly. Men employed putting the boat out. Got the Stream Anchor and Kedge out trying to get her off, when we had to slip the warp of the kedge, and nothing available." — i.e. to no avail.

On the following day, Monday 9th September "at 8 a.m. the water ebbed on the ship to 5 feet. A boat with 4 men came from the shore to assist us to take her off. At 10.30 a.m. made sails and hove away on the Stream Hawser and got her off. Tried the pumps, ship making no water. At noon came to an anchor in New Harbour." The day ended with the inevitable entry — "Pumps duly attended" but this time with the addition "No water". Once more *Cambria* had had a very lucky escape.

A week was spent at Holyhead because of contrary or extremely light winds, before she made the crossing in moderate to fresh breezes in 20 hours, and came to an anchor in Kingstown Harbour. The cargo was unloaded and the ship was cleaned up ready for sea. There is no mention of ballast being taken on board and the next voyage, to Bangor, was made light. With moderate northerly breezes and some squalls she came to anchor in Bangor 16 hours later "and shifted up under Hirael. Furled the sails. So ended the day. Pumps free".

At Bangor the vessel was "put on the Patent Slip and got her up to the yard for repairs". A week later she was got down from the slip and "a block was put under her to fasten the iron keel." On the following day she was hauled to her loading berth and moored alongside. This was extremely quick work compared with the long delays that the less favoured vessels experienced at Port Penrhyn, but it should be remembered that the owners of the vessel were also the owners of the slip and that the owners, Parry and Co., had a close relationship with Arthur Wyatt and John Lloyd, the Port Penrhyn management. Barely a week after coming down from the slip *Cambria* was loaded and hauled out from the quay.

This time the cargo was, of course, slates, the first such cargo since her voyage to Sandwich in June, which emphasises once more the part Port Penrhyn ships played in the general carrying trade of Britain. The destination this time was Silloth, but however efficient the Port Penrhyn management they could not control the weather and it was a further ten days before she got under way from Garth Point on Saturday, September 27th. By "12 a.m. got through the Sound with all sails set . . . foggy weather. At 3 p.m. took in all Light Sails and furled them 4 p.m. hauled topsail back to keep company with another vessel . . . 10 p.m. Morecambe Bay Light Vessel S.E. by E. distance about 5 miles. 11 p.m. set flyn (flying) jib and gaff topsail. *Sunday 28th.* This 24 hours came in wind variable from S.E. to S.W. and moderate; still hazy weather. 3 a.m. Duddon Iron Works Light E.S.E. distance 7 miles. Clear up a little. Wind do. 4 a.m. set square sail and trimmed as requisite. 8 a.m. St. Bees N.N.E. distance 8 miles. Light breeze. S.S.W., all possible sails set. 12 p.m. abreast of Whitehaven. 2 p.m. came on thick fog. Light air S.W. and smooth water. 5 p.m. abreast of Solway Light Vessel distance $\frac{1}{2}$ mile. 8 p.m. Steam Tug *Arabian* took us into Silloth Dock and moor alongside another in dock. So ended this 24 hours. Pumps carefully attended."

The log records the events of the next week at Silloth, including a collision with an Italian barque while being warped into a dock, and then ends abruptly with the entry for October 5th. We know from the Crew Agreement List that from Silloth *Cambria* sailed for Mostyn, and thence to Dublin. At the year's end she sailed from Dublin to Bangor and there she remained.

The remainder of the log records her voyages in February and March 1874 from Portrush to Portmadoc, from Bangor to Alnmouth (as far as Runcorn) in March 1875 and from Bangor towards Belfast. There follow a number of loose pages — 'Port Dinorwic towards Wick', and 'Remarks of the Schooner Cambria at London' for 1875 and then a single sheet, dated November 1884 when she appears to be making passage from the Mersey to the Menai Straits.

The vessel was sold to owners in Port Dinorwic in 1875 and re-registered at the Port of Caernarfon, and this change is reflected in the extant Crew Agreement Lists. Her home port is now Port Dinorwic and she continues to trade mainly with ports on the western side of Britain. In 1900 she was sold to a shipowner in Cricieth and traded from Portmadoc. The series of Crew Agreement Lists ends in 1902 and throws no light on her end. The register merely says that she foundered in December 1903.

A somewhat larger schooner of 74 tons, *Dorothea,* was built in 1862 (10 of that year) for Bangor owners, John Simon, Farmer with 24/64ths, Robert Jones, Master Mariner with 12/64ths, Owen Owen, Master Mariner with 4 and the builders T. T. Parry and R. T. Power 9/64ths each and Samuel

Slate Schooners at Port Penrhyn, c. 1890. (G.A.S. XS 1077/3/2/9.)

Remarks of the Schooner "Cambria" from
September 1872

Friday 6th

Wind S.S.W. fresh breeze and Cloudy weather. At Noon hauled out of Dock got under way all possible Sails set. At 2 P.M. Do Winds and Showery – Abreast of Rock Lighthouse. At 5 P.M wind West to N.W. light airs took in the Square Sail and trimmed the Sails as requisite. At 8 P.M. wind – S.W. fresh breeze and heavy Showers of rain N. West Light Ship bearing E N E distance 9 miles. At Midnight wind from S.W. to N.W. moderate breeze and cloudy. Abreast of Great Ormes Head distance 4 miles off. At 4 A.M. wind N N W fresh breeze and heavy rain. 6. A.M. wind W. N W. fresh breeze and rain. So ended these 24 hours. "Pumps Duly Attended".

Saturday 7th

First part Wind W. N W. fresh breeze At 8 A.M bore up for Moelvre Roads Came to an Anchor in 8 fathoms water furled the Sails. latter part wind drawed to W.S W. moderate breeze and cloudy. So ended this Day. "Pump Free."

Sunday 8th

Wind West fresh breeze and fine clear weather throughout. No work done being Sabbath Day. At Noon wind draw to the Southward, moderate breeze –

Pages from the Log of the Schooner *Cambria* for 6-9 September 1872

(the stranding near the Skerries)

(By kind permission of His Honour Judge Michael O'Donoghue)

Garston Towards Kingston.

September 1872   Mary Prichard

David Jones
Jones

At midnight wind South light breeze
made Sails and got under way. At 1 A.m
Do winds and hazy weather. Abreast of
Lynas Point. At 2 A.M. wind hauled
to S.W. with heavy rain At 3 A.M. Do
wind with thick hazy weather and
drizzly rain. At 3.30 got round Carm.
Head turned into Holyhead Bay —
At 4.30 A.M. wind S.W. and large
rain and thick hazy weather. Ship took
the ground. Rocks Skerries Lighthouse
bearing N by E ¾ E. east end of the —
Breakwater bearing N.W. nearly. Men
employed putting the Boat out got the
Stream Anchor and Kedge out trying
to get her off. when the ~~~ ~~~ ~~~
~~~ ~~~ ~~~ the Kedge and ~~~
available. So ended these 24 hours.
                "Pumps Carefully Attended"

Monday 9th

Wind from S.W. to West with misty
weather. At 8 A.M. the water ebbed on the
Ship to 5 feet. a Boat with 4 men came
from the Shore to assist us to take her
off. At 10.30 A.M. made Sails and hove
away on the Stream Hawser and got her
off. tried the pumps. Ship making no
water. At noon Came to an Anchor in
New Harbour. fresh breeze from W.S.W.
with heavy rain. Men employed at various
Jobs. So ended this Day.
                "Pumps Duly Attended" — No ~~~

Above:

The 71 ton schooner *Sarah Jane* built at Bangor 1861. Sold to Runcorn and lost off Newlyn in 1913. (G.A.S. Henry Parry Collection XS/1279/7/150.)

Right:

Model of the 74 ton schooner *Dorothea* built at Bangor 1862. Sold to Caernarfon and lost in 1900.

(By kind permission of Mr. Denys Owen)

Roberts with 6. Curiously enough, Power, (Parry's brother-in-law) is recorded in this particular register entry as a wine merchant of Liverpool.

The Crew Agreement List[5] for the first half of 1863 has Samuel Roberts, Plas Llwyd, Bangor as her owner and Robert Jones as her master; in the next half year the owner is given as Parry and Co., and that remains until 1868 when the name of Robert Williams, her master at the time, appears. Then for a period the name reverts to Parry and Co., for 1870 it is John Simon, Bangor and thereafter until 1875 it is back to Samuel Roberts. This is mentioned as an example of how many 'owners' a ship could enjoy in the Crew Lists while remaining under substantially the same ownership. In this, as in other respects, the ship's Certificate of Registry was the substantive document.

Dorothea was a typical medium-range Bangor coaster. She was sold to a Caernarfon master mariner in 1886 and re-registered at that port. On January 17th, 1900 she left Caernarfon bound for Silloth. According to the register she 'was totally lost on February 9th, 2 miles S.E. of the Solway Light Ship. Crew appear safe.'

Eliza, a schooner of 101 tons (Beaumaris 1866/10) was built for Richard Williams, Master Mariner of Morfa Nefyn who initially held a 16/64ths share, aided by a mortgage of £250 at 5% from another master mariner of Morfa Nefyn, Robert Williams. The yard was most co-operative; Parry and Power each held 18/64ths and Samuel Roberts 12/64ths and in the course of several years up to 1874 by various transactions they relinquished their holdings to him. He died in the following year and his widow sold half the vessel to yet another Williams, William, Master Mariner of Llanallgo.

Her Crew Agreement Lists from 1867[6] show that she was managed by Parry and Co., and commanded by Richard Williams, Morfa Nefyn. Her crew at this period consisted of Master, Mate 2 A.B.'s, an O.S. and a Boy. She was a long-range trader and made frequent trips to the continent.

The only voyage for which the cargoes carried were recorded began on January 10th, 1872 from Newport with a cargo of coals for Dublin, arriving there on the 12th. She sailed in ballast from Dublin to Bangor on January 26th, arriving the following day. A month later, on February 26th she left Bangor with a cargo of slates for London, which was reached on March 14th. On April 4th she left London with a cargo of superphosphate for Saltney, arriving there on the 23rd. Leaving Saltney on May 8th she arrived at Bangor in ballast on May 16th. On June 21st she left Bangor with slates for Silloth and arrived there on the 26th.

Cargoes are not recorded for the next half-year in the course of which *Eliza* returned to Bangor by way of Newry. She then sailed from Bangor for Harburg returning *via* Glasson Dock, Glasgow, and Holyhead to Bangor

---

[5] L.R.O. W/DB 112 *Dorothea.*
[6] L.R.O. W/DB 126 *Eliza.*

in December. Harburg, Dieppe and Dunkirk are mentioned as destinations as well as numerous ports in England, Scotland and Ireland in the years which follow. She was very much a Port Penrhyn ship until the death of William Williams in 1896; in the following year his widow sold the vessel to Thomas Ingram, Master Mariner of Cork who sold her to Patrick O'Driscoll of Bantry. From 1898 until 1913, when the series of Crew Agreement Lists ends she was employed almost exclusively in the coal trade between Newport and various ports in the south and west of Ireland. She was broken up in 1927 at Skibbereen.

Parry, Power and Roberts had no part in the shareholding of the next ship built in their yard. Aled Eames has recounted in *Ships and Seamen of Anglesey*[7] the history of the schooner *Fomalhaut* from the moment that Captain Owen Williams and his son 'contracted with Samuel Roberts of Plas Llwyd, Bangor, Shipbuilder "on the purchase of the new vessel now on the stocks at the yard of Mr. T. T. Parry at Garth for the sum of £1680" . . . so the *Fomalhaut* was launched into the Menai Straits in 1874.' She was registered (Beaumaris 1874/2) as being 48/64ths in the ownership of William Williams, Edge Hill, Garth, Master Mariner and 16/64ths in the ownership of his father, Owen Williams, who in 1880 transferred his share to his son.

Aled Eames, basing his account on a notebook containing the accounts of the *Fomalhaut* has painted a vivid picture of her activities and the ports she visited which included "Liverpool, Peterhead, Hamburg, Middlesborough, Swansea, Newry, Silloth, Dundalk, Glasgow, Kingstown, Lossiemouth, Thurso, Warrenpoint, Annan, Fraserburgh, Limerick, Nairn, Leith, Dieppe, Weston Point, Birkenhead, Greenock, Porthcawl, Waterford, Poole and Newcastle." Her crews for the most part were drawn from Anglesey. By great good fortune the notebook has survived to give us some of the freights the vessel earned in 1885, when she earned, for instance "May 29 By Freight of Slates from Bangor to Hamburg £26.11.8. and October 15 By Freight of Slates from Bangor to Aberdeen £20.19.4."

October 1902 was a black month for Bangor; *Fomalhaut* and *Lady Louisa Pennant* after loading slates at Caernarfon left Bangor in company on the 14th. Neither was heard of again.

Fomalhaut, a 72t. schooner, built in 1874 was the last vessel of any size to be built at Bangor. During the boom years of the fifties and sixties there had been some over-production of sailing vessels both in Britain and in ships imported from North America; moreover, coastal shipping had to face keen competition for freights from the railways, although it was not until the eighties that the tonnage of freight sent by rail actually overtook that sent by sea from Port Penrhyn. Local investment was going into companies such as the Eryri or Gwynedd Shipping Companies which were ordering from the yards

---

[7] Aled Eames op.cit., pp. 402 ff.

of Liverpool or Sunderland large ocean going ships or barques built of iron or, later, steel which were, at this date, able to compete with steamers for long voyages. With the development of the compound, and later the triple expansion steam engine, steamers were even making inroads on the coastal carrying trade particularly with commodities for which a definite delivery date was desirable such as foodstuffs. Samuel Roberts, who died at the comparatively early age of 56 in 1875 was at least spared the sight of this decline.

It was thus a sign of the times that T. T. Parry's next vessel should have been a steam vessel, the 42 ton *Menai*, built of wood. She was 81.5 feet in length, of which the engine room took up 25 feet. She was a twin-screw vessel, and her engines were supplied by De Winton's, Caernarfon, and described at 20 h.p., direct acting, cylinder diameter 7", stroke 10."

Menai (Beaumaris 1878/7) was owned by a consortium of business men from Bangor and Beaumaris led by Thomas Morgan, Garth Ferry Proprietor, who was the Managing Owner until his death in 1888 when he was succeeded by his son William Morgan.

She plied with passengers between Bangor and Beaumaris from May to October each year. Her crew consisted of a master, an A.B. and an engineer. The Crew Agreement Lists usually record the last ship on which the crew member served; in the case of Henry Jones, Holyhead who signed on as engineer in 1891 it was stated that this was his first voyage but that he was used to managing steam threshing engines! His appointment did not lead to any marine disaster and it continued for another two seasons.

The local press was very appreciative of the ferry service and when *Menai* was sold in 1902 to become a Milford Haven ferryboat, plying between Pembroke Dock and Neyland, she was much missed. The gap was filled when the Bangor Borough Council purchased the steel built steamer *Lady Magdalen* (Beaumaris 1904/2) and became proprietors of the ferry. Although she sailed in distant waters, *Menai* remained on the Beaumaris Register until 1922, when she was converted into a dumb barge.

The very last commercial vessel to be built in T. T. Parry's yard or anywhere in Bangor was the 37 ton smack *Pilgrim*. She was built for Conway owners in 1879 and remained in Conwy hands until she was wrecked on Conway Bar in 1918.

Bangor was not alone in reaching the end of the ship-building road; Porthdinllaen had already built its last ship in 1876, Pwllheli in 1878, Nefyn's last ship was to be launched in 1880 and Caernarfon's in 1884. Even Porthmadog with its strong export trade built only one ship between 1878 and 1891 when there was a resurgence. But there remained the business of ship-repair and ship ownership.

As John Parry had been a shipowner on a considerable scale, so his successors continued with this side of the business. Samuel Hughes Griffith,

Master Mariner of Bangor mortgaged his 69 ton schooner, *Margaret and Anne* (Beaumaris 1856/5) to T. T. Parry, R. T. Power and Samuel Roberts as joint mortgagees for £527 at 5%. She was of foreign build, and was previously the *Nestor* of Nantes and it is possible that the mortgage was raised to pay for some conversion work at the Parry yard.

The mortgage was transferred in 1858 to Thomas Peers Williams and John Williams, Bankers and this marked the end of the firm's involvement with the vessel, but her subsequent history is interesting. After trading for some years in the slate trade, during which she sailed to London, Montrose, Dublin and Hamburg among other places, she was sold in 1875 to two men from Llanaelhaearn and became a stone carrier for the group of quarries at the foot of Yr Eifl, making voyages to the Mersey ports or Ireland for the most part. After a period lying up at Port Dinorwic she was sold in 1912 to a machinery merchant from Stockport and registered anew (Beaumaris 1913/3) 'on conversion to steam' at Port Dinorwic. Her engine of two cylinders (12″ diam. x 20″) was clearly second or even third hand since the maker was not known and she was reduced to one mast 'for derrick purposes only'. She became a salvage vessel but not, seemingly, a very successful one since she was broken up in 1919.

Reference has been made previously to *Ann and Susan* (page 65) and to *Mary Grace* (page 67) both built by John Parry in 1835 and 1841 respectively. In 1857 *Ann and Susan* was re-registered and T. T. Parry and R. T. Power each held 21/64ths and Samuel Roberts 14/64ths. *Mary Grace* was re-registered in 1856 as a result of her lengthening and one of her major owners was Richard Morris Griffith with 32/64ths. These were mortgaged to the builders for £524 in the proportion of 12/64ths each for Parry and Power and 8/64ths for Roberts.

The perceptive reader will have noticed the symmetry of the foregoing shareholdings which are in the ratio of:—

T. T. Parry 3; R. T. Power 3; Samuel Roberts 2

It was remarked previously that the system of ownership by sixty-fourth part shares was still very much alive in North Wales at this time and that there is little evidence for the existence of shipping companies even after the 1862 Companies Act had been passed. Nevertheless, there is a strong presumption that an embryonic shipping company was beginning to form in the partnership of Parry, Roberts and Power, and that Parry and Power each held a $\frac{3}{8}$ interest and Samuel Roberts $\frac{1}{4}$. No formal deed of partnership has been found and these proportions have been inferred from the pattern of the shareholdings recorded in the Registers of Shipping.

Indeed, the same proportions are seen with the share-holdings of ships built in the yard and previously mentioned — *Arthur Wyatt,* where the ratio is 6:6:4, *Dorothea* with 9:9:6 and *Eliza* with 18:18:12. Only

Cambria provides an exception; R. T. Power for some reason did not have any share in her; Samuel Roberts had 10, T. T. Parry had 30, which had they been divided between Power and himself would have given 15 each, entirely in accordance with the formula.

Adieu, a small Conwy built schooner (Beaumaris 1858/6) of 21 tons, again presents the same proportion of holdings. She was altered at the Parry yard and came into the partners' ownership, with Parry and Power each holding 24/64ths and Roberts 16/64ths. Power subsequently relinquished his shareholding to Parry and Roberts so that each now held 32/64ths. *Adieu's* Crew Agreement Lists[8] make somewhat unexciting reading since she ran what amounted to a shuttle service between Bangor and Chester, varying it with an occasional call at Mostyn or Connah's Quay. After Samuel Roberts's death and the bankruptcy of T. T. Parry the vessel was sold to John Hughes, Draper and General Dealer of Red Wharf Bay and she performed the same function between Liverpool and Red Wharf Bay. She was stranded at Hoylake in 1886 and became a total loss.

North American built ships were sometimes purchased by Bangor owners and the 98 ton brig *Emily,* built at Harbour Grace, Newfoundland in 1826, is a good example. She was not a new ship when she was bought by two Bangor men in 1840, Richard Williams, Mariner and Zacharias Roberts, Gentleman, and registered at Beaumaris (25 of 1840). A slight digression on the ownership of *Emily* during the ensuing quarter century is permissible for the light it throws on the wide variety of occupations of those who invested in shipping. Richard Williams and Zacharias Roberts, immediately the purchase of the ship was completed, began to divest themselves of some of the shares. Farmers in general were prominent investors in ships, and it is no surprise to find two farmers, Thomas Jones and John Owens among the first of the new shareholders; others included a draper and a sawyer from Bangor, a gentleman from 'Velin Heli', Richard Edwards, and Edward Ellis, the Bangor shipbuilder, who had a 4/64ths share. True to form, he sold his holding to Henry Ellis, Druggist (his brother?) and Zacharias Roberts two years later.

The vessel was re-registered as a schooner of 88 tons in 1852 with much the same ownership but with the addition of another farmer, Humphrey Ellis of Llanllechid. Nine years later she came into the hands of the 'firm', with T. T. Parry holding 18 shares, R. T. Power 18 and Samuel Roberts 12. The remaining 16 shares were held by her master, Robert Thomas of Bangor. Some of her Crew Agreement Lists for the period between 1863 and 1872 have been preserved[9] and show that her normal complement as a schooner was master, mate and 2 A.B.'s. She was laid up at Bangor until May in 1863, but then sailed to Limerick and Glasgow and back to Bangor. In the second

[8] L.R.O. W/DB 5.
[9] L.R.O. W/DB 146.

half of the year she made three round voyages, to Portsmouth, Plymouth and Bristol, returning direct to Bangor from each place. In 1866 she sailed three times to Glasgow, returning for the first time by way of Liverpool and Dundalk, the second time by Runcorn and the third time by Dublin. The next record is for the year 1872 when the vessel is lying up at Bangor; it says "This vessel has been condemned as not worth repairing" and she was taken off the register in that year.

The 85 ton schooner, *Gazelle,* was built at Berwick-on-Tweed in 1845 and came into the ownership of two master mariners, Edward Owen of Bangor and Thomas Jones of Ysgybor Fawr, Anglesey, a farmer from Llaneugrad and a widow from the same place. (Beaumaris 18 of 1862) Edward Owen owned the whole of the vessel by October 1863, when he sold 4/64ths to Robert Hughes, Gaerwen and 4/64ths to Owen Thomas, Islington, both Ministers of the Gospel. In the same month he sold 3/64ths to T. T. Parry, 3/64ths to R. T. Power and 2/64ths to Samuel Roberts, the same significant proportions indicating that they operated as a firm. Richard Threlfall Power is this time recorded in the register as 'Merchant of Liverpool' rather than 'Shipbuilder' which is perhaps an indication that he did not actively participate in the day to day work of the ship yard. The vessel was lost in the Pentland Firth in October 1866 and the registry closed.

The sloop *Priscilla* of 40 tons (later reduced to 29 tons), built at Pwllheli in 1827 (Beaumaris 30 of 1827) for owners in Aberdaron, was eventually sold in 1856 to Thomas Jones, Diver of Bangor. Her Crew Agreement Lists[10] show that she ranged surprisingly widely with only a crew of one besides the master. Her normal beat was from Bangor to Garston or Runcorn but in 1867 she visited ports as far apart as Silloth and Port Talbot, Dundalk and Bristol, and in 1869 she sailed to Ayr and Dublin. For the first half of 1870 she was recorded as engaged in oyster dredging in Ramsey Bay. Thomas Jones mortgaged the vessel in 1864 to the 'firm' of Parry, Power and Roberts for £100. The mortgage was never discharged and the vessel was bought by Robert Owen, Accountant of Bangor, who promptly sold her to Samuel Roberts for an undisclosed sum, as the newspapers say. For the last two years for which the Lists are available (1871-73) she is recorded as lying up at Bangor, so that it is no surprise that she was broken up in 1879.

At the other end of the scale, as far as Bangor ships are concerned, the 105 ton brig, *Angora,* altered to a brigantine in 1865, (Beaumaris 1862/17) was built at Digby, Nova Scotia in 1853, and was owned in 1862 by David Roberts, Accountant and Richard Owen, Quarry Agent both of Bethesda. They sold her in October 1868 to Robert Owen, Builder of Holyhead who on the same day mortgaged her for £300 at 5% to T. T. Parry, R. T. Power and Samuel Roberts, Shipbuilders, Bangor, probably to pay for work done

[10] L.R.O. W/DB 325.

at their yard. The Crew Agreement Lists[11] show that the vessel was laid up from November 1867 until May 1868, probably for repairs. She ranged widely as the record for the first half of 1870 shows; on March 5th she sailed from Bangor to London, from London she went on to Dublin and Duddon, from Duddon to Swansea, thence to Fècamp and Treport and arrived at the end of June at Runcorn. Owners are given on the Crew Lists variously at T. T. Parry, Robert Owen and Samuel Roberts. In March 1872 she sailed from Irvine bound for Woolwich and she foundered about 18 miles W.N.W. of the Skerries, off the coast of Anglesey. Master and crew were saved. There is no record of the mortgage having been discharged.

As if to emphasise the existence of the firm of Parry, Power and Roberts, the few transactions in the Register in which Samuel Roberts was involved in an individual capacity refer to him as 'Marine Store Dealer'. It seems that the grocer's shop revealed in the 1851 census had long since given way to a handsome house on the corner of High Street and William Street, within sight and easy reach of the port, known then and to this day as Plas Llwyd, and to a shop in Well Street. The extent of the sideline in Well Street may be judged from the flap of an old business envelope (one of the few pieces of paper that have survived) which is embossed 'Samuel Roberts/Merchant/Ship & Boatbuilder/Ship Chandler/ & Sailmaker/ Bangor.'

Nightwatch, a small schooner of 21 tons, built at Holyhead in 1861 (Beaumaris 9 of 1866) was bought by Samuel Roberts from Edward Jones, Pilot Holyhead, in May 1866 and sold in October of the same year to two merchants from Seaforth and was transferred to the Liverpool Registry that month so that her ultimate fate is not known. The old 20 ton sloop, *Jenny,* built at Nefyn in 1787 (Beaumaris 1787/27) came into his hands in February 1867 and was sold to William Evans, Merchant of Menai Bridge in July of that year. Clearly, he had a good eye for a likely vessel for *Jenny* survived until 1919 and was lost at sea; but he did have previous knowledge of her since she had belonged in her time to his old master, John Parry. Clearly, too, in both transactions, Samuel Roberts was acting as a broker independently of the 'firm'.

Samuel Roberts died in December 1875 at the early age of fifty-six, high in public regard for his sincerity in the pulpit and for his integrity in commercial affairs. Accounts of his funeral in the *Life* and in the local press[12] make this very clear. Both the religious and the maritime communities were represented, the former by ministers of different denominations walking two abreast and by deacons walking four abreast, the latter by members of the Bangor Mutual Ship Insurance Society, while all the ships in the port were

[11] L.R.O. W/DB 37.
[12] N.W.C. 25.12.1875.

flying their colours at half-mast. A fellow shipbuilder, the Revd. Rees Jones of Port Dinorwic, offered prayer at the graveside.

His work with the Bangor Mutual Ship Insurance Society, almost from its inception in 1853, will be discussed in a later chapter.

Whether or not Thomas Thomas Parry would have become bankrupt in 1882 had Samuel Roberts survived, is a matter of idle speculation. There was certainly a sharp depression in trade generally and this was not without its effect on coastal shipping, which was also suffering from additional ills of its own, most of which have been mentioned already — competition for freight from the railways and from coastal steamers etc.. The ship-building business itself had come to an end and there were fewer ships to repair and maintain.

On May 6th 1882 'that valuable freehold detached villa residence known as BODIFYR in the occupation of Mr. T. T. Parry . . . with 2 acres of land' was advertised for sale in the *North Wales Chronicle* and a fortnight later the same paper contained a notice 'for the liquidation by arrangement of the Affairs of T. T. Parry, of Bodifyr and of Garth, Bangor, Shipbuilder' and a notification that John Pritchard (an Auctioneer) of Bod Hyfryd, Bangor, had been appointed as Trustee of the property.

The auction was held on June 6th and among the 'valuable effects' are noted 'three large baulks of Greenheart . . . white and red lead . . . about 35 cwt. of nails (iron and copper) . . . powerful winch and patent slip . . . contents of Smithy . . . the hull of the *Eliza Goddard* and the *Louise Clemence* now lying at Hirael . . . 32/64 of the wherry *Adieu*, 24/64 of the flat *Alice Anna* . . . the unexpired term of the lease of the Yard and extensive premises, held at a Rental of £81.10.0 per annum of which £65 is sublet . . .'

This was the sad end of a venture which had started fifty years previously with Captain John Parry and his father-in-law, Robert Thomas. The Liquidator appointed to wind up the concern was that man of many hats, W. J. Parry of Coetmor, at this time of Maesygroes, Llanllechid, quarry-men's leader, store owner, explosives dealer but on this occasion he was wearing his professional hat as an accountant. He appears to have taken over the lease of the premises and to have sub-let them to Owen Roberts, a shipbuilder who was already in business somewhere in Hirael.

Owen Roberts did not build any new ships but it appears from the Registers that he bought and sold vessels possibly, after repairing them in his yard. *Aurora* a 24 ton smack built in Brixham in 1818 (Beaumaris 1856/4) was bought by him and sold to Porthdinllaen in 1883; *Burncoose* a 65 ton schooner built in Swansea in 1840 (Beaumaris 1881/3) was bought in 1881 and sold in the following year to a shipbuilder in Stornoway; *Glynaeron*, a 52 ton schooner built in Aberaeron was bought in 1889 and sold to Aberystwyth in 1894 and the 61 ton schooner *Lewis* built at Three Pines, Prince Edward Island (Beaumaris 1890/4) was bought in 1890 and sold in the same year to a man from Llanallgo. The 45 ton ketch *Margaret* built at Conwy in 1862 (Beaumaris 1892/1) was bought in 1891 and sold two years later to a coal merchant in Wexford.

Although Lloyd's agent for Bangor, Robert Hughes, speaking at an opening ceremony when a new slip was inaugurated at Garth in 1893[13] foresaw a bright future for Bangor as a shipbuilding and ship repairing centre, it was not to be. In the following year Lord Penrhyn ordered his first steamer.

[13] C. & D.H. 13.1.1893.

CHAPTER VII

THE BUILDERS iv

John Roberts

and other builders

It was remarked earlier that the small nineteenth century sailing ship could be built practically anywhere provided that there was access to the sea or a river estuary. The foreshore at Hirael offered an ideally protected site, extending about half a mile in a shallow crescent between Garth Point and Abercegin. Two only of the shipbuilding sites have been identified with certainty, the shipyards of John Parry (later T. T. Parry) at the south end of the bay opposite the Nelson public house, and of Edward Ellis at the other extremity, in Garth Road where the patent slip of Messrs. A. M. Dickie and Sons is situated.

A draft lease from the Bishop of Bangor of an area of waste ground, beach and foreshore extending from Lôn Hirael to a quay in Garth[1] in 1805 to a man called John Roberts does at least give us a name. Included in the lease was a quillet about twelve yards long and eight in breadth adjoining the sea shore with permission to build 'Houses, Baths, Bathing Houses (sea-bathing was at this period all the rage) Wharfs, Quays etc. or

[1] U.C.N.W. Carter Vincent 1196.

for any other purpose'. The lease was for three lives and it is at least possible that the John Roberts who was credited with the building of at least seven ships between 1846 and 1864, was his son or grandson. A rough sketch map with the lease puts the quillet near the mouth of the little River Adda, which is rather nearer Garth than Hirael, and would put John Roberts's yard about midway between the yards of John Parry and Edward Ellis.

There were several timber yards and a foundry in the immediate vicinity so that the raw materials were readily at hand wherever the ships were built, on the foreshore itself or in the fields adjoining. Land could be leased for a short term without necessarily leaving a documentary record.

But before we come to the days of John Roberts the Shipbuilder three other builders must be allowed to make a brief appearance. We have no clue at all as to the precise location chosen by William Williams who according to the Beaumaris Register (18 of 1841) was responsible for the building of the 46 ton smack, *William and Richard,* in which he had a 48/64ths share-holding, with his brother or son Richard, a carpenter, holding 4/64ths. John Williams, a mariner from Bangor, held 6/64ths and the other shareholders were a farmer from Llanfairynghornwy and a spinster from Caernarfon. William Williams does not appear as a shipbuilder in any other Beaumaris registrations, and his name appears later on the same page in connection with a bill of sale as 'Merchant'. It is quite possible, as sometimes happened, that he was not the shipwright but merely the person who organised or financed the building. The vessel was lost in 1860 before the days when the Crew Agreement Lists came into force and nothing more is known about her.

Another shipbuilder about whom nothing is known is Humphrey Roberts who built the 55 ton schooner *Emma Laura* (Chester 1844/3) in 1843. He could be the father or brother of John Roberts since he precedes him in the register (1843) and does not overlap him (John Roberts's name first appears in 1846) but this identification is to be treated with caution. To add to the mystery David Thomas in his list for 1843 has two *Emmas, Emma Laura* of 49 tons and *Emma Louisa* of 55 tons. Humphrey Roberts's name is given as the builder of both ships, but it is given in italics for *Emma Laura* which is an indication that the source is not the registry entry. But, in fact, it is, — in the Chester registry and no entry has yet been found for *Emma Louisa*. One must conclude in the present state of knowledge that the two *Emmas* are in fact one and the same ship, that she was called *Emma Laura* and that she was registered at Chester in 1844.

David Thomas has her, alias *Emma Louisa* of 55 tons, as built for Chester owners and registered at that port, but subsequently sold to Llanelli in 1855. The Chester entry for *Emma Laura* dated 9 April 1844 has a note which indicates that there was a previous registration at Llanelli on May 4 1843 which accords well with the date given for her building, 1843. She was mainly owned by various members of the Bithell family of Chester and Flintshire until 1865 when she was sold and re-registered at Ramsay.

It comes as something of a surprise to encounter the next registration (Beaumaris 1842/2) of the 74 ton schooner, *Mary*, built at Bangor by Nicholas Treweek of Amlwch. The Treweeks were a prominent family in Amlwch as merchants and in connection with the copper trade of Mynydd Parys. She was the only vessel built by Treweek at Bangor in contrast to the several, if not scores, built by the Treweeks at Amlwch. It is possible only to guess why she was built at Bangor at this particular time; the forties were marked by a boom in coastal shipping and it is possible that all the available building sites in the rather cramped harbour at Amlwch were occupied.

With her ownership firmly based in Amlwch's pattern of trading, itself based on the export of copper ore or semi-refined copper, it comes as something of a surprise to find her trading from Bangor for the two years, 1863 and 1864 for which we have her Crew Agreement Lists.[2] Nicholas Treweek had sold the vessel in 1855 to Thomas Davies Griffith, a surgeon, but she still had an Amlwch crew, consisting of a master, mate and one A.B., and occasionally a cook. In the first half of 1863 she sailed from Bangor to Preston, Bangor to Portrush, Ardrossan, Garston, Dublin and back to Bangor. In the second half of the year she sailed from Bangor to Bristol, then Briton Ferry, Liverpool, Dublin, again to Bristol, Swansea, Liverpool again, and Amlwch before returning to Bangor in what seems to have been a very busy year.

In 1864 she sailed from Bangor to Saundersfoot, then Youghal, and on to Bristol and Cardiff. Returning from Cardiff to Liverpool she was lost on Scareweather Banks on September 20 but according to the List 'the crew were saved by the ship's boat and landed safe in Swansea'. A pencilled note adds that she 'struck on a sunken wreck — foundered'.

In contrast to William Williams and Nicholas Treweek who are credited with one ship each, John Roberts built seven ships between 1846 and 1864. He began with the 28 ton smack *Alice and Mary* (Beaumaris 1846/7) built for William Jackson, a railway contractor. She was back in the hands of her builder when she was re-registered in 1862. Her Crew Agreement Lists[3] tell us that she normally carried a crew of three, master, mate and seaman, and that she ran regularly between Bangor and the Mersey ports, Liverpool, Garston or Runcorn — no other ports of call are mentioned. On a voyage from Bangor in January 1869 she was sunk in the Mersey after being in collision with the smack *Eaglet* but her crew were saved.

John Roberts does not appear to have been involved in any new construction for eight years until he built the *Victoria* in 1854 (Beaumaris 35 of that year) for Peter Jones, Master Mariner of Barmouth and a consortium

[2] L.R.O. W/DB 266.
[3] L.R.O. W/DB 25.

116

of merchants and shopkeepers from Dolgellau. Bangor did not see her after her launch since she was employed for the remainder of her life on river navigation on the Mawddach carrying both passengers and goods. She was smack rigged and registered at only 11 tons although she was over fifty-five feet in length and had a beam of 8.6 feet. Her figurehead, incidentally, was a woman's bust. She was, as her registration states, a 'Steam Vessel propelled by paddle wheels', the first of only two built at Bangor. Her comparatively low registered tonnage is explained by the deductions made by the registration formula for the engine room (which measured 15.5 feet by 7.6 feet) and bunkers. Little has been discovered about her subsequent history but she does not appear to have been a successful venture since she was broken up in 1864, only ten years later.

Something of a mystery surrounds the next ship which emerged from John Roberts's shipyard, the schooner *Marion*, built in 1856. A search of the Shipping Registers from Chester in the north to Aberystwyth in the south has failed to reveal any trace of the vessel, and all we have is an account of her launching in *The North Wales Chronicle* of 12 April 1856.

> "LAUNCH: A fine schooner was launched from the shipbuilding yard of Mr. John Roberts, Hirael on Saturday last .She was named the *'Marion'* and is expected to beat, in sailing, every vessel yet launched in Bangor, her sailing qualities being remarkably good. The following are her dimensions: scale 62ft, beam 17½ ft, depth in hold 9ft. She was launched sideways."

By contrast to the last two vessels, much more is known about John Roberts's next venture, the 99 ton *City of Bangor* (Beaumaris 1857/17), and she was more successful than the unfortunate *Victoria*, if success is to be judged by longevity; she lasted until 1894 when she was sunk in an accident.

She was described in a report of her launching in the *Carnarvon and Denbigh Herald*[4] as "a beautifully modelled schooner which during the course of its building, attracted the admiration of several connoisseurs of marine architecture". Lloyds' representatives had inspected her and found her perfect. Her figurehead was unique as it represented "in striking manner, the likeness of the present Bishop of Bangor in his episcopal robes and in the attitude of preaching", — which must have been something worth seeing!

After the inevitable dinner at the Union Hotel, Garth for about forty of the owners and their friends in the large dining room, and about 120 carpenters, joiners, painters, smiths and riggers in an adjoining room, (separate canteens for management and workforce is not a twentieth century phenomenon in Britain!) one of the speakers recalled that thirty-eight years previously, when the *Susanna* was launched, there were only two carpenters and two

[4] C. & D.H. 3/10/1857.

117

apprentices in Bangor; there were now three shipbuilding yards "affording employment to a numerous class of workmen."

The principal shareholder in the new vessel was Meshach Roberts, the druggist with 20/64ths, followed by her master, John Thomas with 12/64ths. The other shareholders were Henry Parry and John Williams, both slate dressers, Mary Willoughby, Hotel Keeper (of the Union Hotel at Garth), Owen Morris, Assistant Overseer, Robert Thomas, Carter and Hugh Pritchard, Butcher, all of Bangor.

Her Crew Agreement Lists[5] for some years from 1863 onwards show a not unusual pattern of trading for a medium range Bangor coaster with regular voyages to London and in particular to Aberdeen which from 1866 onwards appears to have been her first port of call, returning to Bangor in the latter part of 1867, for example, by way of Montrose, Peterhead and Sligo. In the latter half of 1870 and the first half of 1871 whoever was responsible for the Lists chose to include details of the cargoes carried in addition to the itinerary. On July 21st the *City of Bangor* sailed from Port Penrhyn with slates, bound for Aberdeen which was reached on the 28th of the same month. From Aberdeen she sailed in ballast to Peterhead on August 5th, arriving on the same day. She then took a cargo of herrings to Rotterdam, sailing on the 12th and arriving on the 15th August. She left Rotterdam in ballast for Newcastle on August 25th arriving on September 9th. From Newcastle she took coals to Cork on September 21st and arrived on the 1st of October. It was back to Bangor in ballast on the 13th and she arrived on November 2nd.

By the 30th of November she had taken another load of slates on board and was sailing again for Aberdeen which she reached on December 14th. On January 12th 1871 she sailed for St. Andrews in ballast, took on a cargo of potatoes on the 22nd and reached Shields on the 24th. A month was spent in Shields before a cargo of manure was obtained and she sailed for Dundalk on February 24th and arrived there on March 5th. Ten days later she sailed for Bangor in ballast, arriving there on the 19th. On April 19th she again sailed for Aberdeen with a cargo of slates and arrived on May 5th. This time it was with a cargo of oats that she sailed for Yarmouth on the 16th, arriving on the 19th, and she seems to have left immediately in ballast for Bangor. She took yet another cargo of slates to Aberdeen on June 26th but the cargoes carried during the following half-year were not recorded, when she returned to Bangor *via* Sunderland and Plymouth.

The Crew Agreement Lists from 1872 to 1879 are not available and do not shed any light on her sale in July 1875 to Frank and William Turner, slate merchants, Thomas Jones slate agent and others, all from Caernarfon; nor why she returned to the outright ownership of Mesach Roberts in 1878. She remained in his ownership until his death in 1887.

[5] L.R.O. W/DB 84.

The List for the first half of 1880 gives Meshach Roberts as the owner and Robert Jones, Hirael (uncertificated) as master and shows that the *City of Bangor* took slates from Bangor to Limerick and then returned to Bangor by a devious route by way of Littlehampton, Dartmouth, Runcorn, Fraserburgh, West Wemyss, Treport and Weston Point. In the second half of the year Robert Jones signed articles as Purser and Boatswain and Thomas Hughes, of Llandegfan, who had a certificate ,signed as Master for a voyage to Stettin which ended at West Hartlepool.

During the next two years Robert Jones resumed duties as master and made several coastal voyages embracing the whole coast-line of Britain from London in the south (twice) to Kirkwall and Inverness in the north, besides making two voyages to Hamburg. At this time Dieppe, Antwerp and Hamburg were within limits for uncertificated coastal masters. However, this did not apply to the Baltic ports and, as had happened previously in 1880, Robert Jones was temporarily displaced in 1882 and in 1886 for voyages to Danzig, for which he signed articles as Purser; but in between he made several voyages with slates to Aberdeen as well as to other ports including Plymouth, Sligo, Dingwall and London, returning by devious routes and making at the same time substantial contribution to Britain's maritime trade.

After the death of Meshach Roberts the vessel was bought in 1887 by William Parry, Master Mariner of Caernarfon, who commanded her and continued with the same pattern of trading. She was sold again in 1891 to another master mariner, Robert Marks of Llanbedrog, who also commanded her. She is recorded as taking cargoes of slate from Caernarfon and Porthmadog to Jersey, Yarmouth and Hamburg. In August 1894 she was returning from Hamburg by way of Middlesbrough, Topsham and Teignmouth, and while sailing from Teignmouth for Drogheda she was sunk in the English Channel following a collision with the steam trawler *Triton.* Although her papers were lost, the crew were apparently saved.

Grampus, a brigantine of 132 tons, measuring 88.6 feet in length, a beam of 22.5 feet, and a depth of hold of 12.1 feet, with a man's figure as the figurehead, was built by John Roberts in 1859. (Beaumaris 22 of that year). She was initially registered in her builder's name, with Meshach Roberts providing a mortgage of £1260 at 4%. The mortgage was transferred a few months later to John Williams, the Chester banker, and was discharged by March 1860.

In March the vessel was sold to John Millington, junior, Gentleman, Bryntirion, Bangor (22/64ths), John Jones, Port Dinorwic, Agent, (21/64ths) and William Bodelly Buckingham, Port Dinorwic, Accountant, (21/64ths) all men closely associated with the Assheton-Smith interest in the Dinorwig Quarry. Buckingham in later years became a shipowner on a large scale with several ocean going ships. As a consequence of the sale *Grampus* was transferred to the Caernarfon Registry (Carnarvon 1860/7). In 1872 she was sold to two master mariners of Port Dinorwic in equal proportions, Humphrey Jones and Griffith Williams. In December of the same year she was totally lost with all papers off Harwich.

John Roberts next built the small, 29 ton smack, *Pamela Pennant,* (Beaumaris 1860/21) and financed her until her sale in 1862 by means of a mortgage loan from the brothers Robert and Richard Davies, Menai Bridge. We thus have two instances of local business men not only investing in ships (which was common) but also lending the capital to shipbuilders, Meshach Roberts in the case of *Grampus* and the Davies Brothers in the case of *Pamela Pennant.*

The vessel was sold in 1862 to Richard Griffith, Morfa Nefyn, Mariner and she was re-registered at Caernarfon (1862/35). Mortgages play their part again, and this time the joint mortgagees were two of the owners of *Grampus,* W. B. Buckingham, the accountant and John Jones, the building agent from Port Dinorwic. The mortgage was for £240 at 5% and was discharged in January 1871. Another mortgage, this time for £150, was raised in November of the same year from two master mariners of Porthdinllaen and it remained undischarged when the vessel was sold (64/64ths) to a master mariner from Fishguard. All that is known about her subsequent history is that she was sunk by collision off the Breaksea Lightship in March 1895.

Four years later John Roberts appears to have completed another ship, the 53 ton schooner *Charlotte Ann* (Carnarvon 1864/5). At this time the builder's name was not recorded in the Register but John Roberts's name appears as the only Bangor shareholder and as the joint mortgagee (J. and R. Roberts Bangor, Shipbuilders). This was clearly a case of 'easy payments on deferred terms' since the mortgagor was the major shareholder, Lewis Evan Davies, a master mariner from Porthmadog with 30/64ths. With the exception of Robert Rees, Rate Collector, Bethesda, the other shareholders came from Porthmadog. They were another master mariner, a sail maker and a ship chandler and *Charlotte Ann* remained very much a Porthmadog ship to the end of her days since whatever shares changed hands went to other people from Porthmadog, with one exception. John Roberts in 1869 mortgaged his holding of 16/64ths for £200 at 6% to Meshach Roberts, Druggist, Bangor, and this is another indication of the close business association between the two men.

The vessel was totally lost in January 1887 on Harry Furlong's Rocks, off the north coast of Anglesey.

*   *   *   *

There remain another four vessels to be considered, two whose builders are unknown and two whose builders are known or can be safely conjectured. A schooner of 60 tons, *Jane and Elizabeth,* over 68 feet in length and with a woman's bust as figurehead was built somewhere in Bangor in 1859 (Beaumaris 13 of that year). Her principal owner with 56/64ths, Owen Williams, described as Shipowner of Bangor, does not appear elsewhere in the Beaumaris registers so that it is impossible to obtain a hint from the pattern of the shareholdings (as is possible sometimes) as to who the builder was. The other shareholder was her master, Owen Owens, of Bangor, Master Mariner.

Her Crew Agreement Lists for most years from 1866 until 1883[6] are available at the Llangefni Record Office. They are typical of a medium range Bangor coaster, with, for example, 1866 showing that she sailed from Bangor for Poole, then Runcorn, Stirling, Newcastle, Galway, Runcorn again, Wick, Lerwick, Liverpool, Amlwch, and Liverpool for a second time before returning to Bangor.

Owen Williams died in 1866 and in the following year his widow sold her shares, and Owen Owens his, to William Parry, Adelphi Vaults, Amlwch, Master Mariner, who thus became possessed of the 64 parts. The Crew Agreement Lists show that for the next ten years *Jane and Elizabeth* seems to have divided her time between the trade of Amlwch (typically iron ore from Duddon to Swansea and coal from Swansea, Llanelly or Briton Ferry to Amlwch) and the carrying of slate from Port Penrhyn to such various destinations as Poole, Littlehampton, Dover, Drogheda, Belfast and Newcastle, to name only a few, returning by whatever circuitous route offered cargoes.

William Parry came to live in Bangor from about 1876 (at Garth Hill Cottage) and from this time the vessel sailed only from Port Penrhyn. In the first six months of 1876, for example, she was at Fowey at the year's beginning and sailed, one can be sure, with a cargo of china clay for Runcorn; from Runcorn she went to Porthcawl (which nowadays we tend to regard as purely a holiday resort), and to Dublin before returning to Bangor. The second voyage of 1876 took her from Bangor to Newcastle, then to Poole, Runcorn, Dublin and back to Bangor. The third voyage was to Silloth, Newry, Dundalk and back to Bangor, a comparatively short trip, and there was time before the year's end for another west coast voyage, to Greenock, Bowling, Sandicroft and Chester, Dublin and Bangor.

The vessel was sold in 1882 to Thomas Hughes (64/64ths), Master Mariner of Red Wharf who also commanded the vessel. He carried on with the same pattern of trade for a year, but as so often seemed to happen when a vessel changed hands, there was a change of fortune, and *Jane and Elizabeth* was wrecked on Ballarula Sands off Dumfries when bound from London to Dumfries. Although the vessel broke up and all papers were lost, the crew were saved.

The registration of *Sarah Jane* (Beaumaris 1861/12), a 73 ton schooner,

[6] L.R.O. W/DB 208.

does not give the name of the builder, but it can be inferred with fair certainty from the list of the shareholders which contains the name of Henry Owens, Shipbuilder. This is confirmed by Lloyds Register for 1872 which gives the name of her builder as Owens and her owners as Simon and Co. All the original shareholders came from Bangor; they were headed by John Simon, Farmer with 20/64ths, and the others were Richard Jones, Master Mariner (10/64ths) Robert Roberts, Postmaster (14/64ths), Ellis Roberts, Accountant (10/64ths), Thomas Byewater, Shipbuilder (4/64ths) and Henry Owens, Shipbuilder (6/64ths). John Simon and Robert Roberts the Postmaster had shares in several other Bangor vessels.

Henry Owens sold his holding in the same year as she was built to Thomas Jones, Ysgubor Fawr, (Llanfair M.E., Anglesey), Master Mariner, whom we have encountered already as the principal shareholder and master of the Bangor built *Idwal* in which he was to lose his life in 1868.

In 1874 the Bangor shareholders agreed to sell the vessel outright to Samuel Radcliffe Platt of Oldham who was described as a Mechanical Engineer. Three years later, after a series of transactions she was bought by a master mariner from Widnes, a ropemaker and a draper, both from Northwich and was transferred in 1877 to the port of Runcorn.

The 38 ton schooner *Eliza Jane* (Beaumaris 1866/19) was built in Bangor by John Jones, although his name does not appear on her registration entry as her builder but as holding her 64 parts. In an account in the *Caernarvon and Denbigh Herald*[7] of the launching of another vessel, *Dorothea* in 1862 it says "a very beautiful schooner, modelled by Mr. John Jones, foreman to Messrs. Parry and Co. shipbuilders, Bangor was launched . . . on Monday last." Whether or not the identification is certain, there is no doubt that John Jones sold 16/64ths to John Evans, Bethesda, Butcher, 8/64ths to Mary Roberts, Bangor, Spinster, 8/64ths to Thomas Jones, Port Penrhyn, Accountant and 4/64ths to William Humphreys, Bangor, also an accountant. What is more certain is that by 1882 another John Jones, Ambrose Street, Bangor was recorded in the Register as 'Pilot' and can be positively identified as the Captain John Jones, a Swellies pilot and professional diver, whose papers were the subject of an article by Dr. Lewis Lloyd in a recent issue of *Maritime Wales/Cymru a'r Môr.*[8] The papers include a number of receipted accounts from a grocer, a sailmaker, a blockmaker and a butcher for goods received on board the *Eliza Jane*. When John Jones died in February 1885 his 32/64ths of the vessel went to his brother Thomas Jones, Blacksmith of Penchwintan, Bangor.

The Bangor shareholders agreed to sell the vessel 64/64ths to Owen Owens, Morfa Nefyn, Master Mariner in June 1885; in 1890 she was sold again to a master mariner and a timber merchant from Amlwch, and finally

[7] C. & D.H. 23/3/1862.
[8] Maritime Wales No. 9 (1985) pp. 178-181.

in 1902 to owners in Llangrannog. She was wrecked in Llangrannog Bay in November 1913 and afterwards broken up.

Lord Exmouth, a 19 ton smack was built at Bangor and registered in the following year (Beaumaris 1869/2) by an unknown builder. Her original joint owners were John Thomas, Minffordd, Bangor, Slate Merchant and Jane Pritchard, Tanycoed, Bangor, Widow, whose husband, William Pritchard, Slate Merchant had been a ship-owner on a considerable scale. Her Crew Agreement Lists[9] for most years from 1869 until 1898 show a pattern of local trading between Bangor and Chester with an occasional call at Red Wharf and Caernarfon until 1874 when she was sold to Fishguard and the pattern became Milford and Fishguard with occasional calls at Swansea, Hook, Saundersfoot or Porthgain.

The return for the first six months of 1884 is interesting because it states explicity that 14 cargoes, mainly of coal or culm, carried between Swansea and Milford or Fishguard were discharged directly onto the beaches. The end came in October 1898 when, after leaving Milford, she foundered in Ramsey Sound.

*   *   *   *

The vessels built in Bangor from 1830 until 1879 have been presented according to the yard which built them at some cost to their sequence in time. They are therefore summarised in chronological order below:—

Year	Name of Vessel	Tonnage	Rig.	Builder	Ultimate End
1830	Bangor Packet	39	Sloop	John Parry	Hulked in 1887
1832	Anne and Catherine	84	Schooner	John Parry	Foundered 1881
1835	Ann and Susan	60	Sloop	John Parry	Foundered 1865
1837	Eliza and Catherine	54	Smack	Edward Ellis	Lost 1881
1837	Harriet	26	Smack	John Parry	Wrecked 1853
1837	Mona	37	Smack	Edward Ellis	Wrecked 1883
1839	Anne	88	Schooner	John Parry	Lost 1853
1839	Maria and Elizabeth	77	Schooner	Edward Ellis	To Liverpool 1860
1841	Mary Grace	49/65	Sma./Sr.	John Parry	Sunk in collision 1874
1841	Douglas Pennant	100	Schooner	Edward Ellis	Wrecked 1868
1841	William and Richard	46	Smack	William Williams	Lost 1860
1841	*Benjamin Williams* ‡	*70*	*?*	*Edward Ellis*	*Unknown*
1842	Mary	74	Schooner	Nicholas Treweek	Wrecked 1864
1842	Ellen	20	Sloop	Edward Ellis	Broken up 1909
1843	Three Susans	118	Brig'tine	John Parry	Lost 1863
1843	Emma Laura	55	Schooner	Humphrey Roberts	To Chester 1844

[9] L.R.O. W/DB 243.

Year	Name of Vessel	Tonnage	Rig.	Builder	Ultimate End
1844	Port Penrhyn	24	Smack	John Parry	Wrecked 1877
1845	Beatrice Catherine	34	Smack	Edward Ellis	Lost 1859
1846	Alice and Mary	28	Smack	John Roberts	Sunk 1869
1847	Lady Louisa Pennant	73	Schooner	John Parry	Lost 1902
1850	John Parry	56	Schooner	John Parry	Lost 1901
1854	Victoria	11	Smack †	John Roberts	Broken up 1864
1854	Ifor	120	Schooner	Edward Ellis	Foundered 1909
1855	Glanogwen	143	Brig'tine	John Parry	Hulked 1915
1856	*Marion* ‡	*?*	*Schooner*	*John Roberts*	*Unknown*
1857	Idwal	69	Schooner	Edward Ellis	Wrecked 1868
1857	City of Bangor	99	Schooner	John Roberts	Sunk in collision 1894
1858	Arthur Wyatt	96	Schooner	T. T. Parry	Lost 1903
1858	Sarah Bridget	126	Brig'tine	Edward Ellis	Broken up 1936
1859	Blue Jacket	66	Schooner	T. T. Parry	Transferred Ramsgate 1893
1859	Jane and Elizabeth	60	Schooner	Unknown	Wrecked 1883
1859	Grampus	132	Brig'tine	John Roberts	Lost 1872
1860	Cambria	56	Schooner	T. T. Parry	Foundered 1903
1860	Pamela Pennant	29	Smack	John Roberts	Sunk in collision 1895
1860	Heather Bell	257	Barque	Edward Ellis	Wrecked 1891
1861	Sarah Jane	73	Schooner	Henry Owens	Transferred Runcorn 1877
1862	Dorothea	74	Schooner	T. T. Parry	Lost 1900
1863	Mary Edwards	65	Schooner	Edward Ellis	Broken up 1936
1864	Charlotte Ann	53	Schooner	John Roberts	Wrecked 1887
1866	Eliza	101	Schooner	T. T. Parry	Broken up 1927
1866	Eliza Jane	38	Schooner	John Jones	Wrecked 1913
1866	Petrel	15	Sloop	Unknown	Transferred Dumfries 1909
1869	Lord Exmouth	19	Smack	Unknown	Foundered 1898
1874	Fomalhaut	72	Schooner	T. T. Parry	Lost 1902
1878	Menai	42	Steamer†	T. T. Parry	Hulked 1922
1879	Pilgrim	37	Smack	T. T. Parry	Wrecked 1918

‡ Not registered locally; details of launch only from North Wales Chronicle.

† Steam Vessels, *Victoria* propelled by paddle wheels; *Menai* twin screw.

CHAPTER VIII

Mid-Century Owners

The remark was made earlier in this book that in the nineteenth century ownership of ships in Bangor tended to move from the gentry to the people. This remark contained several dangerous generalisations which must be cleared up. By 'gentry' in this context is meant those men who felt themselves entitled to put 'Gentleman' or 'Esquire' behind their names, in particular, in the Registers of Shipping. It is suspected that some of these self-styled gentry would not have passed muster as far as Debrett was concerned, and the definition would hardly satisfy a sociologist of the present day; this may strike some readers as a cowardly evasion of the issue but at least it has the advantage of being precise.

The three generations of the Wyatts, Benjamin, James and Arthur, were all 'Esquires', so were their kinsmen, the Vawdreys. William Baxter of Penrhyn Castle styled himself 'Gentleman' but was in fact the Clerk of Works for building the present castle from 1827 onwards, and James Greenfield, 'Gentleman' of Ogwen Bank was the manager of the Penrhyn Quarry and Benjamin Wyatt's son-in-law. Henry Pace, of Penrhyn Castle styled himself as 'Gentleman' when he bought the small sloop *Ellinor* in 1849 but he was a 'Builder' of Bangor when he sold the vessel in 1854. These men in their different capacities represented the powerful Penrhyn interest. There is little evidence that the indigenous gentry class took an interest in Bangor shipping — a couple of Hampton Joneses from Henllys, Beaumaris in the early years of the century and that is about all. A Zacharias Roberts of Bangor,

125

'Gentleman', was the part owner of the 98 ton brig *Emily,* built at Harbour Grace, Newfoundland, when she was purchased for Bangor in 1840 and he retained an interest in her until 1861. The same 'Gentleman' gives his occupation as a 'Draper' in 1848 when he is one of the shareholders in *James and Maria,* a 46 ton flat, in which he held an interest until 1873 — which only goes to show the pitfalls which await anyone who embarks upon the dangerous topic of class.

Conversely, 'the people' in this context is everyone else. The occupations of Bangor people holding shares in Bangor built or predominantly Bangor owned ships registered for the first time in the decade 1840-50 cover a wide variety; not unnaturally the list is headed by 21 mariners or master mariners. What is surprising is the total absence from this particular count of any member of the professional middle class.

In addition to the 21 mariners the occupations are as follows:

Shipbuilders	4	Shipwright	1	Carpenters	2
Brazier	1	Stonemasons	2	Labourer	1
Druggists	2	Flour Dealers	2	Drapers	4
Baker	1	Grocer	1	Coal Merchants	2
Shopkeepers	2	Farmers	3	Post Master	1
Innkeeper	1	Painters	2	Agent	1
Railway Contractor	1	Slate Merchants	2	Widows	3

This decade also saw the use of the term 'Shipowner' for the first time, as far as is known, in the Beaumaris Registers. In the registration of the 377 ton, ship-rigged *Ann Grant,* built at Whitby in 1806 (Beaumaris 1848/13) we find the name of Edward Ellis, Bangor, 'Shipowner' given as the owner of 28/64ths together with another 'shipowner', John Phillips (also with 28/64ths), a Methodist minister and fund-raiser for the British School Society who later became Principal of the Bangor Normal College.[1] She was engaged in the slate trade between Port Penrhyn and America, but not for long as she was wrecked in Nova Scotia in July, 1851.

Another generalisation; as the century advances the number of share-holders in individual ships tends to decrease, and there is a corresponding increase in the number of shares held by one person, which leads, inevitably, to an increase in sole owner ships (i.e. in 64/64ths ownership). We have seen this trend already in John Parry's sole ownership of the large brigantines (large as far as Bangor was concerned), *Three Susans* and *Glanogwen.* John Parry had prospered and had accumulated a substantial amount of capital. Conversely, ships were getting cheaper and there was plenty of old tonnage around which could be acquired at a reasonable price. The pattern of share-holding was changing; ounces (4/64ths) and half-ounces (2/64ths) were no

[1] See Aled Eames *Ships and Seamen of Anglesey* pp. 256-7.

longer common currency but had given way for the most part to holdings of 16 or 32/64ths, or sometimes to 64/64ths.

A good example is James Jones, Master Mariner of Bangor, who in 1851 bought the old 26 ton smack *Jane*, built in Dumfries in 1812. (Beaumaris 1851/13). He sold her, 64/64ths, to another master mariner from Bangor, Robert Owen in 1857, who in his turn sold her to the port of Holyhead in 1866. James Jones also bought the 54 ton schooner, *County of Cork* (Beaumaris 1851/19) built at Bridport in 1815 and previously registered at Aberystwyth. This was also in 1851 and not surprisingly the vessel was mortgaged in that year to two John Joneses, one a carpenter from Liverpool and the other a mariner from Bangor.

The vessel was sold in 1853 to two Bangor men, Robert and Richard Williams, Coal Merchants, 'co-partners in Robert Williams and Son.' In 1864 they sold her to another sole owner, Evan Evans, merchant of Bangor. Her subsequent history deserves a brief mention; after Evan Evans's death in 1877 she was sold to William Thomas, Shipbuilder of Amlwch who promptly sold her to Thomas Williams and John Edwards, two business men, and to Lewis Hughes, a manager of a chemical works, all from Amlwch. She was bought back in 1882 by William Thomas and his son and remained with them until she was sold in 1907 to the Rea Transport Co. Ltd. She was re-registered at the age of 95 (Beaumaris 1910/2), with her masts removed, as a barge and she was broken up in 1936.

There is no evidence as far as Bangor was concerned of any shipping companies being formed until we come to the Anglesey Shipping Company of the nineties, despite the limited liability status offered by the Companies Act of 1862. Ownership of shipping remained on a personal level; sometimes it was a sole ownership, sometimes a partnership between father and son, as we have seen between Robert and Richard Williams (whose names will recur later), some times it was in an *ad hoc* partnership or consortium. There is evidence, it is true, of a more formal partnership in the shipbuilding and shipowning firm of T. T. Parry, R. T. Power and Samuel Roberts, which was mentioned in a previous chapter but the outstanding example of a partnership involving both kinship and business interests is that between James and Arthur Wyatt and the Port Penrhyn accountant, John Lloyd, who was the junior partner.

This was an historic partnership dating back to the end of the eighteenth century when Benjamin Wyatt was one of the co-owners of *Lord Bulkeley* with William Williams, Llandegai. Of the ships mentioned in the list of Bangor owners up to 1831 (see pages 45-47) three survived until the sixties, *Raven, Penmon* and *Talacre*. Many more vessels were bought by the partnership or ordered from the Bangor builders, John Parry or his successor firm, T. T. Parry and Co., until in the fifties and sixties they presented formidable and much resented competition to other local shipowners.

The fifteen ships are presented in summary form: —

Name	Built or Acquired	Disposal
Penmon 26t. Sl.	1828 b. Bangor by John Jones. Jas. Wyatt 48 1860 Jas. Wyatt 16, Arthur Wyatt 40, John Lloyd 8	Sold T. Parry in 1862 (Broken up 1885)
Talacre 77t. Sr.	1829 from Liverpool. Jas. Wyatt 48, Wm. Baxter 16 1855 Jas. Wyatt 48, Arthur Wyatt 8, John Lloyd 8 1860 Jas. Wyatt 16, Arthur Wyatt 40, John Lloyd 8	Sold R. Lloyd, *et al.* 1867 (Wrecked 1893)
Raven 73t. Sr.	1831 from Worthington/Dale, Bangor 1834 Jas. Wyatt 40, Wm. Baxter 16, John Parry 8 1860 Jas. Wyatt 16, Arthur Wyatt 40, John Lloyd 8	Sold Wm. Dawbarn in 1868 (Hulked 1898)
Ann & Catherine 84t. Sr.	1832 b. Bangor by John Parry, Jas. Wyatt 40, Wm. Baxter 8, H. B. Wyatt 8, John Parry 4 1857 Jas. Wyatt 44, Arthur Wyatt 16, John Lloyd 4	Sold R. Hughes in 1860 (Foundered 1881)
Harriet 26t. Sma.	1837 b. Bangor by John Parry. Jas. Wyatt 32, Wm. Baxter 16, C. Ainsworth 8, John Parry 8	Wrecked in 1853
Robert 43t. Flat	1844 from John Parry etc. James Wyatt 56 1854 Jas. Wyatt 40, A. Wyatt 8, J. Lloyd 8, J. Parry 8	Sold Slater, Bennett & Dornings 1868 (Lost in 1879)
Merlin 51t. Sl.	1857 from Liverpool. Arthur Wyatt 40, Jas. Wyatt 16, John Lloyd 8.	Lost in 1858
Curlew 36t. Sma.	1858 b. Conwy. Arthur Wyatt 48, John Lloyd 16	Sold Slater, Bennett & Dornings 1868 (Sank 1898)
Stag 36t. Sl.	1858 from R. T. & T. T. Parry *et al.* Arthur Wyatt 40, Jas. Wyatt 16, John Lloyd 8	Sold Wm. Dawbarn in 1868 (Lost, n.d. but after 1898)
Blue Jacket 66t. Sr.	1859 b. Bangor by T. T. Parry, Jas. Wyatt 16, Arthur Wyatt 40, John Lloyd 8	Sold Wm. Dawbarn in 1868 (Transferred Ramsgate 1893)

Name	Built or Acquired	Disposal
Penguin 51t. Sma.	1860 from Glasgow, Arthur Wyatt 48, John Lloyd 16	Sold Slater, Bennett & Dornings 1868 (Foundered 1901)
Messenger 28t. Sma.	1860 from J. Hughes, Pilot, Bangor. Arthur Wyatt 48, John Lloyd 16	Sold Wm. Dawbarn in 1868 (Transferred Caernarfon 1886)
John Parry 56t. Sr.	1861 from R. T. & T. T. Parry *et al.* (b. John Parry, Bangor 1850) Arthur Wyatt 48, John Lloyd 16	Sold Slater, Bennett & Dornings 1868 (Lost 1901)
Alexander 96t. Sr.	1862 b. P. E. Island, 1861, Arthur Wyatt 48, John Lloyd 16.	Sold Slater, Bennett & Dornings 1868 (Lost in 1902)
Jane Hunter 63t. Ketch	1864 from Bridport. John Lloyd 32, John Lloyd jun. 16, John Slater 16	Sold to Caernarfon in 1876

To begin at the end, as it were, what is most noticeable about this list is that nine of the ships were disposed of in 1868, (and the Register makes it clear that they were all sold in the same month of January) and a tenth, *Talacre,* was sold in December 1867. Two had been sold in the early sixties, and two had been lost, which leaves one, the *Jane Hunter,* and she was not really a Wyatt ship, being owned by the junior partner, John Lloyd and his son, another John Lloyd.

There had been rumblings in the correspondence columns of the *Carnarvon and Denbigh Herald* at various periods over the previous ten years[2] about the grievances of shipowners in Bangor against the preferential treatment received by some owners. A man signing himself 'A Master Mariner' published a letter in the issue of August 1st, 1857, stating that at Port Penrhyn "there has been a manifest preference extended to certain vessels which make five or six runs while the others have no chance of employment." He goes on to state "that at Port Madoc, Carnarvon and Port Dinorwic every vessel which arrives for a cargo is impartially stemmed according to the acknowledged regulations of the port" and he appeals to the Hon. Colonel Pennant (he had not been ennobled at this time) to see that the spirit of honourable fair play is applied.

A month later, in the issue of September 12th, the same writer alleges that the port management went on the counter-offensive and accused the master mariners of "meddling in matters with which they had no concern"; further-more, it was alleged that the masters were implicated in a fraudulent system of

[2] Again I am indebted to Dr. Lewis Lloyd for drawing my attention to these references.

carrying away" a surplusage of slates, averaging from ten or twenty tons over and above the quantity entered in the bill of lading." Old Spanish customs there may have been at Port Penrhyn a century ago but it is hard to believe that they were on the scale alleged since meticulously careful daily loading ledgers were kept (now to be found at the Caernarfon Record Office of the Gwynedd Archives Service).

Nothing much happened and there followed a period of uneasy peace. Six years later, in the same paper in its issue of April 11th, 1863, a writer who signs himself 'Shipowner', makes substantially the same allegations in a vivid letter entitled "The Monopoly at Port Penrhyn". The situation there, he says, is nothing but "sheer unfairness both to captains and owners who have their vessels for weeks and months together lying on the beach before they can get an offer . . . and are obliged in perfect silence to content themselves with looking at the fleet of vessels that come to this port, the owners of which are so privileged that they never lose sight of their own vessels . . . No matter how often they come, their load and extra gang is in readiness (and a good back freight of coals as a matter of course), and not unusually, when it suits their convenience, any other vessel loading at the time must give up berth and men to serve the so-called 'mails'. Should the above owners referred to continue building and buying vessels at the rate they have of late years, all the other interested vessels in the neighbourhood of Bangor, and depending on Port Penrhyn, will fare badly." This was written towards the end of the dozen years (from 1854 to 1866) which were singled out (see page 91) as being the high-water mark of ship-building in Bangor.

The writer of a lengthy letter in the same paper on December 9th, 1865 is a great deal more specific in his charges. He says that he has been keeping a diary and begs to submit a page from it for Mr. Wyatt's information:—

"Vessels lying at Port Penrhyn about nine days ago:

Catherine and Mary	12 weeks
Jane (flat)	10 weeks
Jane (smack)	10 weeks
Alma (smack)	12 weeks
John Nelson	10 weeks
Alice and Ann	8 weeks
William Edward	8 weeks
Admiral Nelson	8 weeks
Robert Nelson	8 weeks

"Mr. Wyatt's vessels, and number of trips made during the time the above have been lying at Port Penrhyn: —

Alexander	4 times
Blue Jacket	4 times
Penguin	3 times
Robert	3 times
John Parry	3 times
Messenger	4 times
Stag	3 times
Raven	4 times
Talacre	4 times"

Both the writer of this letter and the writers of others which followed are at pains to make it plain that they are not criticising the gallant Col. Pennant, who is, they are sure, absolutely unaware of what his agents, Messrs. Wyatt and Lloyd are up to. But they say that once he has had all the facts, they are confident that he will act honourably.

Much the same complaint was to be heard at that other proprietary port, Port Dinorwic, at this time. One of the letters mentions this and states that "it is significant that the authorities at Ports Penrhyn and Dinorwic have stopped supplying you and your contemporary the *Chronicle* with the shipping intelligence that they formerly furnished, but as they cannot wall up their pocket ports from observation, they may depend upon it that proceedings shall not be unreported." 'Pocket' is here used in the same sense as in 'pocket-borough' rather than in 'pocket-battleship'! It is quite true that the shipping intelligence in the local papers ceases to be of much value as a source of information, particularly in the case of Port Penrhyn, from the late forties onwards when its appearance in the papers concerned tends to be erratic.

Reference to *The North Wales Chronicle* naturally leads to the supposition that all this would have been reported in the Bangor paper as well, but one can comb the columns of that paper for any reference to the complaints of the unprivileged captains and owners (and one has done so!) — in vain. The *Chronicle* was a Tory paper and obediently reflected the views and interests of the great land-owner who owned half the city and the surrounding district besides being the only industrial employer of any size. *The Carnarvon and Denbigh Herald,* on the other hand, had a proud reputation of being in the radical tradition, and as one of the letter writers just quoted puts it "the Northern part of the Principality has cause to be proud of the only paper which does not hesitate to 'tell the truth and shame the devil'. It has experienced many effective gales as a staunch supporter of fair play to the weak, and of sound and growing political principles . . ."

Whether or not it was as a result of the paper's prolonged campaign that an order was given by Lord Penrhyn (as Col. E. G. D. Pennant was now called) we do not know, but it led to swift action and the ten ships were sold within the space of two months. Much the same happened at Port Dinorwic in 1872 when the Vaynol agents were obliged to sell their shares in local ships.

Although it bears no date, a large board which has survived in one of the buildings at Port Penrhyn containing the 'Rules and Regulations to be observed by the Masters of Vessels intending to load at Port Penrhyn' must belong to this period. It is signed by Arthur Wyatt, Agent to the Rt. Hon. Lord Penrhyn and states that "Mr. W. Jones is appointed Harbour Master."

It indicates that there will be a change in the former procedure and that "all vessels coming to Port Penrhyn to load Slates will (as far practicable) be offered cargoes in their turn according to the date of their arrival within the Stemming limits." But this statement of principle is hedged about with so many subordinate clauses, so many provisos and exceptions, and so many reservations that it would take a good sea-lawyer to interpret it. There seems to be a bias in favour of vessels which come in "loaded or part loaded with any kind of Merchandise or other goods . . . for the use of the Concern" i.e. the Penrhyn Estate or Penrhyn Quarry.

There are also sensible regulations for the disposal of ballast, for mooring correctly, for the prevention of fire, for the disposal of rubbish, for stowing spars when alongside the quay, for hauling out when loaded, besides the procedures for reporting arrival and departure to the Harbour Master and for obtaining a cash advance on the freight. This 'document' (which measures about twelve feet by four!) is interesting for the light it casts on the everyday, practical details of running a small port in Victorian times and is reproduced in Appendix II for those readers who wish to study it in detail.

Of the vessels sold *Talacre* had enjoyed the longest *continuous* ownership by the Wyatt family having been bought by James Wyatt and William Baxter in 1829. She was a comparatively new vessel when bought, having been built in 1821 at Tranmere. *Raven* was, of course, a much older ship, built at St. Helen's (Lancs.) in 1788 and first registered in Benjamin Wyatt's name, among others, at Beaumaris in 1800. She, it will be recalled, was bought jointly in 1815 by Samuel Worthington and George Dale, Master Mariner, who acquired her, 64/64ths in 1821. In 1831 George Dale sold a half share to James Wyatt and so she came back into the fold where she remained until 1868. However, *Talacre* was the first to go in December 1867, and she went to three Bangor master mariners, Richard Lloyd, (16/64ths) Edward Jones (16/64ths) and Edward Owen (32/64ths). She remained in Bangor hands until about 1886 when she was sold to two Conwy shipowners. The vessel became a total wreck in Peel Bay and her certificate of registry was lost with the vessel.

The other ships in the fleet were sold to two buyers; William Dawbarn, a Liverpool merchant and a very substantial customer for Penrhyn slate, judging from the daily loading ledgers for Port Penrhyn,[3] bought *Raven, Stag, Blue Jacket* and *Messenger*. The vessels continued to trade in exactly the same way under their new ownership. *Blue Jacket,* for instance, was employed exclusively prior to her sale in trading between Bangor and either Garston or Runcorn; after the sale to William Dawbarn the same pattern continued for some years. Her Crew Agreement Lists[4] show that it was not until 1876 that she visited the Irish ports, Cork, Dundalk, Newry and Waterford and that she made at least one voyage under Dawbarn's ownership to Harburg in 1880. William Dawbarn died in 1881 and the fleet was dispersed; *Raven* was bought by John Pritchard, a master mariner from Brynsiencyn, *Stag* by another master mariner from Moelfre, Joseph Williams, *Blue Jacket* by Thomas Jones, master mariner of Caernarfon who later sold her to a shipowner in Kent, and *Messenger* by a Liverpool labourer called Thomas William Griffith, who, now that he had a ship to manage, moved to Tydweiliog, possibly his old home.

All the other five ships were sold in 1868 to what appears at first sight to be a quite unrelated body of people, who, nevertheless, from the consistency of the pattern of shareholding, must be considered as yet another example of a shipping company in embryo. In the Crew Agreement Lists and in Lloyd's Lists they are generally referred to as Lloyd and Co.

The key member of this group was John Lloyd, junior, who was none other than the son of John Lloyd, the Port Penrhyn accountant. John Lloyd junior's occupation is variously given in the Registers as 'clerk' or 'accountant', and his address is given as 'Old Bank', Bangor. With the exception of *Robert* where the same four participants hold the shares in slightly different proportions, shares in the other four ships were held by John Lloyd, junior, with 16/64ths, John Marsland Bennett, Manchester, Merchant, with 16/64ths, John Slater, Beaumaris, Chemist, with 12/64ths and John Dorning, London, Accountant and William Brundrit Dorning, Bootle, Timber Merchant (or Accountant) with a holding of 12/64ths, held jointly. The remaining 8/64ths were held by the masters of the respective vessels.

Nothing has so far come to light to link Bennett with any other members of the group; an entry in the marriage register of the Parish of Llandygai for 1837-1864 (now in the National Library at Aberystwyth) records the marriage in 1854 of John Slater, Chemist of Beaumaris, with Margaret Lloyd, Spinster of Port Penrhyn, daughter of John Lloyd, Clerk, so that

[3] C.R.O. P.Q. 9ff.
[4] L.R.O. W/DB 61.

John Slater and John Lloyd (junior) were brothers-in-law. Another connection turns out to be 'Mr. Dorning, brother-in-law of Mr. John Lloyd, Manager of the Old Bank' whose obituary notice appeared in the local press[5] in 1882. Further evidence of the connection comes in the register entry for *Alexander,* (Beaumaris Book of Transactions II Folio 78) when John Lloyd's death is recorded and his legatee is named as Ernest Hay Dorning Lloyd, Kensington, Artist. It appears that John Lloyd, junior had married a Miss Dorning. Ernest Lloyd sold his holding of 16/64ths to Hugh Parry, Master Mariner of Hirael. The vessel was totally lost in circumstances unknown in April 1902.

As if to emphasise the purely cosmetic nature of the exercise, John Lloyd, senior, on his retirement in 1871 and styling himself by now as 'Gentleman', bought back from his son his holdings in four of the five ships, *Penguin, Robert, Curlew* and *John Parry.* After 1880 they changed hands for a third time and were bought back by John Lloyd, junior, and shortly afterwards sold. This was a shrewd move as the general depression of trade, and of coastal shipping in particular, had already set in. There remains the question of why these holdings were transferred from father to son and the only explanation that seems to fit this manoeuvre is that in view of the impending sale the son was thought to be able to strike a harder bargain.

The veteran Griffith Williams, mentioned in an earlier chapter, (see page 65) who had bought an 8/64ths share in *Penguin,* retained his command of her until at least 1878, when he was 72 years old, and his holding until 1883, when she was sold to Hugh Roberts, Master Mariner of Llandegfan. She had continued with exactly the same trading pattern with voyages to either Garston or Runcorn as she had prior to her sale in 1868. In 1885 she was sold to two merchants, from Porlock and Plymouth respectively, and from 1886 onwards she traded with ports in the Bristol Channel with an occasional voyage to Ireland. In November 1901 she foundered off Hangman Head in the Bristol Channel. Such was the end of the *Penguin.*

Robert was lost in circumstances unknown in January 1879. Her shares were held at the time by John Slater 12, J. M. Bennett 16, W.B. and J. Dorning 20 and John Lloyd, senior, 16.

Curlew, a 36 ton smack, built at Conwy in 1858 returned to Conwy owner-ship in 1882 after similar manoeuvres by the Lloyds. According to the Register "this vessel was abandoned waterlogged and she afterwards sank 8 miles N.N.E. of the Great Orme's Head on 8th August 1898."

The same cynical disregard of the proprieties is evident in the case of the *John Parry.* Previous to her 'sale' in 1868 she had been employed exclusively between Bangor and Garston; under John Lloyd, junior, as managing owner, exactly the same pattern of trade — slates outwards, coal in — was maintained, and it is not until 1876 that a new pattern of trade emerges, with

[5] N.W.C. 2.9.1882.

voyages to various Irish ports and ports on the south coast of England, according to the Crew Agreement Lists.[6] She was sold to Irish owners in 1885 but returned to Bangor under the ownership of Richard Jones, Surgeon, in 1891 (see page 75). An account of her loss in December 1901 was given by the late Henry Parry, the historian of the lifeboat service in North Wales, thus — "early one morning a message was received from Point Lynas signal station that a vessel was in distress on a reef by Dulas Rocks. At eight o'clock the (Moelfre) lifeboat was launched in a strong north-west gale and after a difficult passage through the scattered rocks with heavy seas breaking over them, reached the vessel — the ketch *John Parry*, of Bangor. She was returning there in ballast from Belfast and after a stormy passage across the Irish Sea, was driven ashore about seven o'clock. Her crew of two were safely taken off and the lifeboat safely negotiated the tortuous return passage through the rocks and landed the men at Moelfre."[7]

There are two points of interest in this account; the vessel is described as a ketch whereas she had been rigged as a schooner when she was built. She had been altered to the ketch rig for reasons of economy as the reduced sail area could be more easily handled by a reduced crew. The second point follows from the first — her crew had been reduced to two, compared with the four men or the three men and a boy she would have carried in 1850 when she was built.

Such, then, is the history of the Wyatt-Lloyd 'fleet' up to 1868 and the Dawbarn and Lloyd-Slater-Bennet-Dorning 'fleets' from 1868 onwards until the vessels were sold in the eighties and the fleets dispersed.

It is time to pause and take stock of the mid-century developments at Port Penrhyn and Bangor in general. The Chester and Holyhead Railway had reached Bangor in 1848 and by 1852 had constructed the Penrhyn siding leading to the port. The port, as we have seen, was considerably enlarged in 1855 by the construction of a breakwater on the eastern side and the formation of an inner basin. It was not, however, until 1876 that the Penrhyn horse tramway which had several inclined planes along its six mile length was replaced by a new track and steam traction.

An important step on the way to eventual municipalisation had been taken in 1848, in response to the fear of an outbreak of cholera, when Parliament was petitioned on behalf of the vestry of ratepayers of Bangor to bring the town under the provisions of the Public Health Act. The result of this was that the Bangor Local Board of Health was established in 1850 with the object of providing a proper drainage and sewerage system, and a piped water supply in place of the many wells and fountains. This was slowly achieved in the course of the next three decades. The Board of Health's

---

[6] L.R.O. W/DB 226.
[7] Henry Parry, 'Wreck and Rescue on the Coast of Wales', Vol. 2, p. 43.

prestige suffered when an outbreak of typhoid occurred in 1882 which led to its abolition and the incorporation of Bangor into a municipal borough.

Substantial, generous even, as was the contribution of Col. E. G. D. Pennant to the Board, particularly in securing an adequate water supply from the slopes of the Carneddau on the Penrhyn Estate, the fact remains that he resisted all efforts to bring Port Penrhyn within the jurisdiction of the board as had been the original intention.

In three successive issues of *The North Wales Chronicle* in 1865 the story comes to its final conclusion.[8] After lengthy correspondence between the Board and Col. Pennant's solicitor, Mr. Henry Barber, a compromise was reached. Pennant's agent, who rejoiced in the name of Pennant Athelwold Iremonger, offered the Board a present (sic) of £4,500 if they would remove all doubts about Port Penrhyn's being in the Bangor Board of Health's district. It was resolved to accept the offer subject to the approval of the ratepayers assembled in vestry meeting. The following issue recorded the overwhelming acceptance of the vestry and a further issue stated that formal agreement had been reached. This curious and half forgotten little episode is further confirmation of what *The Carnarvon and Denbigh Herald's* correspondent had in mind later in that same year (see page 131) when he described Port Penrhyn as a pocket port.

Pocket port or not, there is evidence that the fifties and sixties were a period of high activity for Port Penrhyn. A press report of 1863 of the Parliamentary returns of Pilotage from the Port of Beaumaris[9] states that although one pilot had been 'omitted' (reason not given) from the return, two more, William Edwards aged 23 and William Jones aged 30, were added. In 1862 571 coasters, 16 oversea vessels and 9 foreign vessels were piloted inwards, and 634 coasters, 10 oversea vessels and 6 foreign vessels were piloted outwards, producing a revenue of £445.3s. In addition, from the sea outside the Sound 43 vessels had been piloted to either Beaumaris Bay, Conwy or Bangor, and from inside the Sound 5 to one of the same destinations. The report adds that pilots taken into Conwy were entitled in addition to their pilotage 7s.6d. for their expenses and return to Beaumaris; if they were landed at Great Orme's Head they were entitled to £2.2s., and if carried beyond limits to Chester or Liverpool to £3.3s.

The Port Penrhyn shipping books give a detailed picture of commerce, both coastal and overseas. In addition to the American vessels recorded, such as the *Joseph Howe, Brandy Wind* and the *Callender,* the famous Caernarfon barque, *Hindoo,* belonging to Humphrey Owen, Rhyddgaer, made two voyages in 1860 to Boston and one in 1861.[10] In addition to stating the total amount of the cargo, the books show how each day every ship was loaded;

[8] N.W.C. April 8, 15 & 22 1865.
[9] N.W.C. 10.10.1863.
[10] C.R.O. PQ 65/3 (1857-62).

the larger ocean-going ships did not generally come alongside the quay but lay in Bangor Pool and were loaded by smaller sloops and schooners; between March 2nd and April 4th 1859 *Hindoo* took on board 370 tons of slate from the *Bangor Packet, Susannah, Ann Elizabeth, Jane, Eleanor* and *Aurora.*

In 1860 and 1861 the Bangor owned *Albion,* a 477 ton barque, made two voyages to Boston, carrying 503 tons 12 cwts. and 551 tons 5 cwts. of slates. *Bangor Packet* was again among the vessels supplying lighterage while *Lord Exmouth* was involved twice. Exceptionally in March 1861, it is recorded that *Albion* took on board 152 tons while lying alongside the quay, the remainder being put on board by quite large schooners such as the *Cambria* (loading 118 tons) and the *John Nelson* (loading 110 tons). The delay and the labour involved in these trans-shipments must have added appreciably to the freight charges for voyages to North America. The *Albion* was wholly owned by William Pritchard, Tanycoed, Bangor, a slate merchant and a shipowner on a considerable scale.

Albion was built in Jarrow in 1854 and her registration had been transferred from Liverpool to Beaumaris where William Pritchard registered her. (Beaumaris 1860/7). Her log and crew list for a voyage from London to the West Indies in August 1865 has survived[11] and shows that in addition to her master (Hugh Owen, of High Street, Poplar) she carried 1st and 2nd Mates, Carpenter, Cook, Steward and 8 seamen. The log records that ten days out when they were in Lat.46.2.N. and Long. 10.5 W. they encountered a storm and took in all sails with the exception of the topsails with 3 reefs in the fore topmast staysail and the ship was hove to on the port tack. The vessel was labouring heavily and the galley shifted from its chocks "when the vessel gave a heavy lee lurch and William Edwards, seaman, fell heavily on the weather side of the poop deck and slid across the deck to leeward and fell overboard between the covering board and the lower guard rail; hove him a rope which seemed to be sliding over him as he was dropping astern, likewise the life buoy but he could not get hold in any of them. We could not render any more assistance, (it) being out of reason to get out a boat."

William Edwards, aged 22, born in Anglesey, was only one of many hundreds of seamen who perished but unlike many who left no trace, we at least do know the manner of his death. A list of his clothing and effects follows, and then a pathetic little note; he had worked for 10 days at £2.15 a month and so had earned 18s.4d. But he had been advanced £2.15s of his wages and had received tobacco to the value of 2s.6d. so that the sum of £1.19s.2d. was due to the ship. It would be superfluous to add any comment.

A second voyage is recorded in the log for May to November 1866. *Albion* is returning to London from Jamaica in November and is beating towards Margate and anchors in the road in a heavy gale. The anchors drag

[11] L.R.O. W/DB 14.

and the pilot orders the masts to be cut away "to save cargo, ship and lives" and with the assistance of two steam tugs the ship was got up river as far as Gravesend. The sea pilot then left the ship and the river pilot took over and with one tug she was brought to the West India Docks.

There is no means of telling whether the damage sustained by the vessel in the latter part of 1866 was instrumental in persuading William Pritchard to sell her in the following year, but this is what happened. Her Certificate of Registry was cancelled on 6 April 1867 with the remark that the vessel had been sold to foreign owners.

William Pritchard had other interests besides ships. He was associated with John Thomas in the business of slate merchandising, and as we have already seen, he was the main contractor, together with William Griffith, a mason from Dean Street, for the 1855 extension to Port Penrhyn. Like other successful businessmen he was prepared to lend money on mortgage, and John Hopson, a Master Mariner from Holyhead (later from Bangor) mortgaged his 28/64ths holding in the Nova Scotia built barque, *Glen Tilt*, of 279 tons, to him in 1858. Unfortunately she was lost in the following year, in the Rio Grande de Norte according to the Register.

In 1850 he was one of the original investors, with his business associate John Thomas, in the Bangor built schooner, *John Parry*, and retained his holding of 8/64ths until she was sold to Arthur Wyatt and John Lloyd in 1861. In 1853 he bought a 20/64ths share in the Conwy built schooner, *Sarah Anne*, of 69 tons in which John Lloyd, the Port Penrhyn accountant, also had a 20/64ths share. She foundered in 1875 15 miles north of the Isle of Man.

The 41 ton flat *Sluice*, so called because she had been built at Sluice in Flintshire, was acquired by him in partnership with William Griffith, the mason, and was possibly used for bringing the limestone from Penmon for the extension of Port Penrhyn.

Caradoc, a 224 ton foreign built brig was registered at Beaumaris (1862/22) with William Pritchard as her sole owner. Her origins are a bit of a mystery; the Register states that she was "condemned in the High Court of Admiralty as a prize and taken under the name 'Livonia' ". The Crimean War had ended seven years earlier in 1856, and the name 'Livonia' suggests one of the Baltic provinces of Russia. The balance of probabilities is that *Caradoc* was originally a Baltic trader.

William Pritchard owned her for two years only for she was sold in 1864 to two merchants and one gentleman from Glasgow and her registration was transferred to the Port of Glasgow in that year. It seems unlikely that she was ever in Port Penrhyn during those two years according to the extant crew agreement lists and log books.[12] In the first half of 1863 she sailed from Newport for the West Indies, calling at Grenada and San Fernando.

[12] L.R.O. W/DB 69.

Later in the year foreign articles were signed for a voyage to Malta and any ports in the Mediterranean and Black Sea. *Caradoc* was at Malta in late August and at Taganrog (in the Black Sea) in October, and she called in Malta in December on her way home. In the following spring she went again from Newport to the West Indies, calling at St. Thomas and Trinidad. She carried a large crew for a vessel of just over 200 tons — master (Thomas Griffith of Caernarfon) mate, carpenter, cook and steward, 3 A.B.'s and 2 O.S.'s, but it must be remembered that as a square rigger (a brig) she required a larger crew than a schooner of comparable size.

At the other end of the scale was the diminutive sloop of 15 tons, *Petrel*, built at Bangor by an unknown builder in 1866 (Beaumaris 1866/22) owned jointly by John Thomas, Minffordd, Mary Thomas, Widow, Brynhyfryd and William Pritchard, Tanycoed, Slate Merchants. After William Pritchard's death, when she was owned by the Thomases, she was lengthened and re-registered as a wherry of 24 tons. Sold in 1883 to Scotland she survived at least until 1909 when she was registered anew at Dumfries. When William Pritchard died in November 1868 his legatees were his widow, Jane Pritchard, his business partner, John Thomas and Mesach Roberts, Druggist. What was Meshach Roberts's connection? In his obituary notice in the *North Wales Chronicle* (22.1.1887) it was stated that he was the brother-in-law of William Pritchard, Tanycoed, — yet another example of the often unsuspected marriage or kinship ties, accidentally revealed in this instance, which linked shipowners in the small mercantile community of Bangor.

Which brings us naturally to a consideration of Meshach Roberts's part as a civic leader as well as a shipowner. Born at Holyhead in 1819 he came to Bangor at the age of 14 when he was apprenticed as a druggist. He spent three years in London where he became acquainted with the educational reformer Hugh Owen (later Sir Hugh); he was a life-long supporter of the undenominational schools movement and of the Bangor Normal College. He was a deacon at Tabernacle C.M. Chapel and a Liberal in politics, but these attachments did not deter him from being a member of the Royal Welsh Yacht Club at Caernarfon and a keen yachtsman. On his return to Bangor to take over a business, Thomas Lewis was his first apprentice.

With Thomas Lewis, his fellow Liberal and a fellow ship owner, he was a protagonist in 1886 in the strange episode in Bangor's municipal history when there were two rival mayors. A succinct account is given by Ernest Roberts in *Bargen Bywyd fy Nhaid*.[13] Meshach Roberts resigned his aldermanic seat in order to oppose the Tory, John Pritchard in an election for a councillor. Meshach Roberts headed the poll by 20 votes but the returning officer, Col. Platt declared John Pritchard elected on the grounds that Meshach Roberts was already an alderman. When the council met,

---

[13] Ernest Roberts, *Bargen Bywyd*, Llyfrau'r Dryw, 1963, pp. 31-33. Also P. E. Jones, 'Bangor 1883-1983. A Study in Municipal Government' pp. 108-111.

Meshach Roberts proposed the re-election of Thomas Lewis as mayor, John Pritchard was proposed by the Tories and there was deadlock as the right of the mayor to have a casting vote was disputed with each party recognising its own mayor at different ends of the council chamber. Litigation ensued; Roberts and Lewis lost their case, but won it in the court of appeal and in the subsequent hearing in the House of Lords. Sadly Meshach Roberts did not live to hear the judgement; Thomas Lewis is reputed, falsely, to have built the Town Clock in Bangor High Street as a token of his gratitude.

Meshach Roberts was a director of the Bangor Mutual Ship Insurance Society. In the shift of investment in the seventies from coastal shipping to ocean going vessels, from locally built wooden ships to iron (and later steel) ships built at Liverpool or Sunderland, he was a director of the Arvon Shipping Company (which owned the *Enterprise, Arvonia, Snowdonia, Gwalia, Ogwen, Menai* etc.). But our concern is with his investment in local shipping based on the Bangor slate trade.

Some of Meshach Roberts's holdings in Bangor shipping have already come to light in the chapter about Bangor shipbuilders — his share with Edward Ellis in *Holyhead Trader* (page 95) and his far more significant participation with John Roberts in the building and ownership of *City of Bangor,* the financing of *Grampus* (page 119) and of the same builder's *Charlotte Anne* (page 120). Anywhere but in Wales the fact that they shared the same surname would lead to speculation about kinship; they *may* have been related, but what is certain is that they collaborated closely.

His earliest known holding is in the 128 ton schooner, *Prince of Wales,* built at Cemaes by Ishmael Jones (Beaumaris 1842/5). Her original shareholders all came from Holyhead and district and included two mail guards. In 1846, at the age of 27, Meshach Roberts, who had been born in Holyhead and lived there until he was 14 years of age, acquired 20/64ths and was registered as her subscribing owner. All the other shareholders when she was re-registered in 1846 came from Holyhead and included two Robertses — John, a gentleman and David, a labourer. No conclusions should be drawn! Unfortunately we know very little of the history of this vessel; it appears that she was sold, as she was re-registered in 1851 at Hull (the register entry is not clear).

Nimrod, a 129 ton brigantine was built in River John, Nova Scotia in 1847 and was bought jointly by Meshach Roberts (36/64ths) and Owen Roberts, Master Mariner, Bangor (28/64ths) (Beaumaris 1847/24). In the five years from 1845 to 1849, in the middle of the expansion of the slate trade, no fewer than twenty-one ships were purchased by owners from Bangor. They were mostly small sloops, but among the more substantial vessels were two newly built in the maritime provinces of British North America, *Nimrod* and the 94 ton schooner, *Belt,* which had been built at Beaver Harbour, New Brunswick. (Beaumaris 1847/23). North American ships were cheaper as wood was abundant and were being built in quantity, registered locally, then sent across the Atlantic with a cargo of timber, generally to Liverpool where they found ready buyers and were registered *de novo* in the United Kingdom. *Nimrod* was in Meshach Roberts's owner-ship for only eight years, as she was sold to a Dublin grocer in 1855, but *Belt* continued in Bangor ownership until 1893. Sold to Moelfre she was lost in 1906.

Meshach Roberts was the subcribing owner with 16/64ths together with the master of the vessel, John Jones, Master Mariner of Bangor, with 4/64ths, in the 80 ton schooner, *Ann and Catherine,* (Beaumaris 1848/23) which had been built at Pwllheli in 1840. One owner came from Pwllheli, *Ann* Evans whose occupation is given as Timber Merchant. Three of the other owners came from Holyhead, among them *Catherine* Roberts, Spinster, which leads to the (possibly idle) speculation that perhaps they were sisters and that the vessel was named after them. Meshach Roberts does not seem to have retained his interest in any one ship for any appreciable time. His policy appears to have been to sell and re-invest. The vessel was sold to Amlwch in 1853, but with Ann Evans, Timber Merchant retaining an interest. Nicholas Treweek was a major shareholder by 1867. She was totally lost in 1872.

Although Meshach Roberts's interests in his later years lay more with ocean-going shipping rather than the coasting trade (with the exception of the *City of Bangor*) he gave valuable service to the Bangor Mutual Ship Insurance Society at various times as treasurer, vice-chairman, chairman and long serving director until his death in 1887.

The next link in the chain is totally irrational; Meshach Roberts's name survives at the time of writing above a chemist's shop in Bangor High Street, though there is no longer a family connection; and until recently, at what used to be known as the Penlôn Slate Works, a firm of builder's merchants operated under the name of Humphrey Williams. Humphrey Williams was born in Pwllheli about 1823 so that he would be a near contemporary of Meshach Roberts. Both men, it should be mentioned in passing, were immigrants to Bangor from other parts of Gwynedd in the years of expansion in the thirties and forties which were previously noted.

The name of Humphrey Williams, Bangor, Master Mariner, first occurs in the Beaumaris Registers of Shipping as holding a 16/64ths part of the 79 ton schooner, also called *Ann and Catherine* (Beaumaris 1849/16), newly built at Talycafn on the River Conwy. The major shareholder was William Jones, Talycafn, Timber Merchant who also built the vessel, (there is a close and obvious connection between the two trades of shipbuilder and timber merchant) and the other shareholders were Owen Hughes, Bangor, Farmer and Owen Jones, Conway, Currier.

Humphrey Williams and Owen Hughes retained their interest in the vessel the former increasing his holding to 28/64ths, for another thirty years until she was lost near Leith. Again, in partnership with Owen Jones, the currier of Conwy, Humphrey Williams acquired a half share in the 31 ton smack, *Albion,* (not to be confused with the barque of the same name owned by William Pritchard). This particular *Albion* (Beaumaris 1846/6) had been built at Aberystwyth in 1831 and was formerly registered at that port. Humphrey Williams sold his share in 1859 to John Simon, the Bangor currier or leather merchant, who by 1862 had acquired the whole of the vessel, which he retained until his death in 1875. Afterwards she was wholly owned by William Sutherland, a Master Mariner of Bangor. The Register says of her that 'she foundered off the Copeland 28 June 1883' and that her certificate was lost with the vessel.

We move into a totally different class of vessel with *William Ocklestone,* (Beaumaris 1857/2) a 132 ton brigantine built in 1857 on the River Conwy at 'Eglwysfach'. Once again Owen Jones the currier has 28/64ths to Humphrey Williams' 36/64ths, the remaining 4 being held by Owen Jones, Farmer, Pwllheli, which was, it will be recalled, Humphrey Williams native town. His close business connection with Conwy has yet to be explained. Another mystery is who William Ocklestone was, and why the vessel bore a man's bust, presumably his, as her figurehead.

We have her Crew Agreement Lists for most of the ten years between 1863 and her end in 1873.[14] In the first of these, for the first half of the year 1863 Humphrey Williams is given both as her managing owner and her master, and he holds certificate no. 49354. In addition to the master she carried at this time mate, 3 seamen and 2 apprentices. She sailed from Caernarfon to London, thence by way of Newcastle and Cork to Bangor; from Bangor she again sailed for London, thence by way of Newcastle, Cork and Dublin back to Bangor. The same pattern is repeated in each year until 1868 — first a voyage with slates from Bangor to London, then to Newcastle, possibly in ballast, then a voyage to a port in Ireland, almost certainly carrying coals, before returning to Bangor. Her master in 1866 was David Price (uncertificated), a native of Nefyn, who was succeeded in 1868 by Thomas Jones (certificated) of Ala Road, Pwllheli.

It may be that the change of master took place because Humphrey Williams wished to widen his horizons and a certificated master was essential if the ship was to go foreign; on the other hand there may have been other reasons which we do not know about. In the second half of 1868 *William Ocklestone* made a voyage from Shields to Gibraltar, Cadiz and Huelva, uneventfully, judging from the absence of entries in the log book. She returned to Bangor by way of Newcastle and Dublin. In 1870 she sailed from Bangor for Leith, and obtained a cargo from Alloa to Dieppe, from Dieppe she sailed to

[14] L.R.O. W/DB 412.

Runcorn, thence by way of Dublin to Bangor. There followed two voyages to Hamburg, returning the first time by way of Calais and Runcorn and the second time by Ipswich.

Her master in 1870 was the uncertificated Rowland Williams who was replaced in 1871 by Humphrey Williams himself for a voyage to Stettin for which a certificated master was essential. She left Bangor on March 28. Her log states that on May 1 the 'Master being unwell was discharged at Stettin' and the mate, Thomas Hughes, took charge of the ship for the return to Shields which was reached on the 27th of the same month. For the remainder of the year Rowland Williams took over as master for coastal voyages which included calls at Hamburg, (which was within limits, as previously stated, for uncertificated masters) Middlesborough, Briton Ferry, Dartmouth and Sligo.

In the meantime Humphrey Williams had, in June 1870, acquired Owen Jones's shares and now owned 60/64ths of the vessel. He was to acquire the remaining 4/64ths from John Jones in February 1873.

In 1872 foreign articles were again signed with Thomas Hughes, the certificated mate, as master and Rowland Williams signing on as purser, for a voyage to Stettin, returning *via* Stralsund and Belfast. Later in the same year with Thomas Williams (Cert. no. 48354) of 50 Dean Street, Bangor, as master and Rowland Williams as boatswain she sailed from Newcastle to Ferrol and Bilbao returning to South Shields. Immediately on her return Rowland Williams took over as master. One cannot help wondering what kind of relationship existed between two men in that situation, particularly if the certificated master was an older man who knew that he would be discharged as soon as the vessel arrived at a port in Great Britain.

In the first half of 1873 the Crew Agreement List states that the vessel was "in the coasting and home trade" and that on April 4th she was "lost on Texel Island while on a voyage from Bangor to Hamburg." The official log, ship's log book, certificate and other documents were lost with the ship, but the master, Rowland Williams (aged 33), and the crew consisting of mate, three A.B.'s and one O.S. were all saved.

Humphrey Williams was also part owner with W. A. Darbishire, Gentleman of Bangor, one of the proprietors of the Penrorsedd Slate Quarry in the Nantlle Valley, of the 252 ton barque *Helen* (Beaumaris 1866/1) which had been built at Souris, Prince Edward Island, in 1865. Unfortunately the only extant Crew Agreement Lists are for the last eighteen months of the vessel's life, from June 1871 until January 1873.[15] Her master (Humphrey Jones — cert. no. 28072) and crew signed foreign articles in Antwerp for a voyage to any port in North or South America, the West Indies, Cape of Good Hope and the Mediterranean not exceeding fifteen months. In addition

---

[15] L.R.O. W/DB 252.

143

to the master, mate, boatswain, carpenter and cook/steward, the crew consisted of 4 A.B.'s (born respectively in Norfolk, Va., Norway, Holland and the U.K.) an ordinary seaman from Finland and a boy born in the U.K. — a somewhat different make up from the majority of Bangor ships, the crews of which were mainly locally recruited.

The Log Book records that she was at Rosario for a month in September/October 1871. The cook/steward gave trouble; on four separate occasions his pay was docked for drunkenness or for absence from duty, another of the crew fell foul of the shore authorities for being drunk and disorderly, was disciplined and promptly deserted. The vessel moved down river to San Nicolas where William Banks, a seaman from Dublin, was drowned while bathing. He was seen to be struggling with cramp but before anyone could go to his aid he disappeared. As was usual his clothes and effects were auctioned on board (fetching £3. 15s. 5½d.), more unusually a subscription list was opened to which the master contributed £1 and which totalled £3 12s. 6d., which together with his earnings, less what he had been charged for from the slop chest and for tobacco, was held in the ship's account for his next of kin. He must have been a popular crew member, or his unexpected death in the middle of enjoyment must have struck his mates, who in their precarious calling were not unaccustomed to death, as particularly poignant.

The ship then moved to Montevideo in Uruguay; while she was there a crew member was shanghaied from on board — "Italian boat came alongside and took away Victor Galopia without consent of the mate. At 9 p.m. Master of the Italian barque came and demanded his clothes on the ground that he had signed his articles. He had signed my articles before the Captain of the Port San Nicolas acting counsel (sic) for all nations. I refused his clothes and treat him as deserter and shipped Alfred White at £4.10s. in his stead — the ship having been delayed 24 hours on account of his desertion." A petty annoyance, perhaps, but it had cost the owners 24 hours delay and time spent idle in port meant a loss of money. *Helen* was back at Antwerp in March.

She made another voyage from Antwerp to Havana from May until October, when she arrived at Greenock, which seems to have been uneventful apart from the usual trouble with (another) cook/steward while in port. He was found "intoxicated having stolen some gin". Later he was said to be in a fit, "with black stuff coming out of his mouth — gave him a vomit." It was later reported that he had tried to do away with himself by swallowing gun-powder and trying to jump overboard. Two men were deputed to watch him all night and in the morning he was reported to be better. It seems to have been a permanent improvement since he does not figure in the log for the remainder of the voyage. After reaching Greenock she went to Dublin and thence to Caernarfon.

At about this time William Darbishire severed his connection with the vessel. He had already sold 16/64ths to John Richards, the Bangor surgeon, in 1869 and he sold the remaining 16/64ths to him in November 1872. In the Crew Agreement for her fatal last voyage her managing owner is named as John Richards and her master as the same Humphrey Jones whose address is given as 13 College Road, Bangor. *Helen* was cleared at Caernarfon for a voyage to New Orleans on December 18, 1872 and she was last seen on the 31st January 1873. Her master and nine crew members were recorded as "supposed drowned".

Humphrey Williams and W. A. Darbishire were also joint owners of the 58 ton schooner, *Tay and Tees Packet,* (Beaumaris 1867/20) which had been built at Dundee in 1845. Darbishire did not maintain his interest for more than three years and he sold out to a London merchant in 1870. Humphrey Williams sold his share in 1873 to Frederic Percival, Portmadoc, Gentleman, who also acquired the London interest and became the sole owner. The vessel foundered in September 1886 off Start Point.

The next Bangor owners to be considered present a contrast, and represent the more work a' day aspect of ship ownership. They are the father and son firm of Robert and Richard Williams, Coal Merchants, who progressed to outright ownership by first holding shares with other assorted tradesmen. The 62 ton smack, with one mast and one jigger mast, *Prince of Orange,* (Beaumaris 1837/49) built at Rochester in 1802, was bought in 1844 from her Holyhead owner by nine men, seven of them from Bangor and two master mariners, one from Barmouth and the other from Liverpool. Among the Bangor men were Richard Williams, Master Mariner, who was also in the same year to be associated with Williams and Son in the ownership of the *Union* and of the *James and Maria,* and Samuel Roberts, at this period a grocer (this was one of the first of his shareholdings) who had an interest in the three vessels. Another shareholder was Evan Evans, described as a Master Mariner in 1848 and described elsewhere as 'formely Mariner now Liquor Merchant' who later became a successful merchant and shipowner. These three elderly vessels might well be described as their 'starter kit'! The *Prince of Orange* was lost in December 1852.

Union (Beaumaris 1846/16) was a 55 ton schooner built at Conwy in 1825, and Samuel Roberts, Grocer, Richard Williams, Mariner, and Robert Williams and Son, Coal Merchants each held 10/64ths of her in 1848. By various bills of sale Robert Williams and Son had acquired 40/64ths of the vessel by 1852 but in December of that year she was lost near Holyhead. The fact that she was not written off until 1855 suggests that she may have been driven ashore and there was at one time a prospect of repairing or rebuilding her.

The most elderly of the three vessels, the 45 ton flat *James and Maria* built at Winsford in 1756, (Beaumaris 1848/12) was bought by Robert Williams and Son, and by Richard Williams in his own right, each with

16/64ths, and by Samuel Roberts, with 8/64ths, in 1848. In spite of her age she was making four or five round trips each half year from Bangor to Runcorn, Liverpool or Chester in the first ten years for which we have Crew Agreement Lists (1863-1873),[16] varied in 1869 by voyages to Dumfries, Londonderry, Belfast, Dundalk and Arklow. Her cargoes are not mentioned in the extant Crew Agreement Lists but the fact that her owners included a firm of coal merchants makes it likely that she did not return in ballast to Bangor, especially after her trips to the Mersey or Dee ports. In 1866 Robert Williams and Son sold their share to Samuel Roberts 'formerly Grocer now Shipbuilder', and by degrees he became her sole owner before selling her to Amlwch in 1873. She was broken up in 1877, 121 years after she had been built.

In 1850 Robert Williams and Son bought outright the 38 ton sloop *John Nelson*, built at Kingston, New Brunswick in 1846. (Beaumaris 1850/5). In the same year she was altered to a schooner and her tonnage went up from 38 to 49 tons, and she was re-registered accordingly. (Beaumaris 1850/21). The one extant Crew Agreement List[17] (for the first half of 1863) for the period when she was in the ownership of R. Williams and Son shows Robert Williams, Coal merchant as her managing owner and Griffith Owen, 75 Ambrose Street, Bangor, as her master. She had a crew of three, master, mate and boy. During that time she made three round trips from Bangor — two to Garston and one to Liverpool.

Richard Williams (the son and master mariner) died sometime in the mid-sixties and the vessel came into the hands of Evan Evans, the former master mariner and liquor merchant who now became a coal merchant as well. Evan Evans continued as her managing owner and Griffith Owen as her master until at least 1873 when the series of Crew Agreement Lists is temporarily interrupted. Her usual beat was from Bangor to the Mersey, varied by an occasional voyage to Ireland — Carrickfergus in 1866, Belfast and Dublin in 1872 — and a surprising foray to the south coast, to Shoreham in 1871. In the mid-seventies the vessel was sold to John Owen, Tŷ Hir, Moelfre. He was her master until 1912 when she was reported as lying up at Moelfre. She was broken up in 1916. The next outright purchase by Robert Williams and Son was the 56 ton schooner *John Knox* (Beaumaris 1851/17) built, as one would expect from her naming, in Scotland, at Dumbarton in 1841. So far very little has been discovered about this vessel save that she was lost on 25 October 1862. A letter from Richard Williams, included in the register, states that "John Knox was lost on the Carroner Rock with General Cargo from Glasgow to Dublin."

The next two vessels acquired by the partnership were very different from each other. The 15 ton smack *Pilot* had been built at Kinsale in 1813 and

[16] L.R.O. W/DB 202.
[17] L.R.O. W/DB 225.

was acquired from Cork (Beaumaris 1853/20). She was sold to a mariner from Rhoscolyn in 1855 and according to the somewhat sketchily kept Crew Agreement Lists was employed in fishing after 1863. She was broken up in 1873.

The second vessel was the 104 ton schooner *Louise*, built at Antwerp in 1815, according to the "statement of the late owner Louis Edmond Grousar." Little is known about this vessel except that she was re-rigged as a brigantine in 1858 (the reverse of the usual process — fore and aft tended to gain in popularity at the expense of square sails). In 1858 her registration was transferred to Liverpool when she was sold to another coal merchant, possibly a business associate of the Williamses, Samuel Stocks of Wigan.

To these must be added the schooner *County of Cork*, acquired by Robert Williams and Son in 1853. They mortgaged the vessel to Thomas Peers Williams and John Williams, Bangor, Bankers "as security for floating balance". Eleven years later, in 1864, the bankers sold the vessel to Evan Evans, the rapidly diversifying merchant. The impression one gains overall from the activities of this father and son firm, as revealed by the shipping register, (and this is our only source) is one of upward economic struggle by way of shared ownership at first, then ownership outright of vessels best described as being past their prime, towards a modest success, which came to an end with the probable death of the son in the mid-sixties of the century.

The final 'case history' of this chapter — the other owners will be presented in summary form — is a man who has already been mentioned as a mariner turned merchant, Evan Evans. He first appears in the Register in 1830 as Mariner, holding 48/64ths in the 38 ton sloop *Brothers*, (Beaumaris 1825/56) built in 1817 at Traethbychan. The other shareholder with 16/64ths was Robert Evans, Stonemason. In the entry for 1836 he is described as 'formerly Mariner now Liquor Merchant' and in 1855, when the vessel was sold by him and the executors of Robert Evans, he has become a Wine Merchant, an improvement, perhaps on the faintly raffish associations of the term Liquor Merchant. He is, however, described in 1844 as a Master Mariner when he acquires 4/64ths together with Robert and Richard Williams, Samuel Roberts and other citizens of Bangor in *Prince of Orange*, as previously mentioned: likewise in the registration of the 25 ton sloop *Ann and Elizabeth*, (Beaumaris 1845/17) of which he was the sole owner in 1845.

There is some doubt whether he can be identified with the Evan Evans, Master Mariner of Bangor who in 1855 together with no fewer than four other Evanses, — William, Postmaster, John, Master Mariner; Elizabeth and Jane, both Spinsters, and all from Llanfairpwllgwyngyll — were the shareholders in *Margaret Anne*, a 62 ton schooner built at Caernarfon in 1853 (Beaumaris 1855/25). The doubt arises because of a discrepancy between this entry and others about the date of his death and the subsequent disposal of his shares, and this vessel is best disregarded. She is included in this account for the curious circumstances surrounding her end and the loss of her certificate (one suspects an ingenious excuse!). She lasted until 1888 when she was "stranded on Puffin Island on *25th December* and became a total wreck. Certificate of registry destroyed by drying after being wet."

From 1858 onwards he is described invariably as Merchant, starting with an entry in that year on the page in the register for *Holyhead Trader* (Beaumaris 1849/4). He originally had a 4/64ths share in the vessel, in which Edward Ellis and Meshach Roberts at various times had an interest, and at the time of his death he owned 16/64ths. In 1860 he acquired 16/64ths of the 50 ton schooner, *Richard,* built at Northwich in 1843 (Beaumaris 1860/11) and his holding by 1868 amounted to 48/64ths. The vessel was lost in 1870 in unknown circumstances.

The same tendency to add to his shareholdings and sometimes to become the managing owner of the vessel is apparent in the page recording the registration of *Margaret,* (Beaumaris 1861/6). This schooner of 52 tons had been built at Northwich in 1821 and her registry had been transferred from the port of Chester. In 1861 Evan Evans had a 12/64ths share. (The other shareholders and their holdings were Mary Griffith, wife of Thomas Griffith, Shipwright, Garth 16, Owen Williams, Victualler 8, Mary Jones, Widow 8, Edward Buckland, Agent 8, and John Griffiths, Master Mariner 12, all from Bangor). In 1864 he acquired 4/64ths from Owen Williams, in 1868 8/64ths from Edmund Buckland (who had bought them from Edward Buckland) and in 1877 16/64ths from Mary Griffiths, which gave him 40/64th. He had already been designated her managing owner. Shortly afterwards Mary Jones sold him her 8 shares.

After the death of Evan Evans, — he died intestate — Elizabeth Rowlands, widow of William Rowlands, Wine and Spirit Merchant of Bangor, inherited his portion of *Margaret* and other vessels. Mrs. Rowlands sold her shares to John Griffith who thus became the sole owner of the vessel. The likeliest explanation of her inheritance is that she was his sister — and William Rowlands the wine merchant, his brother-in-law, was probably also his business partner. Though the original William Rowlands has long been deceased, a wine merchant's business bearing his name was, until comparatively recently, a feature of Bangor High Street. (There is one other firm in existence today, John Pritchard and Co., the Estate Agents, which figures marginally in Bangor's maritime history. From the sixties onwards the auctioneer John Pritchard conducted many auction sales of vessels; after the bankruptcy of Thomas Parry he conducted the auction sale of his house, the shipyard and some of the remaining vessels. In the affair of the two mayors John Pritchard was the Tory mayor).

Evan Evans acquired a 48/64ths holding in the 30 ton schooner, *Gipsy,* built at Annan in 1831; 24 of these parts were bought from Richard Morris Griffith, the banker. Mrs. Rowlands inherited this vessel also after the death of Evan Evans. She bought the remaining 16 parts and promptly sold the vessel outright to Hugh Edwards, Master Mariner of Hirael. She was stranded at Llandudno in 1884 and became a total loss.

The next venture was the 54 ton schooner, *County of Cork* which he bought from Thomas Peers Williams and John Williams, the Bangor bankers, the mortgagees of R. Williams and Son in April 1864. Her subsequent history has been recounted briefly earlier in this chapter (page 127). This vessel also came into the possession of Mrs. Elizabeth Rowlands who sold her to William Thomas, the Amlwch shipbuilder.

Similarly the 38 ton schooner *John Nelson* came into his hands in exactly the same way in October of the same year; her trading was discussed earlier in this chapter and it comes as no surprise that she, too, was inherited by Mrs. Rowlands and sold in the following year to John Owen, Tŷ Hir, Moelfre.

Clearly Evan Evans, mariner turned wine merchant, had prospered, but he probably owed his success more to the latter occupation than to ship ownership. He became an important member of the community and was elected to the Bangor Board of Health at its creation in 1850 and also to the Board of Guardians.[18] He built the handsome detached house complete with miniscule entrance lodge overlooking the Menai Straits known then and to this day as Bryn-y-Môr.

*   *   *   *

It would be impossible within the compass of this book — and tedious, too — to mention every Bangor owner of the second half of the nineteenth century, and to mention every ship, some of which, like the *County of Cork* and the *John Nelson,* passed through several Bangor hands or were in multiple ownership. Some of the more prominent Bangor owners have received a passing mention, others have not. They are listed below but first place must be given to Richard Morris Griffith, draper and subsequently banker. Although he has been mentioned several times previously it would not be out of place to draw together the many previous references and to summarise here the contribution made to Bangor's shipping enterprise by him from the late thirties until the sixties of the century.

He was an early supporter of the Bangor shipbuilding industry by his investments, spread equally between Edward Ellis and John Parry. He owned initially 4/64ths of *Eliza and Catherine* when she was built by Edward Ellis in 1837; his portion had risen to 24/64ths by 1850. He maintained and

[18] P. E. Jones, 'The Bangor Board of Health', T.CH.S. Vol. 37 and G.A.S. C.R.O. XM/2765

added to this interest before the vessel was sold in 1862 (page 149). He preserved his impartiality with his 4/64ths share in *Anne,* the 88 ton schooner built by John Parry in 1839, which he held until she was lost in 1853. Also in 1839 he took a 4/64ths share in Edward Ellis's 77 ton schooner, *Maria and Elizabeth,* which he held until 1850. In 1841 he had a 16/64ths share in the 49 ton smack, *Mary Grace,* when she was built by John Parry; his holding had increased to 28/64ths by the time the vessel was lengthened in 1856 and turned into a 65 ton schooner. He sold out to the 'firm' of Parry, Power and Roberts in 1863 (page 66).

The 85 ton schooner *Eliza* was built at Pwllheli in 1839 by Humphrey Griffith (Beaumaris 1839/27) and Richard Morris Griffith was one of the original owners with 4/64ths. John Parry also held 4/64ths. Whether there was a conscious effort on the part of R. M. Griffith to remain impartial between the two competing shipbuilders or whether it was a mere coincidence, the fact remains that he was also the owner of a 4/64th part in the 131 ton schooner, *Splendid,* (Beaumaris 1839/34) built at Pwllheli in 1839, with Edward Ellis holding 2/64ths. Lloyds agent reported from Beaumaris on April 15th 1840 that "the *Splendid,* Owen, from Bangor to London, took the ground in beating out this morning but is not expected to have received any damage." In September of the same year he reported that "the *Splendid,* Owen, from Liverpool to London put in here today, leaking with pumps choked" but it was soon put to rights because the Liverpool agent reported next day that the leak had been stopped and that the vessel was ready to proceed. The vessel was transferred to the Pwllheli register in 1846.

With *Heart of Oak,* an 80 ton sloop built in 1771 at Ipswich (Beaumaris 1843/12) we find Richard Morris Griffith and Edward Ellis each with a 24/64ths holding with her master John Jones of Holyhead holding the remaining 16 parts. Griffith sold his portion to Edward Ellis in 1846. By 1856 she was sold to Thomas Williams, House painter, James Southwell and James Gregory, both Gentlemen. The vessel was lost in 1863.

There is no evidence that Richard Morris Griffith ever took an active part in ship management as ship's husband or managing owner; he was mainly interested in the financial aspects, as is clear when he acted as broker in the sale of *Gipsy* to Evan Evans in 1863. But he certainly performed a service in helping to provide financial stability for the ship building industry in Bangor when it was on the eve of the expansion of the fifties.

The list which follows gives the bare details of ownership and approximate period because it is not easy to determine in every case when an interest began or ended. The list is in alphabetical order and vessels built in Bangor are marked thus ‡

Owner	Vessel	Period & Interest	End
HUMPHREY DAVIES Master Mariner & Farmer	Belt 94t. Sr. b. 1846	1851-1893 16/64-36/64	H. D. died 1893 V. lost 1906
	Holyhead Trader 62t. Sr. b. 1821	1853 briefly 12/64 & 1878-1881 16/64	V. lost 1881
	Thomas Mason 51t. Sr. b. 1838	1868-1893 48/64	V. lost 1894
	Lady Louisa Pennant‡ 73t. Sr. b. 1847	1878-1893 8/64	V. lost 1902
	Elinor 51t. Flat b. 1858	1878-1888 32/64	V. lost 1888
	Maria Catherine 88t. Sr. b. 1841	?1882-1886 32/64	V. lost 1886
	Maria Jane 99t. Sr. b. 1857	?1886-1893 32/64	V. lost 1898
EDWARD ELLIS jun. Ship Carpenter	Caerhun 24t. Cutter b. 1819	1861-1864 32/64	Sold 1864 V. lost 1887
	Mary Edwards‡ 65t. Sr. b. 1863	1863-1864 8/64	Sold 1864 V. broken up 1936
JOHN ELLIS Master Mariner & Shipbuilder	Lady Louisa Pennant‡ 73t. Sr. b. 1847	1865 36/64-44/64 1902	V. lost 1902
	Arthur Wyatt‡ 96t. Sr. b. 1858	1871-1903 16/64	V. lost 1903
	William 50t. Flat b. 1810	1875-1881 16/64	V. lost 1881
	Adieu 21t. Sr. b. 1847	1875 16/64-48/64 1882	Sold 1884 V. lost 1886
	Dorothea‡ 74t. Sr. b. 1862	1875-1877 2/64	Sold 1877 V. lost 1900
	Maria Jane 99t. Sr. b. 1857	?1886-1898 32/64	V. lost 1898
	Maria Catherine 88t. Sr. b. 1841	?1882-1886 32/64	V. lost 1886
ROWLAND EVANS Coal Merchant	Catherine 38t. Sl. b. 1836	1836 briefly 32/64	Sold 1836 V. lost 1852
	Liberty 46t. Sr. b. 1836	1846-?1859 32/64	R.E. died ?1859 V. lost 1860
	Belt 94t. Sr. b. 1846	1847-?1859 4/64	V. lost 1906
	Holyhead Trader 62t. Sr. b. 1821	1851-?1859 36/64	V. lost 1881
JAMES GREGORY Gentleman	Lady Louisa Pennant‡ 73t. Sr. b. 1847	1856-1902 12/64	V. lost 1902
	Heart of Oak 80t. Sl. b. 1771	1856-1860 16/64	Sold 1860 V. lost 1863

Owner	Vessel	Period & Interest	End
ROBERT &	Warren Bulkeley	1849-1858 64/64	V. lost 1858
JOHN HOPSON	53t. Sr. b. 1803		
Confectioner &	Glen Tilt	1856-1859 56/64	V. lost 1859
Master Mariner	279t. Barque b. 1851		
respectively	Boadicea	1859-1861 64/64	Sold 1861
	120t. Sr. b. 1859		
JOHN JONES	Mayflower	1862-1867 64/64	V. lost 1867
Diver & Pilot	26t. Sma. b. 1787		
	Equity	1865-1867 64/64	V. lost 1867
	38t. Sl. b. 1856		
	Eliza Jane‡	1866-1885 32/64	J.J. died 1885
	38t. Sr. b. 1866		V. lost 1913
JOHN JONES	Dart	1847-1848 64/64	Sold 1848
Master Mariner	32t. Sl. b. 1836		V. lost 1888
	Ann and Catherine	1848-1853 4/64	Sold 1853
	80t. Sr. b. 1840		V. lost 1872
	County of Cork	1851-1853 mortgagee	Disch. 1853
	53t. Sr. b. 1815	of 32/64ths of vessel	Broken up 1936
JOHN THOMAS JONES	Argyle	1867-1872 16/64	V. lost 1872
Ship Surveyor	63t. Sr. b. 1802		
	Elizabeth Charlotte	1872-1877 8/64	Sold 1877
	148t. B'g'tine b. 1850		
THOMAS JONES	Sarah Anne	1853-1875 8/64	V. lost 1875
Accountant	69t. Sr. b. 1835		
	Eliza Jane‡	1866-1885 8/64	Sold 1885
	38t. Sr. b. 1866		V. lost 1913
THOMAS JONES	Priscilla	1856-1873 64/64	Sold 1873
Diver	40t. Sl. b. 1827		Broken up 1879
	Equity	1861-1865 64/64	Sold 1865
	38t. Sl. b. 1856		V. lost 1867
EDWARD OWEN[19]	Annie and Jane	1867-1878 20/64	Broken up 1878
Master Mariner	85t. Sr. b. 1867		
	Talacre	1867-1885 16/64	E.O. died 1885
	77t. Sr. b. 1821		V. lost 1893
	John Parry‡	1868-1885 8/64	Sold 1885
	56t. Sr. b. 1850		V. lost 1901
JAMES OWEN	Alert	1859-1860 64/64	Sold 1860
Master Mariner	56t. Sr. b. 1833		V. lost 1867
	Jane and Sarah	1877-1883 64/64	Sold 1883
	43t. Sma. b. 1855		Tr. Barnstaple 1889
	Gleaner	1877 64/64	Sold 1877
	66t. Sr. b. 1820		Broken up 1880

[19] He was one of the captains who benefitted from the compulsory sale of the Wyatt/Lloyd fleet in 1867/8.

Owner	Vessel	Period & Interest	End
RICHARD OWEN Master Mariner	Duchess of Gloucester 78t. B'g'tine b. 1828	1849-1860 40/64	Sold 1860 Tr. Newry 1860
	Wakefield 48t. Sr. b. 1823	1856-1858 32/64	Sold 1858 V. lost 1871
	Eaton 46t. Sr. b. 1832	1856-1875 32/64	Sold 1875 Tr. Wexford 1877
WILLIAM PARRY Brazier	Eliza and Catherine‡ 43/54t. Sma. b. 1837 (lengthened 1855)	1837-1862 4/64	Sold 1862 V. lost 1881
	Mary Grace‡ 49/65t. Sma./Sr. b. 1841 (lengthened 1856)	1841-1871 4/64	W.P. died 1871 V. lost 1874
	John Parry‡ 56t. Sr. b. 1850	1850-1861 4/64	Sold 1861 V. lost 1901
	Cambria‡ 56t. Sr. b. 1860	1860-1871 8/64	V. lost 1903
JOHN RICHARDS Surgeon	Speculation 53t. Sr. b. 1817	1856-1891 32/64	J.R. died 1891 Hulked 1901
	Arthur Wyatt‡ 96t. Sr. b. 1858	1858-1891 8/64	V. lost 1903
	Helen 252t. Barque b. 1865	1869-1873 16/64-32/64	V. lost 1873
MORGAN RICHARDS High Bailiff, County Court	Annie and Jane 85t. Sr. b. 1867	1867-1878 32/64	Broken up 1878
	Argyle 63t. Sr. b. 1802	1867-1872 28/64	V. lost 1872
	Mary Tatham 56t. Sr. b. 1858	1867-1875 64/64	V. lost 1875
	Elizabeth Charlotte 148t. B'g'tine b. 1850	1872-1877 56/64	Sold 1877 Tr. Caernarfon 1877
OWEN ROBERTS[20] Shipbuilder	Aurora 24t. Sma. b. 1818	1877-1883 64/64	Sold 1883 Tr. Cardigan 1886
	Gleaner 66t. Sr. b. 1820	1877-1880 64/64	Broken up 1880
	Burncoose 65t. Sr. b. 1840	1881-1882 64/64	Sold 1883 Tr. Stornoway 1883
	Glynaeron 52t. Sr. b. 1852	1889-1895 64/64	Sold 1895 Tr. Aberystwyth 1895
	Lewis 61t. Sr. b. 1848	1890 64/64	Sold 1890 V. lost 1894
	Margaret 45t. Ketch b. 1862	1892-1894 64/64	Sold 1894 Broken up 1922

[20] Owen Roberts leased the Garth shipyard from T. T. Parry's liquidator, W. J. Parry. He seems to have specialised in repairing and re-selling old vessels.

Owner	Vessel	Period & Interest	End
ROBERT ROBERTS Postmaster	Sarah Bridget‡ 126t. B'g'tine b. 1858	1858-?1880 4/64	Sold ?1880 Broken up 1936
	Sarah Jane‡ 73t. Sr. b. 1861	1861-1874 14/64	Sold 1874 Tr. Runcorn 1877
	Ann and Sarah 34t. Sl. b. 1831	1864 16/64-48/64 1884	Sold 1884 Used as pontoon 1886
	Bangor Packet‡ 39t. Sl. b. 1830	1867 16/64-40/64 1887	Hulked 1887
ZACHARIAS ROBERTS Gentleman, Draper	Emily 98t. Brig. b. 1826	1840 32/64-12/64 1861	Sold 1861 Condemned 1872
	James and Maria 45t. Flat b. 1756	1848 8/64-24/64 1873	Sold 1873 Broken up 1877
WILLIAM ROWLANDS Maesyporth Pilot	Mary Grace‡ 49t. Sma. b. 1841	1841-1846 4/64	W.R. died 1846 V. lost 1874
	Douglas Pennant‡ 79t. Sr. b. 1841	1841-1846 8/64	V. lost 1868
JOHN SIMON Currier/Farmer	Sarah Bridget‡ 126t. B'g'tine b. 1858	1858-1875 4/64	J.S. died 1875 Broken up 1936
	Albion 31t. Sl. b. 1831	1859-1875 32/64	V. lost 1883
	Sarah Jane‡ 73t. Sr. b. 1861	1861-1875 20/64	Tr. Runcorn 1877
	Dorothea‡ 74t. Sr. b. 1862	1862-1875 24/64	V. lost 1877
	Samuel 359t. Barque b. 1866	1867-1874 16/64	Sold 1874 ('to foreigners')
JOHN THOMAS Minffordd Hall Slate Merchant	John Parry‡ 56t. Sr. b. 1850	1850-1861 16+4=20/64	Sold 1861 V. lost 1901
	Petrel‡ 15/24t. Sl./Wherry b. 1866	1866-1883 32/64	Sold 1883 Tr. Dumfries 1909
	Sluice 41t. Flat b. 1838	1868-1873 jointly 32/64	Sold 1873 V. lost 1883
	Lord Exmouth‡ 19t. Sma. b. 1869	1869-1874 32/64	Sold 1874 V. lost 1898
THOMAS WILLIAMS House Painter	Prince of Orange 62t. Sma. b. 1802	1844-1853 4/64	V. lost 1853
	Dart 32t. Sl. b. 1836	1848 48/64-64/64 1871	Sold 1871 V. lost 1888
	Concord 45t. Sr. b. 1776	1851- ? 32/64	No further record
	Heart of Oak 80t. Sl. b. 1771	1856-1863	V. lost 1863

Owner	Vessel	Period & Interest	End
W. FRANCIS WILLIAMS	Samuel	1867-1874 16/64	Sold 1874
Ironmonger	359t. Barque b. 1866		('to foreigners')
	Dorothea‡	1875-1875	Sold 1876
	74t. Sr. b. 1862	31/64 held jointly	V. lost 1900
	Albion	1875-1876	Sold 1876
	31t. Sl. b. 1831	64/64 held jointly	V. lost 1883
	W. D. Potts	1878-1901 8/64	Sold 1901
	111t. Sr. b. 1878		V. sunk by
			U-boat 1917

If nothing else, this list, taken together with the names of those previously mentioned at length, shows the wide variety of occupations among the ship-owners of Bangor. Again, as previously noted, the professional, as distinct from the commercial middle class, is sparsely represented — one doctor, one accountant, one gentleman — and Morgan Richards, the High Bailiff of the County Court, a man of many parts, an inveterate publicist and author of 'Slate Quarrying and how to make it profitable'.

Since our main concern is with coastal shipping no mention has been made of the comparatively few ocean-going vessels owned at Bangor but registered at Liverpool or elsewhere. The deficiency, if such it is, is splendidly filled by Aled Eames' recent book, *Ventures in Sail*,[21] which deals comprehensively with the ocean-going ships of Gwynedd from 1840 until 1914, their masters, builders and managers and with Gwynedd's close connections with the port of Liverpool.

Meshach Roberts's directorship of the Eryri Shipping Company has already been mentioned. The most important shipping magnate who lived in Bangor was Charles Pierce, a cousin of the Davies brothers of Menai Bridge, who took over the management of the firm with its worldwide interests in the eighties. Like Meshach Roberts he made a valuable contribution to the municipal life of the city of Bangor, but unlike him he had no holdings in local vessels. Two men who combined local interests with interests in large ships were John Lloyd, junior, who owned the barque *Alice Platt,* and John Richards, the Bangor surgeon, who owned the barque *Lady Penrhyn* in addition to their holdings in the local vessels listed above.

If there is any one man in the list who deserves a special mention it is William Parry, the brazier. His holdings were modest, it is true, but over a period of thirty years or more, he gave faithful backing to the products of the Bangor shipbuilders' yards and to none other. He impressed his con-

---

[21] Published jointly by Gwynedd Archives and Museums Service, Merseyside Maritime Museum, National Maritime Museum, London (Gee and Son, Denbigh 1987).

155

temporaries, too; despite the fact that many other members had considerably greater holdings in Bangor ships than he had, the Annual Reports of the Bangor Mutual Ship Insurance Society for 1854 and 1859 show that William Parry, Brazier was one of the three trustees of the society, together with such substantial figures as Rees Jones, Shipbuilder of Felin Heli and Robert Thomas, Shipbuilder of Nefyn. It is now time to consider this aspect of Bangor's maritime and mercantile life.

CHAPTER IX

Ship Insurance

The term 'Insurance Clubs' really says it all; they were formed by shipowners, initially, to protect themselves against the exorbitant charges of the monopolists, the London Assurance Society and the Royal Exchange Society, a monopoly which came to an end in 1824. But there were so many advantages in these voluntary self-help associations that they persisted, and indeed, proliferated in all parts of Britain, and especially at first in the ports of the north east of England, for the greater part of the nineteenth century, and they declined only as coastal shipping itself declined.

The movement reached North Wales in 1841 with the establishment of the *Portmadoc Mutual Ship Insurance Society* in 1841, but it was another twelve years before the second such 'club' was established, at Bangor in 1853.[1] Shortly afterwards a similar club was founded at Nefyn, the *Pwllheli and Nevin Mutual Marine Insurance Society,* and the little town of Nefyn thereafter became a nest of insurance clubs, among them the *Ancient Briton Mutual Marine Society* of 1868 and an offshoot, the paradoxically named *Ancient Briton Iron Sailing Ships Mutual Marine Insurance Association Ltd.* of 1877. The proliferation of clubs was caused by the extension of local investment from coastal shipping into ocean-going vessels, and later into large iron vessels, since the early clubs placed a limit of £1,000 or £1,500 on the amount covered. A large vessel such as William Thomas's famous *William*

[1] D. Thomas 'Hen Longau etc.' Ch. 11 and pp. 237-8.

Melhuish, valued at £5,000 was covered by the Bangor Society for £1,500 and the remainder was placed elsewhere.

Instead of paying a substantial premium members of a club paid an entrance fee (£2 10s. per £100 covered in the case of the Bangor Mutual Ship Insurance Society — B.M.S.I.S. henceforth) and an annual subscription of £1 per cent. Calls for losses were then made on members in proportion to the sums they themselves were held insured — expressed as £s or parts of a £ per cent. The entrance fees and the annual subscription went into a general fund from which the salaries and expenses of the secretary, the surveyors and the directors were paid. There was also an insurance fund into which the sums accruing from the calls were paid and from which members were compensated for their losses.

There were many advantages for shipowners from such a system; there were no premiums to be paid in advance, only, after the first year, the very moderate annual subscription, neither were there agents' commissions. But the chief advantage for the owners was that they were dealing with officials who lived locally, spoke Welsh and were aware of local difficulties, not with some faceless bureaucrat in Liverpool or London. Fraud and swindling were almost impossible because there were strict regulations and powers of expulsion for anyone bold enough to disregard them, and in a small community everyone was known to everyone else. For all that, it is sad to have to record that after nearly half a century of success the B.M.S.I.S. was compulsorily wound up in 1897 after its secretary had been convicted at the Caernarfon Assizes of forgery, not in connection with the B.M.S.I.S. but with a local building and friendly society of which he was also the secretary.

Evidence about the B.M.S.I.S. is fragmentary. The original Deed of Settlement of 1853, and the Annual Reports for 1872 and 1879 are to be found at the Caernarfon Area Record Office of the Gwynedd Archives Service[2] while the Annual Reports for 1854, 1859, 1878, 1885 and 1886 and the Society's Rule Book of July 1858 with amendments up to March 1869 are kept at the Library of the University College of North Wales at Bangor.[3] The Rule Book bears the inscription "To be kept on board *Lady Louisa Pennant.*" This is a coincidental reminder that the Secretary of the B.M.S.I.S. from 1854, the year after it was founded, until his death in 1875 was a man who probably had a hand in her building in 1847 (when he was employed by Captain John Parry) and held from that time a 4/64ths share in the vessel which rose to 8/64ths in 1865 — Samuel Roberts. Fragmentary though the evidence is, it is sufficiently spread about over the years to enable us to form an adequate general picture of the 'club's' activities.

The Deed of Settlement lays down that the management is to be in the hands of the Directors, not less than 12 nor more than 14 in number, "each

[2] C.R.O. XM/55/21, XM/804/9, & XM/499/3.
[3] U.C.N.W. KI 715.

of whom shall be interested in his own right in some Vessel or Vessels insurable by the Society to the extent of £100." The Directors were to be elected at the Annual General Meeting at which members could vote in person or by proxy, and for every additional sum of £100 insured by them in the Society beyond the first £500, they had an additional vote with an upper limit of 20 votes.

There were some familiar names among the Directors in the 1854 Annual Report, which, unlike the other reports that have survived, was printed in both English and Welsh. As has been mentioned previously, the Trustees were Rees Jones of Port Dinorwic, Robert Thomas of Nefyn, both shipbuilders and William Parry, brazier of Bangor. The Bangor directors were — Richard Williams, Coal Merchant, Rowland Evans, Coal Merchant, William Pritchard, Tanycoed 'Superintendent' (of what it is not stated — but we know that he was a slate merchant and shipowner), Meshach Roberts, Chemist, Robert Hopson, Confectioner, Thomas Williams, Painter, John Jones, Coal Merchant, John Owen, Pen-y-dref, Master Mariner, Zacharias Roberts, Hirael, Shipowner and the secretary, Samuel Roberts who was also a director. The other directors were Hugh Roberts and Robert Thomas, both shipbuilders and both from Nefyn, and a Caernarfon flour merchant by the name of Thomas Davies. The Report also gives the names of the Surveyors appointed for the several ports — Bangor (3), Caernarfon (2), Nefyn (2), Amlwch (2) and one each for Port Dinorwic, Conwy and Holyhead.

The original Deed of Settlement of 1853 stated that insurances were to be confined to vessels 'registered or belonging to Conway, Bangor, Carnarvon, Nevin, Holyhead, Amlwch and Beaumaris, except in the case of any vessels of any other port whose owner is already a member of the Society by virtue of some other insurance.' The loophole provided by the last clause was later widened by a resolution giving the Directors discretion to admit vessels of which not less than $\frac{1}{8}$ belonged to a person resident within 60 miles of the City of Bangor. This provision was to lead to the introduction later on of some large ocean going ships registered at Liverpool and, as we shall see, caused some dissatisfaction among the owners of smaller coastal vessels.

All vessels were to be regularly surveyed and were divided into two categories. First Class ships were not to be insured beyond $\frac{3}{4}$ and Second Class ships beyond $\frac{2}{3}$ of their value. No person whose competency was not approved by the Directors could be the master of any vessel insured by the Society. 'Passing the Club' was a qualification of some value. In the early years of the Society the task was probably delegated to a master mariner who was also a director, but at some time in the seventies Examining Masters were appointed for the ports already mentioned with the significant addition of Liverpool. (In 1878 Capt. R. T. Power was appointed for Liverpool).

In the column entitled 'Log Book' in the *Weekly Post* in November 1934 Captain David Roberts, then retired, had this to say about 'passing the

Club'.[4] 'The only qualification then aimed at with the great majority of us was to pass the Club, as it was termed, and qualify to be skipper. That meant undergoing an examination, the examiners being the directors of the Club (Insurance Society) composed of practical old skippers and some of them used to be pretty keen and severe. Of course they used to question you in their own way.

The best of it was that one always realized that he was examined by men who had gone through hard, practical, rough experience. But should you get through successfully one or other of them would give you good sound advice and information that would stick to you for the rest of your life, such as the following "Should you be embayed in so and so bay, always remember so and so" . . . They taught you something — besides passing your examination you as a rule collected more knowledge than ever you had, and all this from practical old warriors'.

Insurances in 1853 were confined to the coasting trade and to continental voyages between Ostend and Cape La Hogue but in the years that followed the limits of voyages were extended; but there were still restrictions — "ships shall not be, or continue to be insured when sailing to or from or while at any port or place on the coast of Labrador to the North of Cape Charles nor when sailing to or from or while at Hudson's Bay, Davis's Strait, Greenland, Iceland, Spitzbergen or north east of the entrance to the White Sea." Other constraints there were, with close definitions and restrictions on the dates between which voyages could be made. There are pages and pages of these in the Rule Book of 1869 but one example should suffice. Penalties are expressed in deductions from any claim varying from 5% up to 25% or in some instances ships forfeited all insurance cover.

> "Ships sailing for the lower ports of the Baltic not higher than Memel (inclusive) and for any port or place in the Belt Sound or Cattegat except Gothenburg after the 5th of November and before the 20th of November shall be subject to the deduction of 10% and later than the 20th November of 20% . . ." etc. etc.

The list includes 'the British Colonies in North America', the U.S.A., the Baltic (as we have seen) and the White Sea, (dangers of icing) the Black Sea, the 'West Indian Islands or Spanish Main', the Bay of Honduras and the Gulf of Mexico (during the hurricane season) and there is also a penalty of 25% for "vessels sailing out over the Bar of the Rio Grande without the assistance of a steamer." This is not to say that vessels insured with the B.M.S.I.S. had faced each and every risk contained in the rules. These are clearly model articles and this is borne out by the fact that when an Amlwch 'club' was established it followed the Bangor rules almost word for word.

---

[4] Reproduced from the appendix to the Captain's manuscript autobiography. U.C.N.W. 15085.

THE COMPANIES ACTS, 1862 to 1880.

𝔐emorandum and Articles of Association

OF THE

BANGOR AND NORTH WALES
MUTUAL MARINE PROTECTION ASSOCIATION

LIMITED.

ESTABLISHED 1870.

Incorporated the 24th day of December, 1881.

REGISTERED OFFICE:

PLAS LLWYD, BANGOR,

IN THE COUNTY OF CARNARVON.

LONDON:

RICHARD JORDAN, Public Companies' Registration Agent, Printer, and Stationer,

120, Chancery Lane, W.C.

1881.

The cover of the Articles of Association of the *Bangor and North Wales Mutual Marine Protection Association.* (G.A.S. XCV 303.)

THE BANGOR MUTUAL SHIP INSURANCE SOCIETY.

LIMITED.

PLAS LLWYD,
BANGOR, N. WALES.

Whereas *Capt Griffith Thomas*
25 Chapel St Carnarvon
has become a Member of the Bangor Mutual Ship
Insurance Society, Limited, and in respect of the
ship hereinafter named entitled to this policy,

No. 181

£ *300 - 0 - 0*

Now this Policy of Insurance Witnesseth, that in consideration of the
premises, and of the observance by the assured of the provisions of the Articles
of Association of the said Society, the said Society hereby agrees with the
insured, to pay and to make good according to the said provisions, all such
losses and damages, as according to the same it shall be liable for in respect of
the sum of £ *300* hereby insured, which insurance is hereby declared to
be upon the Ship called the *"Napoleon"* valued at £ *450*
whereof is at present master, or whoever
else shall go for master of the said Ship, lost or not lost. And the said
Association promises and agrees, that the insurance aforesaid shall commence
upon the said Ship at and from noon of the *1st* day of *Jany* 1889
until noon of the 1st day of January 1890

In witness whereof, the Common Seal of the said Society hath been hereunto affixed, and is
authenticated by the signature of the Secretary and two Directors of the said Society, this *Second*
day of *Feby* 1889

Humphrey Davies
Robert Thomas Parry Directors.

Robt. Hughes Secretary

Insurance certificate of the schooner *Napoleon* for 1889. (G.A.S. XM/546/99.)

The Fancy Dress Competition held to celebrate the opening of Bangor Pier in May 1896 may interest the social historian; in the background, besides numerous small craft, five schooners at anchor in Hirael Bay and several on the beach show that the port was still fairly busy at this date. The hulk at the centre of the picture was used by Thomas Lewis as a warehouse.

(By kind permission of *Mr. W. Richard Thomas*)

PLAS LLWYD TODAY

Samuel Roberts lived here, and it also housed the offices of the Bangor Mutual
Ship Insurance Society and its subsidiaries.

S.S. BANGOR AT BRISTOL

(By kind permission of Mr. Eifion Buckland)

There were strict prohibitions against smuggling and illicit trade. In time of war vessels were allowed to carry arms and ammunition. In 1853 the possibility was remote but in 1854 the Crimean War broke out.

Masters of shipwrecked vessels were to be directed by the Society on any course of action, and if a vessel was run down, the Society, on indemnifying the owner, reserved the right to sue in his name for damages. The Annual Reports of the B.M.S.I.S., such as they are, are a valuable barometer of the state of the shipping industry in Bangor, indicating a period of fair weather in the fifties and sixties, changeable in the seventies and then the onset of a prolonged depression in the eighties.

The Annual report for the year 1854 shows that there were 170 vessels with an insurable value of £84,404 11s. in full or part membership of the Society, an increase of 52 vessels since the previous year. The great majority of the vessels were small coasters and of the 170 there were only 21 registered as over 100 tons and they included one of 255 tons, *Bell,* (John Hopson, Master) and the 237 ton *Caradoc,* (Samuel H. Griffith, Master). The accounts show that entrance money at 50s per cent amounted to £902 0s. 9d., considerably more than the annual subscription of 20s per cent of insurable value which amounted to £419 16s. 4d. This is a clear indication of a society expanding rapidly in its early years. Although during the year there had been four total losses it had not been necessary for the Directors to issue any calls but a call for subsequent losses would be made early in 1855. Claims for losses had been met by transferring £1,800 from the General Fund to the Insurance Fund.

The next report is for the year 1859, issued in March 1860; no fewer than 295 vessels with an insurable value of £196,829 15s. 6d. were on the books of the Society on 22 March 1860 but there had been 16 total losses in the previous year which had "proved an unprecedented one for disasters among shipping". There is an echo of the loss of the *Royal Charter* in a later reference to the "memorable terrific gale of 25th October last" which did not leave Bangor shipping unscathed. The accounts of the Insurance Fund show that there had been calls in May for 40s per cent and in November for 20s per cent and that there would be a further call in the spring to cover the previous autumn's losses. Claims for nearly £9,000 for 1859 had already been met by these calls and the transfer of £3,500 from the General Fund. Quite clearly the Society had weathered a financial storm of some magnitude.

Unfortunately there is a gap of thirteen years before the next report, that for the year 1872, but we catch a revealing glimpse of the kind of life that the Secretary of the B.M.S.I.S., Samuel Roberts led from a letter written to his wife from the island of Skye in September 1863, which is reproduced in 'The Life'. There is a great deal about Samuel's religious observances — the letter starts off with the remark that there is no chapel or service of any kind within 8 miles of the place and that it is a strange place to spend the

161

Sabbath. He was asked by the Collector of the Custom House to preach in English, which he appears to have done with some success (despite the fact that the language of Heaven is undoubtedly Welsh!). In the evening he conducted a Sunday School for the Welsh sailors. It is only at the end of the letter that a little light is shed on why he is on the island at all. He says that he was up by 6 a.m. on Monday to take the men to the ship and put the gear on the rocks, and he hopes to get her off today. Everything has been prepared ready, with the exception of the tides which are unfavourable — but they are out of his control! The ship is not named and we do not know if the attempt to refloat her was successful. But this little extract shows that the secretary was no mere back-room boy but was prepared to roll his sleeves up when there was a job to be done.

In 1872 the Society's offices were still at Plas Llwyd (the house, which stands on the corner of High Street and William Street, still bears that name) and Samuel Roberts was still the Secretary. His remuneration had risen to £150 per annum — it had been £40 in 1854 and £80 in 1860 — which is an indication of the esteem in which he was held by the Directors. He also drew annually a further £30 as manager and secretary of the associated *Bangor & North Wales Mutual Marine Protection Association* which with its office also at Plas Llwyd had been established in 1870. This association, whose membership was much the same as its parent body, the B.M.S.I.S., offered shipowners protection against claims from third parties for damage caused rather than sustained by their own vessels. The Report of the association, which was printed and bound together with the Report of the B.M.S.I.S. states that in the previous year there had been no claims and consequently no calls.

What immediately strikes one on reading the B.M.S.I.S. report for 1872 is the vast difference in the list of ships insured between the reports of 1859 and 1872. There were now 309 vessels on the Society's books — a modest increase of fourteen ships since 1859 — but it is the size of some of the ships that matters. Twenty-one ships were over 500 tons and ten of these were over 1,000 tons. Very few of these were registered at the Port of Beaumaris and reference to Lloyd's List for 1872 gives Liverpool as the home port of the majority of them. Of the twenty-one no fewer than sixteen had been recently built in North America, seven of them within the last five years and the oldest was only nine years old. W. B. Buckingham owned four of these, including the largest, *Northern Empire* of 1327 tons; all four had been built at Quebec between 1863 and 1870, so that it is possible to date the entry of North Wales owners to this market with some precision. William Thomas, Liverpool had two large vessels insured with the Society, *North Star* (718 tons) and *Sappho* (707 tons), and William Thomas, Amlwch one, the famous *William Mellhuish* (707 tons).

The total value of the *Northern Empire* was given as £8,500 and of *William Mellhuish* as £5,000, but the Society had placed an upper limit of

£1,500 on any one vessel insured with it. The remainder would have been laid out with other societies, such as the *Pwllheli and Nevin Mutual Ship Insurance Society* or one of the other four which at this date had been established at Nefyn. (A total of eleven societies was established at Nefyn between 1859 and 1880; most of them were dissolved about 1890.)

The Report states that the calls made by the B.M.S.I.S. in the previous year for the losses sustained by its members amounted to *"Four Pounds* per cent — the latter part of the year proved one of the most disastrous on record to Shipping and this Society has had its share of the losses." Members were informed that there would be a further call of £3 per cent to meet the losses sustained in November and December but they were reassured that the year 1872 had been exceptional in the history of the Society. "The average premiums of this Society from its formation in 1853 (including the £2 10s. Entrance for the first year and the Annual Subscription) up to December last are £3 16s. 6d. per annum."

The Secretary of the Society, Samuel Roberts, died in December 1875. An account of his funeral in the *North Wales Chronicle* (25.12.1875) makes it clear that he was held in the highest esteem by his fellow citizens. The hearse was preceded by ministers of various denominations, walking two abreast and numbering about a hundred, by deacons walking four abreast and by members of the B.M.S.I.S., and "all the ships in the port were flying colours at half mast." There is no doubt that his sincerity in the pulpit and his strong religious convictions contributed in no small way to the reputation for integrity that he gained in his commercial activities.

His biographer makes this judgement on his work with the Bangor Mutual Ship Insurance Society.[5]

> "His word was law among the directors particularly when tricky issues arose involving the law of the sea . . . He was considered by many to be an oracle on maritime law. He was often approached in the fullest confidence for his opinion and advice when a dispute arose between one shipowner and another about some mishap at sea, and he frequently brought the dispute to an end through his wisdom and mature judgement. Parties often went to him for his arbitration rather than resort to litigation. No-one knows how much good he did for small owners by restraining them from squandering their resources in courts of law."

(Translation)

("Yr oedd ei air yn ddeddf ym mhlith y cyfarwyddwyr, yn enwedig pan y deuai amgylchiadau dyrus ger bron ynglŷn â chyfraith y môr . . . Ystyrid ef gan lawer yn oracl ar gyfraith morwriaith. Llawer tro yr aed ato, gyda'r ymddiried llwyraf, am farn a chyngor, pan gyfodai cweryl rhwng meddianwyr llongau a'u gilydd oblegid ryw anhap ar y môr. Nid anfynych y rhoddai derfyn ar yr ymryson trwy ei ddoethineb a'i farn aeddfed. Gwelwyd pleidiau yn myned ato gan ymfodloni i'w farn ef yn hytrach na myned i ymgyfreithio. Ac nis gŵyr neb pa faint o ddaioni a wnaeth i berchenogion bychain, er eu rhwystro i wario eu meddiannau mewn llysoedd gwladol.")

[5] 'Life' p. 52.

This some what fulsome tribute could be dismissed as mere hagiography had not a small bundle of correspondence between him and another ship-owner survived. The letters exhibit a capacity for lucid exposition of maritime law, a strong desire to achieve settlement by compromise rather than by litigation and his undoubted skill as a negotiator. They also, by a strange coincidence, provide another instance of the Calvinistic Methodist connection since the letters are to be found among the Glanrhyd Papers, now held at the Caernarfon Area Office of the Gwynedd Archives Service.[6]

The Revd. Griffith Hughes, son of Captain John Hughes of the *Palmyra,* was a Methodist minister who was associated with Glanrhyd Chapel and lived at Edern. Like the Revd. Rees Jones and the Revd. Samuel Roberts, he, too, had another occupation. He was a partner in the firm of G. & W. Hughes, Timber Merchants. He also had a 4/64ths share in the 39 ton sloop, *Gomer,* (Pwllheli Reg. 1841/25 and Caernarfon 1855/11 and 1858/22) which had been built at Nefyn in 1841. Jointly with William Hughes, his partner in the timber business, he had a 2/64th share in the 88 ton schooner, *Maria Catherine,* also built at Nefyn in 1841. (Pwllheli 1842/7). Another share-holder in the vessel was John Parry, Shipbuilder, Bangor with 4/64ths.

In 1851 Evan Ellis built for him at Porthdinllaen the 88 ton schooner *Luther* in which he held a 44/64ths share. (Pwllheli 1851/1). Her master — and he was to continue to be her master until 1870 — was John Williams, of Edern who held 16/64ths. The Register entry is endorsed "This vessel was totally lost by collision with a steam boat in Liverpool River on the 4th of February, 1870. Certificate of registry lost with the Vessel." Fortunately no lives were lost.

The first indication in the Glanrhyd papers of the sinking is a telegram from William Thomas, Liverpool addressed to "Hughes, Luther, Plas Llwyd, Bangor" — the wreck of the *Luther* must be blown up as it is a hindrance to navigation. This is followed by a letter from William Thomas advising that Captain John Williams (of the *Luther*) should go with some suitable person from the 'Club' to investigate the circumstances of the sinking.

It is plain from the letters that Samuel Roberts himself visited Liverpool several times and with William Thomas tried to get witnesses of the collision. In the account of the final settlement £11 18s. is deducted for expenses. "Paid Mess. Pritchard and Son, Proctors for opinion on case and correspondence, Mr. W. Thomas for services, and his men employed with the Secretary looking out for evidence and Secretary's expenses five days at three different journeys to and at Liverpool and Cheshire side of the Mersey." Samuel Roberts had acted conscientiously and energetically since receiving notifica-tion of the sinking, and nothing illustrates this better than a letter to Griffith Hughes a bare ten days after the event.

[6] C.R.O. XM/4889/81 ff.

Samuel Roberts says that he has received a favourable reply from the Proctors in London. They confirm his own opinion that according to Captain Williams's testimony the blame lies squarely on the steamer *Bonny*. They do not know what line of defence the steamer will take —

> "but it is possible that they will try to prove that the *Luther* was on the larboard tack and that she went about on to the other tack so to cause the collision. But if we can prove that *Luther* was on the starboard tack for some minutes before the collision the blame will lie entirely on the steamer as a sailing vessel should not give way under such circumstances."

(Translation)

("Nid ydynt yn gwybod dim pa linell o amddiffyniant y dichon y steamer gymeryd ond dyfalant yr ymdrechant brofi fod y Luther *ar y* larboard tack *a darfod iddi fyned o gwmpas ar y* tack *arall fel ac i achosi y* collision, *ond os gellir profi fod y* Luther *ar y* Starboard tack *am rai munudau cyn a tarawiad, y bydd y bai yn hollol ar y* steamer *gan nad yw llong hwyliau i roi i ffwrdd am y fath amgylchiad."*)

The proctors advised them to obtain independent evidence from eye witnesses to the collision and to try to discover what the pilot of *Bonny* would say. If the owners of the steamer could put the blame on him they could clear themselves. But if it could be shown that some of *Bonny's* crew were at fault, either in not keeping a good look-out or in failing to carry out the pilot's instructions, that would make the steamer responsible. In the busy activity of getting under way it is quite possible that the crew were pre-occupied with other tasks instead of keeping a proper look-out.

In a second letter to Griffith Hughes four days later Samuel Roberts says that he has heard from the solicitors for *Bonny's* agents; they have advised the owners to oppose any claim on the grounds that *Luther* was solely to blame, but that the owners, to avoid litigation, were prepared to pay half the value of the ship, but they thought that a valuation of £600 was excessive. Arbitration by a disinterested and qualified person was suggested. This letter was to be regarded as being without prejudice, but in spite of this declaration it is clear that the owners did not feel that they were on very safe ground. Samuel Roberts tells Griffith Hughes that he has not replied to the solicitors' letter and seeks his reaction but adds, (and this bears out what was said in *The Life* about his reluctance to resort to litigation) "it has truly been said that there is glorious uncertainty in the law" *("ansicrwydd gogoneddus mewn cyfraith")* and if it is possible to come to some agreement about some proportion of the loss, this would be the best course.

There was a further complication in arriving at a settlement because the harbour authorities at Liverpool were claiming £70 from the owners towards the expense of blowing up the wreck. Among the papers is a copy of a letter from Griffith Hughes to his agent in Liverpool, Graham H. Hills, authorising him to sell the materials saved from the wreck of *Luther* and apply the proceeds towards the claim for blasting the wreck.

On March 8th Samuel Roberts wrote again; the Directors (of the B.M.S.I.S.) had discussed the case. The agents of the *Bonny* had offered half the value of the *Luther* at a lower valuation than the Directors had asked. They were anxious to know whether Griffith Hughes would be satisfied with a lower proportion than was claimed for the freight and for the captain's clothes and effects if they could reach agreement *without going to law.* Of course the Society would do its best to get as much as it could. If he and Captain Williams were unwilling, then the Directors would try to come to an agreement for the ship alone and it would be up to them (Griffith Hughes and the Captain) to do the best they could. There is more than a hint here of gentle pressure being applied to effect a compromise.

A copy of Griffith Hughes's reply has been written on the back of this letter. He says that he is willing to accept what they can get for the freight, the victuals and the captain's effects —

> "for I can do nothing apart from you. I believe you will do your best for the extra as well as for the old ship, and I hope that you can obtain half of what she was valued by the Club and not by her murderers."   (Translation)

> (*"Canys nis gallwn wneuthur dim ar wahan oddiwrthych chwi. Credaf y gwnewch eich gore am yr extra, fel am yr hen long, a gobeithiaf y bydd i chi gael hanner yr hyn a priswyd gan y Clwb ac nid gan ei llofryddion."*)

One wishes that the other side of the correspondence, between Samuel Roberts and the agents of the *Bonny,* had survived or that one could have been a fly on the wall during the verbal negotiations, but the correspondence with Griffith Hughes suggests that Samuel Roberts was a skilled negotiator. His next letter reveals that the owners of the steamer had raised their offer to 15s in the £ on condition that they have a valuation of the other claims. He suggests that Captain Williams produces an affidavit for the amount of his losses, money, clothes, provisions etc., and also a bill of lading for the freight. One senses already a successful outcome.

The total amount of the claim eventually made by the B.M.S.I.S. in the *Luther v. Bonny* affair was £560 4s. which was made us as follows:—

	£	s.	d.
Vessel value agreed for compromise	420	0	0
Freight	34	4	0
Ship's Victuals	8	10	0
Expenses blowing up nett	70	0	0
Captain's effects &c.	27	10	0

Luther was valued on the Society's books at £600, to cover £400, in other words, she was a vessel of the second class and insured to two thirds of her value. Samuel Roberts expressed some satisfaction in his letter:—

166

"I think that, taking everything into consideration, we have come out of it fairly well, if not very well."   (Translation)

("Yr wyf yn meddwl, a chymeryd pob peth i ystyriaeth, ein bod wedi dyfod allan yn weddol dda, os nad da iawn.")

In the next letter he says that the 'Club' has not yet put in a claim for the crew and the boy but it is unlikely that there will be any difficulty now that the first matter is settled. He asks for the owners' authority for him "to receive and pay all claims in respect of the Schooner *Luther* as far as it relates to the collision in the River Mersey with the *Bonny*" and he provides this form of words (in English) for Griffith Hughes to sign. All the correspondence between the two preacher shipowners apart from this one item was in Welsh.

The owners of *Bonny* had paid 75% of the £560 4s. claimed value and this amounted to £420 3s. of which £306 1s. 10d. was the apportionment for the vessel. Two thirds of this would be paid in the first instance to the B.M.S.I.S. and one third to the owners. After deducting the Society's costs, (£11 18s) and a proportion for blowing up the wreck, and adding the adjustments for the loss of victuals and captain's effects, he encloses £204 3s. 9d. and adds that the balance of the £400, the sum for which *Luther* was insured, would follow in due course.

The way this money was sent offers a curious sidelight on the banking facilities or lack of them in the remoter areas of Lleyn, and on the lack of confidence in the safety of money sent through the post. Samuel Roberts sent with the letter the halves of two Bank of England £100 bills and a postal order for £4 3s. 9d. and says that he will send the other two halves of the bills when he has been notified of the safe arrival of the first two pieces.

Luther was sunk on the 4th of February; by mid-April the insurance claim had been settled by the B.M.S.I.S., or rather by its energetic Secretary without resort to litigation and without the dubious benefit of telephone, telex or word processor. The mode by which the settlement was reached bears out to the smallest detail the tribute paid in *The Life* to Samuel Roberts's knowledge of maritime law, his judgement and skill as an arbitrator and negotiator and his reluctance to go to law. There is no doubt that he played a considerable part in the development of Bangor as a maritime mercantile centre, both as a proprietor and as a leader in the insurance industry.

An account in the *North Wales Chronicle* on April 3rd 1875 of the Annual General Meeting of the B.M.S.I.S. stated that after the previous year's meeting a "Special General Meeting had been held, at which the opinion was expressed by the majority that a separate society for vessels of 150 tons and upwards would be more advantageous than keeping large and small together, and in pursuance of such opinon, the new society was formed on January 1st taking 34 vessels from the old society thereby considerably reducing the insurable value on the books." Thus the *Bangor and Provincial Ship Insurance Company Ltd.* came into being but no annual reports of this society have so far come to light, nor is it known what part Samuel Roberts played in its formation. He became seriously ill in July 1875 and died in December of that year.

The same newspaper account records "that a long and animated discussion" arose on the right of directors and other officials to act in a similar capacity for both societies. The directors proposed that a rule forbidding them to have an interest in another society should be repealed, but this was defeated.

A table, compiled by the late David Thomas from the annual reports and from press reports,[7] showing the number of ships on the books of the B.M.S.I.S. and their insured value for some of the years between 1853 and 1879 makes clear the decline in both the number of ships and their insurable value; in 1874 there were 310 ships on the books with an insurable value of £166,183 compared with the 1876 figures of 244 and £114, 685. There are no figures for the *Bangor and Provincial Mutual Ship Insurance Society* until 1877 and 1878 when they are, respectively, 104 ships at £123,450 and 128 ships at £142,090. The figures for both present a clear reflection of the difference in size of the ships insured by either society.

The Annual Report of the B.M.S.I.S. for 1878 shows that Rees Jones of Port Dinorwic was still a trustee of the society together with C. B. Dyer, an Amlwch shipowner and T. T. Parry of Bangor. The Chairman of the Directors was Thomas Jones, a shipowner from Menai Bridge with Meshach Roberts as Vice-chairman, the other directors being drawn from Bangor, Amlwch and Caernarfon. The Nefyn interest had at last disappeared following the establishment there of several societies. Robert Owen of James Street, Bangor was the Secretary and Robert Roberts, the Bangor post-master, was one of the auditors.

If one were to enquire the reasons behind the sudden and almost simultaneous decline of ship building in the ports of North Wales — Bangor built its last sailing ship in 1879, Caernarfon in 1884, Nefyn in 1880, Porthdinllaen in 1876, Pwllheli in 1878 and Porthmadog in 1878 (though there was to be a revival in 1891) — one need look no further than the B.M.S.I.S. report for 1878, which begins eloquently : —

> "The unparalleled depression which has overtaken the commerce of this country has not weighed with greater severity upon any branch of industry than upon the shipping trade. In North Wales this has been further intensified by the extraordinary stagnation in the demand for slates, this necessitating the production to be reduced, and a consequent decrease in the tonnage

---

[7] U.C.N.W. 19078.

168

available for shipment, which besides necessarily throwing many vessels altogether out of employment, has likewise depressed freights to a most unremunerative figure so that at this period ship-owning is a business which, in the vast majority of cases, not only yields the capitalist no return upon his investment, but to the contrary frequently results in actual loss."

The writer of that purple passage was not to know that the same 'unparalleled depression' would affect Britain continuously for over a hundred years, being lifted temporarily by short-lived 'recoveries', most of them stimulated by wars. That passage sets the tone for future reports.

A small symptom of this depression, and an incidental confirmation of the B.M.S.I.S. report, is to be found in report in the *Caernarvon and Denbigh Herald* of April 13, 1878 which reads —

"BANGOR, SEAMEN'S WAGES. Shipowners have intimated that they intend reducing seamen's wages from £3 10s. to £3 a month. This step has been necessitated by the state of trade, and the reduction of freights at Port Penrhyn."

Nothing came of it and the same paper reported a month later (18 May) that

"The scheme for the reduction of seamen's wages seems to have fallen through."

However, a letter in the June 15 issue from Captain Humphrey Williams, the shipowner, who gave his address as Penlôn Slate Works, states that "he shipped three men at Liverpool to proceed with the *Foyle Packet* from Bangor at £3 per month" and that these men had gone to sea on those terms. He dismissed allegations that a threatening crowd of 250 sailors had assembled intent on making the men return "bag and baggage" to Liverpool and said that there were not, throughout that day, more than a dozen people in the vicinity of the vessel. But this seems to have been an isolated incident.

The trade recession caused much discontent among workmen in Gwynedd since it affected the only industry of any size, the slate industry, and this in turn had widespread effects on other trades. Another extract from the same paper for 18 January, 1879 has this to say —

"BANGOR. STRIKES. — On Monday, the mechanics in the foundries and smiths' shops at Bangor and the surrounding district turned out against a reduction in wages of 1s. per week, and later in the day the men employed in the building trade struck against an order for extended hours of work. The ship-builders are also on strike, and the quarrymen, owing to the bad state of trade, work but for four days weekly."[8]

The Report of the B.M.S.I.S. for 1879 begins —

"In face of the continued badness of trade it is a source of great satisfaction . . . that it was found necessary in the course of the year to make only two calls of 25s and 30s per cent."

[8] I am again indebted to Dr. Lewis Lloyd for drawing my attention to these extracts from the *Caernarvon and Denbigh Herald*.

169

It was also doubtless, a source of satisfaction for the Directors that compared with 1876, the year following the split into two societies, the number of ships on the books had increased by ten to 254 and their capital value by £10,000 to £125,267.

In 1881, as is apparent from a Rule Book of the Society marked "To be kept on board the *Napoleon* for the use of the Master and by whom it should be carefully studied,"[9] the Society having been registered in 1862 as a company with unlimited liability now became "a company limited by guarantee but not having a capital divided into shares . . . for the objects and purposes mentioned in the Articles of Association." The liability of members in the event of winding up was limited to "Two Pounds per cent upon the amount such Member has insured." The Society no longer relied upon its own surveyors to determine the class of a vessel. "Vessels A1 at Lloyds will be placed in the First Class" and could be insured up to $\frac{3}{4}$ of their value; other vessels remained in the second class and could be insured up to 2/3 of their value. No ship or part of a ship which was over 150 tons register was to be insured by the Society and £1,500 was set as the limit for which any one ship could be insured. A member — "not being an infant, lunatic or married woman" — still had additional votes for every £100 over £500 of insurance held, with an upper limit of 20 votes. A member who was a spinster or widow thus forfeited her membership on marriage and her new husband had a mere month to take up what had been his wife's insurance; such was the plight of the married woman under the property acts of the last century.

Napoleon, a well known Caernarfon schooner, owned in 1889 by Capt. Griffith Thomas, 25 Chapel Street, Caernarfon was valued at £450 and insured for £300 according to the policy at the Caernarfon Record Office[10] (see illus. facing page 161). The Directors in 1889 included Robert Thomas Parry, Capt. John Ellis and Captain Humphrey Davies of Bangor whom we have encountered previously, and W. E. Jones of Port Dinorwic, the son of Rees Jones and the designer of such fine vessels as *Moel Tryfan* (1,691 tons). The secretary in 1889 was Robert Hughes and one of the auditors was the Bangor postmaster, Robert Roberts.

There had been a steady decline in the eighties. In 1879 the number of vessels insured with the B.M.S.I.S. was 254 with an insured value of £125,267. By 1885, the next year for which we have an Annual Report, the number of ships insured had fallen by almost half to 132, and the amount covered fell drastically to £55,692. The annual report no longer contains a list of the vessels insured, their ship's husbands, their value and the amount for which they were insured, and it merely contains a statement of the accounts, a list of the directors and other officials and a brief report about the business

[9] C.R.O. XM/546/72.
[10] C.R.O. XM/546/99

of the year. The report for 1885 states that the directors had declined to accept a number of risks offered to them.

The tone of this report and the one for the following year is rather dispiriting — "Now that shipping has become so unremunerative a property . . ." (1885) and ". . . the Board of Directors regret that it cannot congratulate them (the members) upon any increase in the Society's capital. Owing to the depressed state of Shipping several members deemed it advisable during the past year to make considerable reductions in their insurances, and, with due regard to the interests of the Society, the Board revised the amount insured upon several vessels insured and made very large reductions, thereby lessening the Society's risk." (1886) Nevertheless the Directors were at pains to point out in 1885 that the calls for the past year had amounted only to £4 per cent of the amount for which each member was held insured, and this compared very favourably with "the Calls made by other similar institutions in the Kingdom," and they pointed out that the average percentage of the Society's premiums, including all fees and subscriptions since its foundation in 1853, had been only £4.10s per annum.

It would be rash to diagnose a serious malaise in the Society's affairs on the basis of one set of annual accounts only, but the accounts for 1885 reveal that in a total turnover of £3,252 the uncollected calls (i.e. arrears) for the previous financial year amounted to nearly £170, which is surely a significant symptom. Some members were clearly not living up to their obligations but the directors did not feel strong enough to discipline them, nor in the precarious trade conditions could they afford to expel them. The Society's bank overdraft at the end of the year was £141 19s. 5d.

Little has so far come to light about the final years of the B.M.S.I.S. A brief report in the *North Wales Chronicle* of May 15, 1897 stated that "on Wednesday last in the Chancery Division before Mr. Justice Vaughan Williams, the petition for the winding up of the Bangor Mutual Ship Insurance Society Ltd. under a supervision order came in for hearing. Counsel stated that the necessary meeting of shareholders had been held and that Mr. W. J. Parry had been appointed liquidator. There was no opposition and his lordship granted a supervision order."

However, a bundle of legal papers[11] has survived which shows that in a case involving the parallel Bangor and North Wales Mutual Marine Protection Association (which was located at the same office and had the same secretary as the B.M.S.I.S.) the Association had been sued in 1896 in the Queen's Bench by Mr. John Thomas Jones for £165 16s. 3d. due to him for services rendered as a ship surveyor and for his travelling and incidental expenses. A petition for winding up was granted by Mr. Justice Vaughan Williams in April 1897 and Mr. W. J. Parry was also appointed liquidator.

[11] C.R.O. XCV 303.

It is a fair assumption that the state of affairs that W. J. Parry found applied to the B.M.S.I.S. as well.

A submission by him for the opinion of counsel revealed that the last *signed* minutes of the Directors Meeting had been for 1892 and it was doubtful if any Directors Meetings had been held since that year. Several calls to cover losses had been made since then and it was impossible to say which of them were fictitious. The Association's books were 'in a deplorable state' and several owners claimed that they had given notice to withdraw their vessels but they were still nominally on the secretary's books. One such vessel, it was claimed by an owner (Owen Roberts) had been sold to an Irish owner and another owner (John Coppack of Connah's Quay) claimed that his vessel, the *Not Forget,* had been condemned by the Board of Trade in 1892. The liquidator was having the utmost difficulty in proving who was and who was not a member of the Association.

Later in that same year (1897) the secretary of the B.M.S.I.S. absconded and was eventually arrested in Antwerp and charged with forgery in connection with the Bangor and Arvon Permanent Benefit Building Society of which he was also the secretary.

The subsequent trial took place at Caernarvon Assizes[12] in October at which he pleaded guilty to charges of forgery and embezzlement. It was claimed on his behalf that of the two marine insurance societies of which he was the secretary one owed him £200 and the other £1200, and he stated himself that he had paid some of the calls of the societies out of his own pocket. He was sentenced to five years penal servitude.

It was on this tragic note that the Bangor Mutual Ship Insurance Society ended its forty-four years of mostly efficient service to the maritime enterprise of Bangor and the surrounding district.

---

[12] See the *North Wales Chronicle* of 4th September, 2nd October and 30th October 1897 for details of his arrest and trial.

CHAPTER X

The Decline of Sail

It was earlier stated, possibly rashly, that ship ownership in Bangor in the course of the nineteenth century tended to move from the gentry to the people. In support of this assertion, the withdrawal in 1868 of the Wyatts from ship ownership was the most prominent feature though the Penrhyn interest was probably safeguarded by the nominees who bought their ships. As we have seen there was a sudden decline in wooden shipbuilding throughout Gwynedd in the late seventies and early eighties (it was true also of most parts of Britain) and this is directly reflected in the small number of new registrations in the Beaumaris shipping registers. Most of the vessels registered were re-registrations of old vessels, and Owen Roberts who leased what had been the yard of T. T. Parry and Co. from the liquidator, W. J. Parry after T. T. Parry's bankruptcy, was involved in several of these transactions.

In 1877 he bought the old Nefyn built schooner, *Gleaner,* (Beaumaris 1877/1) for breaking, and in 1881, when he was still established in Hirael, he bought the 65 ton schooner *Burncoose,* (Beaumaris 1881/3) built at Swansea in 1840. It is a matter of speculation but the likelihood is that he repaired her with a view to re-sale. He raised a mortgage of £60 at 6% in October 1881 which was discharged in February 1882 and in the same month the vessel was sold to Aeneas Mackay Mackenzie of Stornoway. In 1889 he bought the 52 ton schooner *Glynaeron,* which had been built at Aberaeron in 1852 and sold her to a master mariner from Aberystwyth in 1895. Similarly in 1890 he bought the 61 ton schooner *Lewis,* (Beaumaris 1890/4) built at Three Pines, Prince Edward Island in 1848 and sold her later in the same year to a Robert Owen of Llanallgo whose occupation was given as Car Proprietor. In 1892 he was registered as the owner of the 45 ton ketch, *Margaret,* built at Conwy in 1862. She was the vessel previously mentioned as being on the books of the B.M.S.I.S. in 1897 though she was sold in 1894 to Simon Roche, a coal merchant of Ballygow, Co. Wexford. She was not de-registered until 1922 when the register is endorsed "Certificate cannot be found. Owner died 10 years ago. Vessel is out of repair and not worth repairing and registration is no longer required." These are only the instances recorded in the Beaumaris register and there may well be others at present unknown. The fact that the patent slip was renewed in 1893 suggests that this may well be the case.

On the other hand there were several registrations of new and old steamships. We have already encountered Thomas Lewis, the Flour Merchant and radical, in connection with the saga of the two mayors. He had served his apprenticeship as a druggist with Meshach Roberts and like him, was a shipowner, but unlike him, he put his faith in steam power.

The first of Thomas Lewis's vessels was the little schooner rigged steam coaster *Medway* (Beaumaris 1880/3) of 54 tons, built at Hackneywick, Middlesex in 1866 which traded between the Mersey and Bangor with grain and other foodstuffs. Thomas Lewis owned a jetty and warehouse at Garth *(Cei Thomas Lewis)* on the west side af T. T. Parry's shipyard and the lane leading to it from Beach Road was known then and to this day as Medway Road. The photograph of Hirael Bay and Port Penrhyn (bet. pp. 176-177) gives a glimpse of *Medway's* stern and Thomas Lewis's jetty. (The other boat in the photograph, which is the true subject of a picture which bears all the hallmarks but not the signature of the artist-photographer John Wickens of Bangor, is the sand-boat *Flatfish.* There were several of these boats at Hirael; they supplied the builder's merchants of Bangor and district with sand from the Lavan Sands right up to the second world war.) *Medway* was involved in a collision with the steamer *Alexander* in the Mersey in November 1896 and declared a constructive total loss. However she was salvaged after the wreck and received the Board of Trade's Certificate of Seaworthiness and re-registered in Thomas Lewis's name two years later. (Beaumaris 1898/1). She was now flat rigged and the photograph appears to date from this period. Thomas Lewis sold the vessel in 1907 to a shipowner in Belfast and she survived until 1920 when she was broken up.

The ketch rigged steamer *St. Seiriol* of 67 tons built by C. P. Swan and Hunter of Wallsend on Tyne in 1886 (Beaumaris 1886/3) was registered in the name of Thomas Lewis, Gartherwen, Bangor, Shipowner. She had compound engines each of 30h.p. and remained in Thomas Lewis's service until her sale in 1905 to Messrs. Reavely Ltd. of Cardiff.

174

Thomas Lewis went to the same builder for his next vessel, the schooner rigged steamer *St. Tudwal* of 107 tons. (Beaumaris 1895/4). Her two 35 h.p. compound engines were capable of driving her along at 9 knots. She was sold in 1909 to the Bristol and Cardigan Trading Co. of Cardigan, thus ending Thomas Lewis's career as a shipowner.

Another steamer of this period was the *Prince Ja-Ja,* built by William Thomas, Amlwch, which traded extensively between Liverpool and the Menai Straits ports. Although she was never in Bangor ownership she gave her name, unofficially, to a wooden jetty, now demolished, on the west side of Bangor pier which was known as the Ja-Ja pier.

The small steamer *Menai,* built at Bangor in 1878 for the Bangor — Beaumaris passenger service has already been mentioned (page 107). She was owned by a consortium of local business men and run by Thomas Morgan and after his death by his son, William, as the lessees of the Porth-esgob/Garth Ferry. In 1895, in anticipation of the opening of the municipally owned Bangor pier in the following year, the Borough of Bangor acquired the ferry rights[1] and bought the ketch rigged steamer *Torbay* of 19 tons (Beaumaris 1895/5). She was a wooden vessel, built at Paignton in 1892, and powered by a single compound engine. She lasted until March 1918 when the Register says that she foundered in the Irish Sea. The presumption is that she had been requisitioned for war service as a tender or a patrol vessel. A larger steel built vessel was bought by the Borough Council in 1904, the 44 ton screw steamer *Lady Magdalen* (Beaumaris 1904/2). She had been built in Port Glasgow in 1896 and her two sets of compound engines gave her a speed of 10 knots. She was sold to Middlesborough in 1919. The *Cynfal* (Beaumaris 1917/1) which in time replaced her was built by Yarwoods of Northwich. She remained in service until 1929 when she was sold to the James Dredging, Towage and Transport Co., Westminster and re-registered at the Port of London. Both the *Cynfal* and her successor, the motorboat *Nantlys,* were named after the houses of the mayors of the years in which they were acquired, Sir Richard Williams and Dr. J. E. Thomas respectively. The *Nantlys* survived until the mid-seventies. As the last ferryboat of the six ferries whose history dates back to medieval times she was bought and restored by the National Museum of Wales in conjunction with the Seiont II Maritime Trust of Caernarfon where she is now exhibited.

Apart from Owen Roberts's acquisitions which were mentioned earlier in this chapter, there were only six registrations of sailing vessels by Bangor owners in the twenty years from 1880 to 1900 in the Beaumaris Registers of Shipping compared with the eight steamers registered within the same period. They were —

[1] H. R. Davies 'The Conway and the Menai Ferries' pp. 285-7.

Cousins 43t. Sr. (1881/1) b. Preston 1813	Hugh Roberts, Bangor, Master Mariner 64	Lost 1893 Leasowe
Confidence 75t. Sr. (1881/2) b. Aberystwyth 1862	John Jones, Bangor, Master Mariner 64	Sold Arklow 1902
Silvia 153t. Sr. (1883/1) b. Appledore 1871	Hugh Evans, Bangor, Master Mariner 64	Sold St. Austell 1902
Valiant 19t. Sma. (1889/2) b. Peel 1860	Charles Freeman, Bangor, Fishmonger 64	Sold Pwllheli 1899
Syren 38t. Sr. (1890/5) b. Annan 1856	Thomas Hughes, Bangor, Master Mariner 32 John Owen, Beaumaris, Gardener 32	Broken up 1909

and

Mary B. Mitchell (1892/3) 195t. 3 masted Sr. b. Carrickfergus 1892	W. M. Preston, Lleiniog Castle, Beaumaris, Gentleman 32 S. T. Chadwick, Haulfre, Beaumaris, Gentleman 32	Sold Arklow 1919

During the same twenty year period 39 ships wholly or partly in Bangor ownership were lost at sea, 8 were broken up or hulked and 7 sold to other ports, — 54 in all. This is consistent with the decline in the number of ships insured with the B.M.S.I.S. which was mentioned in the last chapter, and bears out the Directors' gloomy prognostications about the unprofitability of local shipping.

Of the six ships mentioned above five were old ships and only one, *Mary B. Mitchell,* was new construction. It is perhaps worth noting that the four of the five were owned outright by master mariners who also commanded them. Crew Agreement Lists show that *Confidence* in her time took Port Penrhyn slate to ports in almost all parts of the United Kingdom as it then was, from Jersey to Aberdeen, and from Sligo to Newcastle on Tyne. *Silvia* ranged more widely in the general trade particularly between Newcastle and London and ports in Ireland; she made two voyages in 1883/4 to Spain and Portugal and to the Baltic port of Riga under the command of her owner, Captain Hugh Evans.

Lest it should be thought that the eighties saw the virtual disappearance of the sailing ship and its replacement in the coasting trade by the steamship, it would be well to look at the Crew Agreement Lists relating to *Silvia* in some detail.[2] She went again to Riga and Hamburg in 1886. 1887 was a very active year; she sailed in the spring to Stettin, returning *via* Dunkirk, in the summer to Hamburg and in the autumn to Mogador and Saffi in Morocco. In the course of the next year she made voyages from Glasgow in the general trade to Lannion (Britanny), Seville, and twice to Saffi. In 1889 she made

[2] L.R.O. W/DB 359.

LOADING AT PORT PENRHYN

The short lived S.S. *Linda Blanche* in the foreground and the *Mary B. Mitchell* in the background. *c.* 1914.

(G.A.S. XS 1077.)

PORT PENRHYN FROM GARTH

In the foreground the sandboat *Flatfish* with the small steamer *Medway* unloading
at Lewis's jetty. *(Cei Thomas Lewis)*.

(By kind permission of Mr. W. Richard Thomas)

Another view of Lewis's Jetty, with one of his steam-wagons letting off steam.
The vessel is probably either the *St. Tudwal* or the *St. Seiriol*. The slipway on the
left is at the yard of Edward Ellis, later T. T. Parry and Co.

(G.A.S. XS 1077/3/2/11.)

The 195 ton three masted schooner *Mary B. Mitchell* of the Anglesey Shipping Co.,
built at Carrickfergus in 1892. (G.A.S. XS 1942/3.)

Not Lord Penrhyn's private yacht! The *Mary B. Mitchell* with auxiliary engine
and patched sails under her later Irish ownership. (G.A.S. XS 1297/135.)

The *Mary B. Mitchell* as H.M. Q Ship No. 9 in the 1914-18 War. (G.A.S. Henry Parry Collection XS 7/1279/237.)

two voyages from Porthmadog to Harburg and one to Drammen (Norway). In the spring of 1890 she went from Runcorn to Isafjorde and other places in Iceland and in that summer she took a cargo of slates from Bangor to Stettin. In 1891 she took slates twice to Harburg, once from Porthmadog and once from Bangor. There is a gap in the records until 1894 when she made two voyages from Porthmadog to Harburg; in 1896 she went from Bangor to Stettin, in 1897 from Port Dinorwic to Hamburg and in 1899 from Bangor to Harburg. In the same year she made a voyage from Porthmadog to Stettin, Swinemünde and St. Petersburg. On her return trip she was wrecked on Scoughall Rocks, but apparently repaired, her next trip began in Dysart to Altona on the Elbe. After two more voyages from Porthmadog to Hamburg in 1901 and one in 1902, punctuated by coastal trips, calling among other places at Glasson Dock, Connahs Quay, London, Drogheda and Waterford, she was sold to F. W. Mutton of Charlestown (Cornwall) in March 1902.

She remained in his ownership at least until 1913 when the series of lists comes to an end, and in 1915 her registration was transferred from Beaumaris to Fowey. Her beat was now between Charlestown and the other china clay ports and Ghent and Antwerp on the continent, and London, Liverpool, Preston and Runcorn, to mention only a few of the ports visited.

Although by the turn of the century their numbers had been drastically reduced the coastal sailing vessels of Bangor were still performing a useful and efficient service.

*   *   *   *

It was remarked at the beginning of this chapter that ship ownership in nineteenth century Bangor tended to move from the gentry to the people; now, in the closing years of the century, the wheel was beginning to turn full cycle with the ordering in 1890 of the steamer *Anglesey* by Mr. O. T. Jones of Bangor for two gentlemen who formed the Anglesey Shipping Company. They were, in fact, two Lancashire business men who had settled in Beaumaris, William Henry Preston of Lleiniog Castle and Samuel Taylor Chadwick of Haulfre, but in 1894 and 1895 they were joined in the company and in the purchase of the steamers *Bangor* (Beaumaris 1894/2) and *Penrhyn* by a man whose claim to high social status could not be doubted, Sir R. H. Williams Bulkeley, Bart., of Baron Hill, Beaumaris. Associated also with 2/64ths and 3/64ths in the respective vessels was the above mentioned Owen Thomas Jones of Erw Fair, Bangor, described in the shipping register as 'Ship Manager'. O. T. Jones also managed the *Mary B. Mitchell,* and the steamers *Harrier, Penrhyn, Bangor* and *Pennant* after their transfer to the ownership of E. A. Young, the Penrhyn agent in 1897/8. After Young's death in 1911 the vessels were registered in Lord Penrhyn's name but the polite fiction that they belonged to the Anglesey Shipping Company was maintained.

But to return to 1890; the *Anglesey* was ordered from the Carrickfergus ship-yard of Paul Rodgers which was one of the few yards (including the yard of William Thomas, Amlwch) which had made the successful transition from building wooden schooners to building them in steel. *Anglesey* was never registered at Beaumaris but she appears to have been of about 130 tons register. Neither does she appear to have satisfied her owners; her boiler was too small and she was sent back to Glasgow, where her engines had been fitted, in 1891 for modification. She was sold by the company in 1893. Nothing more is known of her history save that she foundered in 1912 while on a voyage from Minos to the Piraeus in 1912.

However, in 1891 O. T. Jones on behalf of the Anglesey Shipping Company placed another order with Paul Rodgers & Co. for a sailing ship, which is, perhaps, an indication that their dissatisfaction with the *Anglesey* related solely to the machinery and not to the hull. Thus, on the 22nd of April 1892 the *Mary B. Mitchell* (Beaumaris 1892/3) sailed on her maiden voyage from Carrickfergus to Bangor with a cargo of rock salt.

Mary B. Mitchell is the most famous of the Port Penrhyn ships and it is not surprising that her story[3] has acquired a patina of legend. Her lines were so beautiful that there was a strong and insistent oral tradition in Bangor that she was intended as Lord Penrhyn's personal yacht even though she had been ordered by Preston and Chadwick for the Anglesey Shipping Company and immediately began her lengthy service as a slate carrier.

She was a steel built three masted schooner 129 feet in length and with a beam of over 24 feet. Her depth of hold was a little over 12 feet and she carried a figure head of a female bust. She was named after Mary Brasier Mitchell whose memorial, after her death in 1895 at the age of seventy-nine, was erected in Penmon churchyard by "her sincere and sorrowing friend W. M. Preston."

Her crew was normally Master, Mate, 2 A.B.'s 2 O.S.'s and a Cook. Her voyages in the nineties were mainly to London or to Hamburg, returning to Bangor generally by way of Newcastle, Aberdeen or Sunderland, London, Dublin or another Irish port. On December 26th 1896, under the command of G. H. Preston, a native of Trefnant, she was stranded on Texel while carrying slates from Port Dinorwic, probably for Hamburg, and abandoned

---

[3] For her detailed history see Aled Eames, *Ships and Seamen of Anglesey* pp. 501-505 and pp. 517-8 and the same author's *Meistri'r Moroedd* pp. 210-219 which contains a list of her voyages between 1893 and 1913 extracted from her Crew Agreement Lists.

Her service as a Q-Ship during the 1914-18 War is described by E. Keble Chatterton in *Q-Ships and their Story*, Chapter VI.

Maritime Wales/Cymru a'r Môr No. 4 (1979) has several photographs of the *Mary B*, as she was affectionately known and a brief note by Aled Eames, No. 7 (1983) has an article by Michael McCaughan on Paul Rodgers and his Welsh connections, including 'Ship No. 38' which became the *Mary B. Mitchell*.

by her crew on the following day. She was repaired on the continent and in August of the following year a new crew was signed on at Amsterdam, Master, Mate, 3 A.B.'s, one O.S. and a Cook/Steward. She was under the command of David Davies, a native of New Quay who thus began an association with the vessel that lasted with brief interruptions at least until 1913 when the series of Crew Agreement Lists comes to an end.[4]

The lists show that the vessel made only one more voyage to the continent, to Harburg in November 1901, but there were not many ports in Great Britain and Ireland at which she did not call at least once in the period up to 1907. In Ireland she frequently visited Dublin, Belfast, Cork, Queenstown and Youghal; on the west coast of Britain, Bristol, Cardiff, Llanelly, Swansea and Lancaster (Glasson Dock); in the south-east, London, Gravesend, Rochester, Shoreham and Folkestone; Newcastle on Tyne, Sunderland, Stockton, Middlesborough, Hull and Grimsby on the east coast; and most frequently the Scottish ports of Stranraer, Irvine, Bowling, Kirkcaldy, Inverness, Burghead, Aberdeen, Arbroath, Leith and Broughty Ferry.

After 1907 the pattern changes; she made many more voyages to London and then directly back to Bangor and some voyages with only one intervening call, for instance at Dublin or Pembroke Dock. The reason behind this changed pattern is to be found in the ledger for the *Mary B. Mitchell* which is among the Penrhyn Quarry records at the Caernarfon Area Record Office of the Gwynedd Archives Service.[5] From 1907 onwards the vessel carried a regular back-cargo of cement from London to Bangor and in her accounts for the year 1908-9 the 'Profit on cement' is recorded separately from the other freights, but in subsequent years is incorporated with them. Among the customers for cement we see some familiar names — Humphrey Williams, Penlôn, Watkin Jones, Bangor, besides the regular users, Penrhyn Quarry and Penrhyn Estate.

There is little in the log to indicate much change in this uneventful pattern — it might almost be described as the Port Penrhyn — London shuttle service. An entry for October 1909 records that after taking shelter in Milford Haven for a week the vessel sailed but "when about mile and a half inside of St. Anne's Point the wind fell to a dead calm with a little swell from the S.W. We drifted against a Schooner *Esmeralda* of Bridgewater and done some damage to her gear also damaging our steering wheel." In a tape-recorded interview the late Richard Dop of Port Dinorwic, whose brother Robert served aboard *Mary B.* and who himself had served on the Penrhyn steamers *Bangor* and *Penrhyn*, said that the steamer sailors hated the sight of the *Mary B.* since they were often diverted by the office in Bangor to tow her through calms.

During the 1914-18 War *Mary B.* continued for some time to sail between

[4] L.R.O. W/DB 271.
[5] C.R.O. P.Q. 92/71.

Port Penrhyn and London but in the spring of 1916 she was requisitioned by the Admiralty and armed with three hidden guns to serve as a decoy ship. In a variety of disguises she was to invite U-boat attack in the western approaches and at the very last moment to reveal that she had teeth. She was twice involved in engagements with U-boats and inflicted such damage that they were afterwards possibly sunk. She survived in this hazardous trade and returned to Port Penrhyn after the war.

In 1919 she was re-registered (Beaumaris 1919/2) "in consequence of a change in propulsion" as she had been fitted with auxiliary motors — twin screw, but she was still rigged as a three masted schooner. She was sold to Job Tyrrell of Arklow in 1919 and her registration was transferred to the port of Dublin in 1933. She almost survived the second world war since she was wrecked in the Solway Firth in December 1944.

Shortly after ordering the *Mary B. Mitchell* the Anglesey Shipping Company, as already recounted, ordered the screw steamer *Harrier* (Beaumaris 1894/1) of 94 tons net, 204 tons gross, from the yard of Scott and Sons, Bowling, on the Clyde. She was followed in quick succession by *S.S. Bangor* (Beaumaris 1894/2), 119 tons net, 340 tons gross, *S.S. Penrhyn,* (Beaumaris 1895/3) 127 tons net, 355 tons gross and *S.S. Pennant,* (Beaumaris 1897/5) of 266 tons net, 648 tons gross.

In March and April 1898 Emilius Alexander Young, Lord Penrhyn's agent, acquired these four steamers and the *Mary B. Mitchell* from their share-holders in a clean sweep, and in 1903 he bought *S.S. Pandora* (Beaumaris 1903/2) of 79 tons net, 203 tons gross, which had been built in 1892 at Wallsend by Schlesinger, Davies and Co. She was the only Penrhyn steamer not to have been built by Scotts of Bowling.

Ours is not the only age which complains that the accountants are taking over our hospitals, universities and social services, — the entire country, if you are so minded — it was beginning to happen a hundred years ago. Young, a London accountant, had been brought in by the second Lord Penrhyn to manage his estate and his quarry on businesslike lines. Soon the regime of the first Lord Penrhyn, the Wyatts and Pennant Lloyd was to appear positively benign compared with Young's invariably hard line which led to the labour troubles of 1896 and 1900 in the quarry, from which, consequentially, the shipping interests of Bangor never fully recovered.

Young succeeded in out-Wyatting the Wyatts; single handed, he owned and controlled the Anglesey Shipping Company's fleet of one three masted schooner and five steamers — and he did not meet his 1868 in the form of being obliged by Lord Penrhyn to sell them. When he died in 1910 the ships were inherited jointly by his widow, Elizabeth, of Blackheath, his sons, L. A. Young, Gentleman, of Blackheath and Reginald Young, Solicitor of London and by M. C. Matthews, a London solicitor and probably his son-in-law. In 1911 the vessels were all sold to the Rt. Hon Edward Sholto, Baron

Penrhyn, whose address was given as Wreken Park, Stony Stratford, Northants.

The fleet remained firmly in the hands of successive holders of the title until it was finally dispersed after the Second World War. Up to 1914 it consisted of the six vessels already mentioned with the addition in 1914 of *Linda Blanche*, (Beaumaris 1914/2) of 199 tons register, 369 gross, built by Scotts of Bowling. She did not have a long life for she was sunk by the German submarine U-21 in the Irish sea in January 1915. The other vessels all survived the war. Two new vessels were ordered from Scotts of Bowling in 1921 to replace the *Linda Blanche* and the *Mary B. Mitchell,* which by this time had been sold. They were *Pamela* of 147 tons net, 408 tons gross and the smaller *Sybil Mary* cf 270 tons gross.

Harrier was sold back in October 1926 to Charles Wood Scott of Bowling, Shipbuilder, who sold her six months later to an owner at Cape Town. She was eventually sunk by a U-boat in the Second World War while on passage from Durban to Mombasa. *Bangor* was sold to a Belfast owner in 1933 and foundered in the following year. Her crew were saved.

Pennant was sunk with some loss of life after being run down in thick fog off Southend by an oil tanker, *S.S. Acasta*, in 1925. The wreck was subsequently raised and broken up in 1926. *Penrhyn* was sold to a Lancaster shipowner in 1937 and she was eventually broken up in 1951.

By the time of the Second World war the fleet was down to three vessels — *Pandora* (built 1892), *Pamela* and *Sybil Mary* (both built 1921). The register records that *Pandora* was sold to the Ministry of Transport in 1947 who sold her to an Edinburgh shipowner in the same year. While in the hands of the Merchiston Steamship Co. of Edinburgh she foundered in a gale off Whitby and was lost with all hands in October 1951. *Pamela* was lost with all hands in October 1944 while on a voyage from Sharpness to Liverpool and it was presumed that she had struck a mine. The Register records the vessel as "lost by marine perils." *Sybil Mary* was broken up at Dublin in 1951.

Penrhyn slate no longer went by sea to the quarry's customers and the railway took over — but only briefly, for the Port Penrhyn standard gauge branch, constructed in 1852, was reduced to the status of a siding in 1954 and finally closed in 1963, in the same year as the Bangor — Bethesda branch of the L.M.S. The great Penrhyn Quarry passed into the hands of Messrs. McAlpine and the whole of the production now goes by road with the exception of an occasional shipment of fullersite (granulated slate) from Port Penrhyn in mainly foreign ships.

To go back briefly to the days of *Mary B. Mitchell* and the first generation of the Penrhyn steamers, the Caernarfon Record Office of the Gwynedd Archives Service contains, among other Penrhyn records, the ledgers, cash books etc. of most of their ships for most of the years from the nineties to the twenties of the present century. It would be impossible within the compass of this book to examine all the ledgers in detail but a sample of the accounts of two ships over a period of five years is instructive.

The two ships selected are *Mary B. Mitchell* and *Bangor* for the years 1908 to 1913 for which ledgers for both ships are available.[6] Further reasons for their selection are that both ships were of a similar age, that each had a similar carrying capacity of some 340-350 tons and that Crew Agreement Lists giving details of their voyages as well as of their manning are available for most of the relevant years at the Llangefni Area Record Office.[7] By collating these two sources it is possible to build up a picture of the commercial merits of both types of vessel. What is unfortunately not available is the comparative capital cost of each vessel but it can be safely assumed that the steamer was easily the more expensive.

It would be rash to form any definite conclusions about the comparative economics of sailing vessels and steamers on the basis of this single instance but there are certain pointers here.

Firstly, there is the number of round voyages from the Menai Straits (each ship made an occasional trip from Caernarfon or Port Dinorwic) to be considered. The Crew Agreement Lists show that *Mary B.* made 32 in the course of five years, an average of 6.4 voyages per year (and it should be remembered that the majority of these voyages were to London and straight back to Bangor with a cargo of cement); *S.S. Bangor* performed 72 voyages in four years (the Crew Agreements for 1910 are missing), an average of 18. This average would have been higher but for the fact that the vessel spent some weeks in the summer of 1911 salvaging goods from *S.S. Ivernia* and ferrying them from Queenstown to Liverpool.

Secondly there is the whole question of manning and wages to be considered, and in these matters there is a complete contrast between the two ships. Both ships were of similar size and carrying capacity; the sailing vessel employed seven crew members, — master, mate, cook/steward and four seamen (sometimes 3 A.B.'s and an O.S. or boy, sometimes 2 A.B.'s and 2 O.S.). The steamer employed ten — master, mate, engineer, second engineer, 4 seamen and 2 firemen. Occasionally one of the four seamen would be designated as A.B./boatswain and another as A.B./cook. Besides the handwritten endorsement on the Crew Agreement, common to both sailing and steam propelled vessels sailing from Port Penrhyn, to the effect that the crew were required to work cargoes and ballast, there was commonly a second endorsement for steamer crews that they consented to assist each other in their respective tasks as ordered by the master (or at least in one case, by the mate or engineer as well), i.e., there were to be no demarcation disputes.

While the sailing vessel's crew were paid in the traditional way — per month and all found, the steamer's crew were paid on the 'weekly boat'

[6] C.R.O. P.Q. 92/71 *(Mary B.)* and P.Q. 92/1 *(S.S. Bangor).*
[7] L.R.O. W/DB 271 *(Mary B.)* and W/DB 52 *(S.S. Bangor).*

system — a weekly wage out of which they had to supply their own food. Thus a direct comparison of wages would be meaningless. Crew Agreements rarely record the wages of the master but we know that the master of the *Silvia*, (pages 176-7) a vessel of comparable size, was drawing £6 per month. The highest paid crew member on the *Mary B.* after the master was the mate (£4 – £5), followed by the boatswain and cook (each on £3. 10s. – £4), A.B. (£3 – £3. 5s.), O.S. £2 – £2. 5s.) and boy (£1. 5s. – £1. 10s.). On the steamer the highest paid after the captain was the engineer on £2. 10s. – £3 per week, followed by the mate and second engineer on a par at £1. 12s. – £1. 15s., seamen and firemen on a par at £1. 7s. It was worth paying a little extra for a good cook and the A.B./cook was generally paid £1. 10s.

In the summary annual account in the ledgers (reproduced for 1908/9 – 1912/13 in Appendix I) there is no consistency between the heads of expenditure and income between the *Mary B. Mitchell* and the *Bangor*. Wages and victualling expenses of the *Mary B* are concealed within the omnibus title of 'Loading expenses and dues, until we come to 1912/13 when they are given separately. Comparison with the same items for *S.S. Bangor* is now possible.

The relevant items are £346. 13s. 10d. for wages and £140. 1s. 2d. for victualling for seven men on the sailing vessel, a total of £486. 15s. compared with a wages bill of £865. 19s. for ten men on the steamer, (out of which, of course, they had to provide their own food). The average cost per man on the sailing ship was approximately £69. 10s. and on the steamer £86. 12s. In the following year the figures are respectively £388. 16s. 4d. and £152. 13s. 10d. making a total of £541. 10s. 2d. and an average per man of £77. 7s. for the *Mary B.*, and for the *Bangor* a total of £912. 1s., giving an average of £91. 4s. per man. Taking into account the higher wages paid to the engineers on the steamer the old system of payment by the month and all found was the more economical for the owners.

One of the largest items of expenditure for the steamer was coal which in most years was not far short of £1,000. Repairs were usually more expensive and the re-boilering of 1908/9 cost over £800. Not unnaturally in view of her annual mileage the item for loading expenses and dues was considerably higher than *Mary B.'s* but her freight earnings over the years were three or four times greater. Which brings us to the question of profits. We only have the gross profit as a percentage of the annual turnover, without any deductions for depreciation or taxation.

On this basis, and on this alone, the sailing vessel is consistently more 'profitable', and even more so when her smaller capital cost is taken into consideration but the 'profit' is on a greatly reduced turnover because the steamer is capable of earning many more freights within the same period. This is shown below (amounts rounded to nearest £): —

	Mary B. Mitchell			S.S. Bangor		
Year	Turnover	Gross Profit	% Profit	Turnover	Gross Profit	% Profit
1908/9	£1,414	£526	37.2	£4,560	£430	9.4
1909/10	£1,237	£346	28.0	£4,208	£783	18.6
1910/11	£1,054	£169	16.0	£4,697	£1,198	25.5
1911/12	£1,525	£561	36.8	£4,014	£926	23.1
1912/13	£1,260	£383	30.4	£4,197	£956	27.8
Total of 5 years	£6,490	£1,985	30.6	£21,676	£4,293	19.8

That a sailing ship could be a sound economic proposition in the coastal trade during this period is borne out by the success of the Bangor schooner *Silvia* over a number of years. Sailing vessels presented a real source of competition to steamers with their low labour and capital costs, the fact that they did not need elaborate port facilities but could be unloaded if need be at convenient creeks or on open beaches. Had the First World War, which showed up the vulnerability of the sailing ship to submarine attacks, not occurred when it did, the coastal sailing ship, particularly in its steel-hulled form, might have been a common sight for at least twenty years longer.

As with the Bangor schooners, brigs and brigantines, the Port Penrhyn steamers also played their part in the general mercantile trade of Britain. The Crew Agreement Lists of *S.S. Bangor* record that during the first half of 1909, under the command of Richard Owens of Amlwch Port, her master since 1897, she sailed from Port Penrhyn with cargoes of slate to the following ports — Middlesbrough, London, Cork, Newcastle on Tyne with part cargo for Berwick, Sunderland, Inverness and Hamburg. Ports visited on the return voyages to Bangor included Bristol, Rainham, Dublin, Dundalk, Limerick, Stranraer, Kirkcaldy, Greenhithe, Dover, Rochester and Llanelly. From the ledger we can gain some idea of the variety of cargoes carried — railway chairs, scrap iron, stone, coals, flour, manure — and the staple back-cargo to Port Penrhyn, or occasionally to Deganwy, cement.

In the five years under review besides being re-boilered at Bowling *S.S. Bangor* was dry docked annually at Port Dinorwic. The accounts for her repairs were naturally higher than *Mary B.'s* and as well as the boiler renewal on 1908 the donkey pump had to be renewed in 1910. In the same period there was little expenditure on repairs to the sailing vessel apart from her annual docking and the renewal of a spar and a few sails. The account for her repairs in 1912 actually showed a profit; in July *Mary B. Mitchell* sustained damage when she was in collision with the steamer *Hawkswood* in London. She was temporarily repaired there and the probability is that she was towed to the dry dock at Port Dinorwic. Her bow plating was repaired there by E. Neele who was paid £90. A further £33. 15s. had been spent on temporary repairs, surveyors' fees etc. The owners of the steamer had paid £279. 15s. in settlement of the claim. Thus in the accounts for the year 1911/12 the item 'By Repairs' appeared not as an expense but as an income, and made a substantial contribution towards the gross profits for the year. (See Appendix I).

The study over a period as short as five years of the accounts of only two ships engaged in the trade of only one port cannot, as previously pointed out, be regarded as in any way conclusive evidence about the economics of sail as opposed to steam, but in the present context it has served to throw a little light on the conditions under which the ships of the period operated and what kind of lives the men who served in them led. In brief it is of more value to the social than to the economic historian.

*   *   *   *

To the majority of Bangor citizens the sea means nothing today, except, perhaps in a recreational sense as the element one swims in or sails upon. It is a source of livelihood for a few, mostly in its recreational aspects of catering for the needs of yachtsmen and tourists. It is as if the clearance of the Hirael area — and no-one doubts the desirability of clearing away the huddled, hastily built and unhygienic houses of 150 years ago — had at the same time swept away the folk-memory of the days when most of the houses in the Hirael and Garth areas contained someone whose livelihood was connected with the sea — as a seaman, fisherman, pilot or diver, as a ship-wright, carpenter, rigger or sailmaker, as a slate stower, engine driver or port labourer. The commercial middle classes were also involved; chemists, grocers, accountants, drapers and many other occupations are to be found among the shareholders of ships and directors of insurance clubs.

The process began in the early years of the nineteenth century when Robert Thomas of Abercegin, John Jones the shipwright and their associates contested with the Penrhyn interest, in the form of the Wyatts (and their kin!) and the Worthington consortium, for a share in the maritime trade of Port Penrhyn. With the expansion of the slate industry in the middle years of the century, the native contribution to the shipowning concerns became an increasingly significant proportion of the whole, particularly after Worthington's retirement; the shipbuilding business itself, as has been shown, was wholly indigenous, as was the later marine insurance business which was under the joint control of the shipbuilders and owners. The men who manned the ships that went out from Port Penrhyn with slates and played their part in the general mercantile life of Britain by taking cargoes to practically every port in the kingdom were Welshmen from Bangor and the immediate locality, as the Crew Agreement Lists preserved at the Caernarfon and Llangefni Record Offices of the Gwynedd Archives service amply bear out.

The Wyatts were persuaded, if not ordered, to give up their shipping interests in 1868 but their nominees, William Dawbarn, the Liverpool merchant and the John Lloyd junior clan continued with exactly the same pattern of trading for some years. Formally, at least, the Penrhyn interest was not represented in the shipping world.

All that changed in the years of the trade depression which began in the eighties. The wooden sailing ship was finished; the future lay with the steamers, but up to the 1914-18 War large sailing ships, and some coasting schooners continued to be built — but they were built of iron and steel. (The perfection of the design and construction of the wooden schooner came in the so-called Western Ocean yachts of the nineties and early years of this century, but they were an anachronism, and they were confined to the hardest of all trades — with the Labrador fishing ports and the phosphate rock trade of the Dutch West Indies.) All this is symbolised by the acquisition by the Anglesey Shipping Company in 1892 of the steel three masted schooner, *Mary B. Mitchell* and in 1894 of the steamship *Harrier*. The 'gentry', in the form of Sir R. H. Williams Bulkely, Bart, and his associates had the capital resources necessary to finance such major projects which were beyond the reach of the local middle class. What a pity from the point of view of Bangor, that William Thomas who at this very time was building iron or steel schooners and brigantines, (which in the opinion of some knowledgeable people rivalled the Western Ocean yachts both in beauty and efficiency) besides being a builder of small steamers, was established in Amlwch and not in Bangor! But William Thomas was connected not with the slate interests of Gwynedd but with iron and steel trade of Millom in Cumberland.

Nevertheless, the achievements of the Bangor middle class, under the leadership of men like Robert Thomas, John Parry, Edward Ellis, Samuel Roberts, Meshach Roberts and others, even though they failed to make the transition into iron and steel, were by no means inconsiderable. They were competing in a region dominated by the arch-capitalists, the Penrhyn family, who had sufficient substance to weather trade depressions and economic storms, such as the strikes and lock outs of 1896 and 1900, which brought disaster to the working communities of Bethesda and Tregarth where most of the Penrhyn quarrymen lived, and to a lesser extent to the maritime interests of Bangor. When the quarry reopened in 1903 with a much reduced working force, many of the Bangor schooners had left Port Penrhyn to seek work elsewhere, many at Port Dinorwic, Caernarfon or Porthmadog, many at more distant ports. Many of the seamen, too, moved to other ports, like Captain David Roberts of the *Lady Louisa Pennant* who after his ship had lain idle for some weeks sought, and obtained another command at Fleetwood. Some of the schooners gradually returned to Port Penrhyn but of the greatly reduced output of the quarry which went by sea, the greater part was carried in the holds of the Penrhyn steamers and the schooners competed for what was left. After the 1914-18 War the occasional schooner still called at Port Penrhyn and the present writer recalls watching one being warped into a loading berth in the summer of 1931 from the view point of the grounds of the old Penrhyn Arms Hotel where the National Eisteddfod was being held at the time.

Despite the fact that there was only one shipment of slate by sea from Port Penrhyn after the second world war and that the production of the Penrhyn Quarry was now distributed by rail and increasingly by road transport, transhipment (if that is the correct word to use) of slates from the Penrhyn narrow gauge railway to the main line of the L.M.S. or to road transport still took place at the sidings of Port Penrhyn until 1962 when the Penrhyn Railway was closed. In the following year the connection with the main L.M.S. line was taken up, and in 1964 McAlpine and Company acquired a controlling interest in the Penrhyn Quarry and began a programme of drastic reconstruction based on the construction of roads connecting all the old galleries which enabled heavy machinery to be used. The connection between the quarry and the port was broken not only by the severing of the railway link but also by this transfer of ownership; the quarry belonged to McAlpines but the port remained under the control of the Douglas-Pennant family.

Since then it has been adapted for a number of different purposes. There are a number of inshore trawlers based in Bangor and a depot and ice plant has been established at the seaward end of the inner basin. There are also a growing number of boats engaged in sea angling which is gaining in popularity. From time to time ships are laid up here and the inner basin is a base for an interesting mix of yachts and work boats; on the quayside yachts are wintered and 'old-timers' are lovingly rebuilt and restored by optimists whose time scale is measured not in years but in decades — the salt of the earth.

From time to time the Port has been used as a base for specialised vessels engaged in civil engineering operations off the North Wales coast, at the oil terminal and associated works at Amlwch, the Rhos on Sea breakwater and the exploratory drilling by the Coal Board off the Point of Air, to mention only a few. In the seventies the 2,000 tonners *Aberthaw Fisher* and *Kingsnorth* were frequent visitors bringing heavy components for the C.E.G.B.'s pumped storage scheme at Llanberis on heavy roll-on roll-off trailers. *Aberthaw Fisher* has recently been seen in the port. A special ramp was built at their intended berth in the inner basin and the graceful wrought iron bridge in the foreground of the illustration (facing page 104) had to be demolished and replaced by a more substantial concrete structure to accommodate the heavy loads carried.

187

One of the tugs belonging to the Carmet Tug Company of Bromborough Dock, Wirral, is based on Port Penrhyn and a tug towing a barge or lighter is not an infrequent sight at Bangor, and it is expected that it will be an even more frequent sight when the biggest civil engineering contract in Wales, the Conwy tunnel, gets under way.

There is also the regular trade, both inwards and outwards; no longer do the sand boats tide out of Hirael to the Lafan Sands and tide back to Hirael on the flood but instead the sand dredger, *Hoveringham V*, fulfils the requirements of the local builders' merchants and the ready-mix concrete plant on the adjoining quay with sand from the Constable Bank, off Prestatyn. Recently there was an import of pumice for the Penrhyn Quarry (for the manufacture of breeze-blocks) in a large Icelandic vessel. There are also regular exports from the Penrhyn Quarry of rock stone (for the building trade) and slate granules and Fullersite (for the manufacture of plastics and other products).

For the last two years the tonnages were[8] : —

	Inward			Outward	
	1984	1985		1984	1985
Sand	66,907	46,800	Slate Products	8,236	5,818
Pumice	—	1,060	Rock Stone	3,476	4,916

Of the four slate ports of Gwynedd, Porthmadog and Port Dinorwic have become marinas and have no commercial shipping, the famous slate quay at Caernarfon is the base for a few fishing and angling boats and lots of yachts, but at the other end of the waterfront the oil dock still receives cargoes from the Shell and Rowbotham Bros. coastal tankers. Port Penrhyn manages to maintain a well balanced variety of activities — between fishing and angling, towage work, providing services for laid up vessels and the regular trade in sand and slate, besides catering for yachtsmen. Capt. Ian Metcalfe, the Harbourmaster, believes strongly that it has a future as a working port and not a mere pleasure centre, and devotes his energies to this end.

Until the coming of the railway in 1848 the sea was Bangor's most potent link with the commercial world outside, and the maritime connection, though greatly diminished, persisted until the first world war. An example of this vestigial connection with the sea is that when Bangor's first petrol driven bus service was inaugurated it ran between the pier, via the Town Clock, to the railway station — not for the benefit of tourists who wanted a breath of sea air, but for the very practical purpose of enabling ferry passengers

[8] I am indebted to Capt. Ian Metcalfe for these figures and for much of the information about the present day activity at the Port.

from Beaumaris and south-east Anglesey to catch trains from Bangor station and to return by the same route.

The Bangor pier and ferry undertaking never made a profit for the City Council but for thirty years or more it performed a valuable social and economic service. It brought the farmers of Llangoed and Pentraeth or their wives to Bangor market on Fridays and to patronise the city's tradespeople in their turn. In fact several of the Straits ferries survived until the outbreak of the second world war because of the heavy toll charged for the crossing of the Menai Suspension Bridge. With the abolition of the toll in 1940, the coming of the motor bus and the popularity of the family car, the ferries came to an end as a serious economic proposition, but the Beaumaris and Llandegfan ferries survived during the summer months as a tourist attraction until about ten years ago, when Bangor pier was declared unsafe. The pier has now been restored at a cost which would have staggered the city fathers who built it. The restoration of the ferry service also would be a token recognition of Bangor's debt to communication by sea.

Appendices

APPENDIX I

Mary B. Mitchell

1908/09

	£ s d		£ s d
Insurance a/c	38. 5. 7	Profit cement	9.16.10
Loading, dues &c.	655.13. 8	Freights	1403.18. 1
Sundry a/cs.	191.17. 0		
Gross Profit	525.13. 9		
Bank. Comm.	2. 4.11		
	1413.14.11		1413.14.11

1909/10

	£ s d		£ s d
Insurance	40.11. 0	Freights	1237. 6. 4
Loading, dues &c.	739. 3. 0		
Repairs	18.17. 7		
Sundries	91. 5. 6		
Gross Profit	346. 2. 7		
Bank Comm.	1. 6. 8		
	1237. 6. 4		1237. 6. 4

1910/11

	£ s d		£ s d
Insurance	51. 7.11	Freights	1054. 0. 2
Loading, dues &c.	631. 9.11		
Repairs	66.14. 9		
Sundries	134. 7. 4		
Gross Profit	168.13. 9		
Bank Comm.	1. 6. 6		
	1054. 0. 2		1054. 0. 2

S.S. Bangor

1908/09

	£ s d		£ s d
Coal	1037. 6. 3	By Freights	4330.13. 6
Gross profit	430. 3. 7	Sundries	229. 9. 3
Insurance	70. 4. 5		
Loading, dues &c.	1194. 6. 0		
Repairs	939. 5. 6		
Wages	885. 6. 4		
Comm.	3.10. 8		
	4560. 2. 9		4560. 2. 9

1909/10

	£ s d		£ s d
Coal	992. 7. 3	By Freights	4208. 8. 5
Gross Profit	783. 6. 3		
Insurance	63.11. 3		
Loading, dues &c.	1222. 3. 3		
Repairs	55.17. 1		
Wages	850. 0. 0		
Comm.	3.18.10		
Sundries	237. 4. 6		
	4208. 8. 5		4208. 8. 5

1910/11

	£ s d		£ s d
Coal	956.15.10	By Freights	4431.13. 6
Gross Profit	1198. 9. 2	Salvage of 'Wellsed'	265.16. 5
Insurance	82.15. 4		
Loading, dues &c.	1206. 0. 9		
Repairs	119. 7. 2		
Wages	901. 0. 0		
Sundries	230. 1. 7		
Commission	3. 0. 1		
	4697. 9.11		4697. 9.11

Insurance	49.10. 0	Freights	1369. 4. 4		
Loading, dues &c.	807.19. 8	‡ Repairs	156. 0. 0		
Sundries	106. 3. 7				
Gross Profit	561. 0. 6				
Bank Comm.	10. 7				
	1525. 4. 4		1525. 4. 4		

Coal	790. 1. 1	By Freights	4014. 6.10
Gross Profit	926.13. 3		
Insurance	80. 6. 5		
Loading, dues &c.	1045. 7. 5		
Repairs	48. 9. 2		
Wages	901. 0. 0		
Sundries	219. 5. 6		
Commission	3. 4. 0		
	4014. 6.10		4014. 6.10

1912/13

Repairs	16.13. 0	Freights	1259.13. 4
Insurance	53.12. 9		
Sundries	57.14. 4		
Loading, dues &c.	259.13. 6		
Wages	346.13.10		
Victualling	140. 1. 2		
Gross Profit	383. 9. 3		
Bank Comm.	1.15. 6		
	1259.13. 4		1259.13. 4

Coal	831. 8. 0	Freights	4196.17.10
Gross Profit	956.13. 3		
Insurance	85.12.11		
Loading, dues, &c.	1150. 3. 5		
Repairs	114.12. 3		
Wages	865.19. 0		
Sundries	188.19.11		
Commission	3. 9. 2		
	4196.17.10		4196.17.10

‡ C.R.O. P.Q. 92/71 Folio 69 (Repairs) shows receipt of cheques from owners of 'Hawkwood' in settlement of claim for damage to bow, surveyor's fee, towage etc. amounting to £279.15. The repairs, fees, etc. cost £123.15; hence the profit on repairs!

APPENDIX II

Rules and Regulations to be observed by Masters of Vessels intending to load at Port Penrhyn.

1

All orders for Slates are now stemmed to take regular turn in loading instead of the Vessels as formerly. All Vessels coming to Port Penrhyn to load Slates and reported as herein after mentioned will (as far as practicable) be offered cargoes in their turn according to the date of their arrival within the Stemming limits; but the Agents reserve to themselves the power of loading any Vessel or Vessels with the orders coming on turn that they may think proper, whether such Vessels have arrived after those already waiting for charters or otherwise, provided they come in ballast, or loaded, or part loaded with any kind of Merchandise or other goods for the said place for the use of the Concern, or they do not lay under repairs for a longer period than three weeks from the date of their arrival, without consent as under; but any Vessel loaded or part loaded for any place between Menai Bridge and Beaumaris, otherwise than for the Concern unless upon being reported to the Harbour Master within 24 hours after her arrival and being discharged and afterwards brought within the Stemming limits within 5 running days immediately following the same, will, after that period not be stemmed until discharged and brought within the Stemming limits; and any Vessel remaining under repairs for a longer period than three weeks as above stated (unless upon application to the Agents previous to such Vessel going under repair permission is given by them to the Harbour Master allowing a longer period) such Vessel will not be Stemmed until clear of the Carpenter's hands; no newly launched Vessel can be stemmed to take her turn until completed and ready for Sea, without the consent of the Agents at Port Penrhyn.

2

No Vessels will be chartered unless in a good state of repair.

3

Masters of Vessels are required to report themselves to the Harbour Master within 24 hours after their Vessel became entitled to be stemmed, and in neglect thereof such vessel will only be stemmed from such a day as she is afterwards reported.

4

Loaded Vessels coming to discharge at the Crane or Coal Yard the Masters thereof cannot be allowed, without leave, to bring their Vessels within the line of the pier until there is sufficient water at the point of discharge.

194

5

The Master or other person having charge of any Vessel in Ballast shall discharge the Ballast in such place as the Ballast Master shall direct and when done shall get his crew to spread the same on the Ballast Bank.

6

All Vessels intending to load must be moored to West of the Buoys or Dead-man's Bank, with not less than 10 fathoms Chain or Rope from the mooring Buoy, and cannot be allowed to have any Anchor cast, or any Cable, Chains, Ropes or other Tackle moored to the East of the said Buoys as the same will obstruct the Channel and free Navigation of the Port.

7

No Master or other person having the charge of any Vessel can be allowed to bring his Vessel to the Quay, or within the line of the Quay and mooring buoys before the order he is engaged to load is on turn, and until a Berth is fixed for him by the Harbour Master.

8

The Master or other person in charge of any Vessel, when bringing the Vessel to the Quay shall run up the Jib-Boom, top up the lower Yards, hoist up the Topsail yard (if required) and take off her Boom Irons and keep the Flukes of the Anchors in board.

9

Masters of Vessels, whilst alongside the Quay, not to suffer their crew to throw anything over board but water, but may remove anything into the Waggons to be conveyed thence to the Ballast Ground, with the permission of the Harbour Master.

10

Masters of Vessels, or the crew, not to heat any Pitch, Tar, or Tallow on board whilst moored alongside the Quay, but to make a fire in some convenient place on the Quay to be fixed on by the Harbour Master.

11

Masters of Vessels to slack down their mooring Ropes when required to allow another Vessel to come to her loading berth and to haul to another Berth (if required) and to haul out when loaded.

Masters of Vessels requiring any Money on account of Freight must give six days previous notice thereof in the Office.

13

Every Master of a Vessel will be required to clear out his Vessel at the Office as soon as loaded and before his Vessel leaves the Quay, unless otherwise arranged; and any Master of a Vessel not being here when she is three parts loaded, her loading will be stopped until his arrival.

N.B.   Any Master of Vessel or other person in charge of the same willfully neglecting to comply with any of the foregoing Rules and Regulations, or refusing to comply with the same when required by the Harbour Master, his Vessel shall be immediately taken off the Books, and will not be entered afresh until he complies with the Rules and Regulations. If such Vessel has commenced loading, she cannot be proceeded with until the Master or person in charge complies with the Rules and Regulations, unless the Agents shall upon the recommendation of the Harbour Master and a review of the matter consider it a case deserving of mitigation.

ARTHUR WYATT

Agent to the

Rt. Honble. LORD PENRHYN.

Mr. W. JONES is appointed Harbour Master.

APPENDIX III

Beaumaris 1800/26 RAVEN   73t. Sl.
b. St. Helens 1788
(Former registry London 1793/103)
63.9 x 16.9 x 9
    William Thomas, Mariner, Cadnant   John Roberts, Gentleman, Bangor
    William Jackson, Bangor Ferry Inn, Innkeeper   (S.O.'s)
    Thomas Jones, Esquire, Bryntirion   Benjamin Wyatt, Esq., Lime Grove, Bangor,
    Mary Williams and Mary Williams *(sic)* both of Bangor   (N.S.)
Endorsement 1815 Samuel Worthington, Merchant and George Dale, both of Bangor are
    the sole owners.
Beaumaris 1815/30
    Samuel Worthington, Esquire, Llwynon, Llandegai   George Dale, Mariner, Bangor
Beaumaris 1817/4   73t. Altered to Schooner
    Samuel Worthington, Esquire, Llwynon, Llandegai   George Dale, Mariner, Bangor
    Memo: Samuel Worthington sold all his shares to George Dale, 14 April, 1821.
Beaumaris 1825/140
    George Dale, Mariner, Bangor 64/64
Beaumaris 1831/3
    George Dale, Mariner, Bangor 64/64
    Feb. 1831 George Dale b.o.s. 32/64 to James Wyatt, Gentleman, Lime Grove
    Jan. 1834 Mary Dale, widow of George Dale, b.o.s. 8/64 to James Wyatt, 16/64 to
    William Baxter, Gentleman, Penrhyn Castle and 8/64 to John Parry, Shipwright, Bangor
Beaumaris 1834/3
    James Wyatt, Esquire, Lime Grove 40/64   John Parry, Shipwright, Bangor, 8/64
                                    (S.O.'s)
    William Baxter, Gentleman, Penrhyn Castle 16/64 (N.S.)
Beaumaris 1836/22 68t.   Sr.   (Admeasurement)
    As above.
    Jan. 1844 Legatee of Wm. Baxter, dec. b.o.s. 16/64 to James Wyatt, Esq., Lime Grove
    Aug. 1854 James Wyatt b.o.s. 8/64 to Arthur Wyatt, Esquire, Lime Grove
Folio 79 New Form
    John Parry dies Apr. 1855: Robert Thomas Parry and Thomas Thomas Parry jointly 8/64
    Mar. 1857 R. T. Parry and T. T. Parry b.o.s. 8/64 to James Wyatt
    Jan. 1860 James Wyatt b.o.s. 32/64 to Arthur Wyatt, Tanybryn, Gentleman
    — — — do — — — — 8/64 to John Lloyd, Accountant, Port Penrhyn
    = James Wyatt 16, Arthur Wyatt 40 and John Lloyd 8

    Jan. 1868 Arthur Wyatt 40, James Wyatt 16 and John Lloyd 8 b.o.s. to
    William Dawbarn, Merchant, Liverpool.
Beaumaris 1868/3
    William Dawbarn, Merchant, Liverpool 64/64
    May 1881 Wm. Dawbarn dies: William Turner, Merchant, Liverpool 64/64
    July 1882 William Turner b.o.s. 64/64 to Robert Thomas, Ship Broker,
                                 Brunswick Street, Liverpool
    Dec. 1883 Robert Thomas b.o.s. 64/64 to John Pritchard, Master Mariner,
                                 Brynsiencyn

Converted into a hulk.   Registry cancelled Feb. 1896.

Beaumaris 1817/15   SUSANNA   80t.   Sl.
b. Bangor, 1817 (? John Jones)
56 x 18.9 x 10.6
No figurehead.
    Thomas Lewis, Mariner, Bangor   John Jones, Shipwright, Bangor
    Robert Thomas, Farmer, Llandegai   Abel Davies, Merchant, Abergele   (S.O.'s)

SUSANNA — *Continued*

Lewis Hughes, Merchant
Robert Jones, Smith
Evan Evans, Brazier
Richard Jones, Ferryman,
David Williams, Llandegai

Robert Williams, Land Surveyor
Robert Hughes, Grocer
Henry Morris & William Price, Mariners
 all of Bangor
  Thomas Edwards, Merchant, London (N.S.)

Beaumaris 1825/7   79t.   Sl.

Thomas Lewis, Mariner, Bangor   4/64
Robert Thomas, Farmer, Llandegai 6/64

John Jones, Shipwright, Bangor   10/64
 (S.O.'s)

Abel Davies, Merchant, Abergele 20/64
Robert Jones, Smith   4/64
John Nanney, Shipbuilder   2/64

Robert Williams, Land Surveyor   4/64
Robert Hughes, Grocer   2/64
Richard Jones, Ferryman   2/64

Catherine Hughes, widow administratrix of Lewis Hughes and Rev. John Hughes also a legatee jointly 4/64
Eleanor Williams, widow of David Williams 2/64, all of Bangor.
Thomas Edwards, Merchant, London 4/64   (N.S.)

Lost and Register (No date — but between 14 May 1827, when there was a change of Master (William Edwards), and the compulsory re-registration of 1836).

Beaumaris 1820/15   JANE ELLIN   113t. Brig.
b. Bangor, 1820 (?John Jones)
65.1 x 20.11 x 11.10

Hugh Pugh, Mariner, Carnarvon
Edward Thomas, Maltster, Bangor

Robert Thomas, Farmer, Llandegai
 (S.O.'s)

Robert Williams, Land Surveyor
William Jones, Farmer
Robert Jones, Smith
John Roberts, Surgeon, Carnarvon
Jane Jones, Spinster, Baron Hill

Lewis Roberts, Infant
Charles James, Innkeeper
Evan Evans, Merchant, all of Bangor
Griffith Hughes, Farmer, Monachdy, Llanfair-
           ynghornwy.

 (John Parry becomes Master, 4th September, 1823)

Beaumaris 1824/20

Robert Thomas, Farmer, Llandegai 12/64
John Parry, Mariner, Bangor   22/64

Edward Thomas, Maltster, Bangor 8/64
 (S.O.'s)

Robert Williams, Land Surveyor   4/64
Charles James, Innkeeper   4/64
Griffith Hughes, Farmer, Monachdy 4/64

Lewis Roberts, Infant   4/64
Robert Jones, Smith, all of Bangor 2/64
Jane Jones, Spinster, Baron Hill   4/64

Beaumaris 1836/163   106t.   Brig
(Admeasurement)

John Parry, formerly Mariner, now Shipbuilder   16/64
Robert Thomas, Farmer, Llandegai 12/64   Jane Jones, Spinster, Baron Hill   4/64
               (S.O.'s)

Edward Thomas, Maltster   8/64
Charles James, Innkeeper   4/64
Lewis Roberts, Infant, now Denbigh 4/64
Catherine Hughes, Widow, Monachdy 4/64

Robert Williams, Land Surveyor   4/64
Robert Jones, Smith, all of Bangor 2/64
Ann Griffiths, Widow   6/64

Wrecked on 23rd February, 1840 at St. Helen's, Scilly. Registry cancelled 4 May 1840.

[This transcript nicely illustrates John Parry's progress from Mariner to Shipbuilder and his association with Robert Thomas. See also Ann Parry's letter about the conduct of Hugh Pugh, Mariner, reproduced on Pages 39-40]

198

Beaumaris 1827/38   ABEL   113t.   Snow
10613. b. Bangor, 1827, by John Jones
65.5 x 20.4 x 11.2
Man's bust figurehead.

Thomas Lewis, Mariner, Bangor	8/64	John Jones, Shipwright, Bangor 4/64
Robert Thomas, Farmer, Llandegai	8/64	(S.O.'s)
John Parry, Mariner, Bangor	4/64	Robert Williams, Land Surveyor,
Thomas Jones, Farmer, Llysfaen	4/64	Bangor 4/64
Thomas Brown, Gentleman	4/64	Thomas Edwards, Wine Merchant 4/64
William Evans, Mariner, Barmouth	4/64	both of Cripplegate, Middx.
Abel Davies, Merchant, Abergele	16/64	Jane Jones, Spinster, Beaumaris 4/64

Beaumaris 1826/209 (Admeasurement)   94t.   Brig

Thomas Lewis, Mariner, Bangor	8/64	William Evans, Mariner, now of
Jane Jones, Spinster, Beaumaris	4/64	(S.O.'s) Bangor 4/64
Trustees of John Jones dec.	4/64	Robert Thomas, Farmer, Llandegai 8/64
John Parry, Shipbuilder, Bangor	4/64	Robert Williams, Land Surveyor,
Thomas Brown, Gentleman,		Bangor 4/24
Cripplegate	4/64	Exors, of Abel Davies, Merchant 24/64

Beaumaris 1854/5   94t.   Brigantine
    William Edwards, Master Mariner, Bangor 24/64   John Parry, Shipbuilder, Bangor 16/24
    John Tyrer, Draper, Beaumaris (trustee for Mary, dau. John G. Jones, Bodorgan, dec.)
                                                                        8/64
    Mary Davies, Aberdovey, legatee of William Edwards, Master Mariner, Bangor   8/64
    Robert Thomas, Farmer, Llandegai   8/64
    Dec. 1854 Mary Davies b.o.s. William Edwards, Master Mariner, Bangor   4/64
    — — — — do — — — — Samuel Roberts, Grocer, Bangor   4/64

Folio 109 New Form
    Aug. 1858 William Edwards b.o.s. William Roberts, Master Mariner, Bangor   20/64
    May 1866 William Edwards dies; Mary Williams 8/64
    Dec. 1866 Mary Williams b.o.s. Edward Edwards, Master Mariner, Bangor   4/64
    — — — — do — — — — William Pritchard, Master Mariner, Bangor   4/64
    Apr. 1855 John Parry dies; Robert Thomas Parry and Thomas T. Parry jointly 16/64
    Dec. 1854 Robert Thomas dies; R. T. Parry and Anne, wife of W. Thomas, Farmer,
            Port Penrhyn, jointly 8/64

Transaction Book II Folio 12
    June 1871 R. T. Parry and Ann Thomas b.o.s. Rd. Threfall Power, Litherland, Shipowner
                                                                        8/64
    June 1871 R. T. Parry and T. T. Parry b.o.s. Robert Owen, Accountant, Bangor   16/64
    June 1871 Robert Owen, Accountant b.o.s. Robert Thomas Parry, Gentleman,
                                                            Llandegai 8/64
    — — — — — do — — — — — Thomas Thomas Parry, Shipbuilder, Bangor
                                                                        8/64

Folio 16
    1859   John Tyrer dies; Daniel Delamon and Anne Tyrer 8/64
        Daniel Delamon and Anne Tyrer b.o.s. Thomas Owen, Farmer, Rhyddgaer 8/64
    Dec. 1866 William Roberts dies; Jane Roberts 20/64
        1872 Thomas Owen, Rhyddgaer b.o.s. Thomas T. Parry, Shipbuilder, Bangor   4/64
        — — — — do — — — — Samuel Roberts, Shipbuilder, Bangor   4/64

Folio 17
    April 1871 Jane Roberts (20) b.o.s. Thomas T. Parry, Shipbuilder   8/64
    — — — — do — — — — — Robert Thomas Parry, Gentleman   8/64
    — — — — do — — — — — Samuel Roberts, Shipbuilder   4/64

ABEL — *Continued*

Sep. 1874 Edward Edwards   b.o.s. Robert Owen, Accountant, Bangor   4/64
— do — William Pritchard — — — — — do — — — — — —   4/64
— do — Robert Owen — — — —Thomas T. Parry, Shipbuilder   4/64
= Nov. 1874 Samuel Roberts 16, R. T. Power 8, R. T. Parry 16, T. T. Parry 24.

Folio 18

Jan. 1875 Thomas T. Parry   b.o.s. Samuel Roberts, Shipbuilder   24/64
Feb. 1875 Robert T. Parry — — — — — do — — — — —   16/64
= Samuel Roberts 56, R. T. Power 8.

Vessel broken up; Certificate of Registry cancelled 21 February 1879.

Beaumaris 1840/25   EMILY   98t.   Brig
b. Harbour Grace, Newfoundland 1826.
Formerly reg. St. John's 1834/65
63.2 x 16.7 x 11.5
Scroll head

Richard Williams, Mariner, Bangor   32/64
Zacharias Roberts, Gentleman, Bangor   32/64
Sep. 1840 Richard Williams b.o.s. Thomas Jones, Farmer, Bangor   8/64
— — — — do   — — — — William Roberts, Mariner, Bangor   4/64
— — — — do   — — — — Thomas Roberts, Draper, Bangor   4/64
Sep. 1840 Zacharias Roberts b.o.s. Richard Edwards, Gentleman, Velin Heli   16/64
— — — — do   — — — — Edward Ellis, Shipbuilder, Bangor   4/64
Jan. 1841 William Roberts   b.o.s. John Owens, Farmer, Bangor   4/64
May 1841 Thomas Roberts   b.o.s. Robert Roberts, Sawyer, Bangor   4/64
May 1842 Edward Ellis   b.o.s. Robert Robers, Sawyer, Bangor   2/64
— — — — do   — — — — Henry Ellis, Druggist, Bangor   2/64
Feb. 1850 Richard Williams (8), Z. Roberts (6), H. Ellis (2) to Samuel Griffith, Mariner,
                                      Llaneilian   16/64
Jan. 1852 Samuel Griffith   b.o.s. Richard Williams, Master Mariner   10/64
— — — — do   — — — — Zacharias Roberts, Gentleman   6/64

Beaumaris 1852/1   88t.   Sr.
Zacharias Roberts, Gentleman, Bangor   12/64
Thomas Jones, Printer, Bangor   8/64
John Owens, Farmer, Bangor   (S.O.'s)   4/64

Richard Williams, Mariner, Bangor   18/64
Richard Edwards, Gentleman, Velin Heli   16/64
Reps. of Robert Roberts, Sawyer   6/64

Folio 136 New Form

Mar. 1852 Richard Williams dies: Margaret Williams, widow   18/64
May 1859 Margaret Williams dies; Humphrey Ellis, Farmer, Llanllechid and
        Richard Williams, Coal Merchant, Bangor, jointly   18/64
May 1853 Richard Edwards dies; Ann Edwards, Widow   16/64
— do — Ann Edwards, b.o.s. Robert Thomas, Mariner, Bangor   16/64
May 1861 Thomas Jones (8), John Owens (4), reps. of Robert Roberts (6)
        b.o.s. Thomas Thomas Parry, Shipbuilder, Bangor   18/64
May 1861 Zacharias Roberts b.o.s. Samuel Roberts, Shipbuilder, Bangor   12/64
May 1861 Humphrey Ellis, Llanllechid and Richard Williams, Coal Merchant
        Bangor b.o.s. Richard Threlfall Power, Master Mariner, Liverpool   18/64
        = Robert Thomas 16, T. T. Parry 18, R. T. Power 18, Samuel Roberts 12.

Registry closed   Vessel condemned 1872
(*Note:* This North American built vessel passed through the hands of a fair cross section
of Bangor shareholders in 32 years, including both Edward Ellis, Shipbuilder and the other
Bangor shipbuilders, Parry and Co. The ratio of the three partners' holdings in that firm is,
as usual, 3.3.2. (see page 108).

Beaumaris 1843/12   HEART OF OAK   80t.   Sl.
b. Ipswich 1771. Former cert. Ipswich 1836/28
57.3 x 17.5 x 10
No figure head.
    Richard Morris Griffith, Jun., Draper, Bangor   24/64
    Edward Ellis, Shipbuilder, Bangor   24/64
    John Jones, Mariner, Holyhead (& Master of vessel)   16/64

    Oct. 1846 R. M. Griffith b.o.s. Edward Ellis, Shipbuilder   24/64

Beaumaris 1847/5   77t.   Sl.
    Edward Ellis, Shipbuilder, Bangor   48/64
    John Jones, Mariner, Holyhead   16/64

    May 1847 John Jones, b.o.s. Edward Ellis, Shipbuilder   16/64

Carnarvon 1848/32   77t.   Sl.
    WilliamWilliams , Mariner, Morfa Bychan   4/64
    Edward Ellis, Shipbuilc'er, Bangor   40/64

    Griffith Jones, Draper   8/64
    Morris Davies, Schoolmaster   8/64
    John Henry Williams, Blacksmith, all of Portmadoc   4/64
    [Oct. 1846 Edward Ellis b.o.s. Griffith Jones, Draper   16/64
    — — — — do — — — — Morris Davies, Schoolmaster   8/64
    Nov. 1846 Griffith Jones b.o.s. William Williams, Mariner   4/64
    — — — — do — — — — John Henry Williams, Blacksmith   4/64]
    March 1852 Edward Ellis, mortgage to Thomas Peers Williams and
              John Williams, Carnarvon, Banker and co-partners   40/64

Transaction Book. Folio 79.
    T. P. Williams and John Williams, discharge of mortgage   40/64
    Apr. 1854 Wm. Williams dies intestate; John Williams, Widow   4/64
    Apr. 1856 Jane Williams b.o.s. David Jones, Farmer, Morfa Bychan   4/64
    Apr. 1856 David Jones b.o.s. James Southwell, Gentleman, Bangor   4/64
    Apr. 1856 Edward Ellis b.o.s. Thomas Williams, House Painter, Bangor   32/64
    — — — — do — — — — James Southwell, Gentleman, Bangor   8/64
    — do — Griffith Jones b.o.s. James Gregory, Gentleman, Bangor   8/64
    — do — Morris Davies — — — — — — do — — — — — —   8/64
    — do — J. H. Williams — — James Southwell, Gentleman, Bangor   4/64

Beaumaris 1856/10   71t.   Sl.
    Thomas Williams, House Painter, Bangor   32/64
    James Southwell, Gentleman, Bangor   16/64
    James Gregory, Gentleman, Bangor   16/64

    May 1857 James Southwell b.o.s. Thomas Williams, House Painter   16/64
    Aug. 1860 James Gregory — — — — do — — — — —   16/64
    Mar. 1862 Thomas Williams b.o.s. John Henry Williams, Iron Founder,
                                     Portmadoc   32/64
Registry closed.   Vessel lost 1863.

Beaumaris 1855/26   GLANOGWEN   143t.   Brigantine
10,608 b. Bangor 1855
82.6 x 2 x 12.8
Woman's bust figurehead
    John Parry, Shipbuilder, Bangor   64/64
          (Owen Jones Master)

Folio 64
    Apr. 1855 John Parry dies; Robert Thomas and Thomas T. Parry jointly   64/64
    May 1856 R. T. & T. T. Parry b.o.s. Richard Threlfall Power, Master Mariner, L'pool
                                                                       20/64
    — — — — do — — — — Owen Jones, Master Mariner, Bangor   4/64
    May 1867 R. T. Power mortgages 20/64ths. to Jas. Leach, Liverpool for £400 at 5%
    Apr. 1871 Owen Jones b.o.s. Robert Thomas Parry, Gentleman, Llandegai   4/64
    Apr. 1871 Jas. Leach, Palm Oil Refiner, Liverpool discharges mortgage:
                                                      R. T. Power   20/64
    May 1883 R. T. Parry & T. T. Parry b.o.s. R. T. Power, Master Mariner, Liverpool 40/64
    June 1883 R. T. Power b.o.s. Robert Thomas Parry, Gentleman, Llandegai   60/64
        = Robert Thomas Parry 64/64, June 1883.

Folio 118 Book 2
    June 1890 Robert Thomas Parry dies: Anne Thomas, Widow, Abercegin   64/64
    July 1891 Anne Thomas b.o.s. Robert Parry Thomas, Farmer, Talybont Isaf   32/64
    — — — — do — — — — John Parry Thomas, Fisherman, Abercegin   32/64
    May 1893 Robert Parry Thomas dies; Catherine Thomas, Widow, Ty Mawr,
                                                     Talybont   32/64
    June 1893 Catherine Thomas b.o.s. John Parry Thomas, Shipowner, Abercegin   32/64
    J. P. Thomas mortg. 64/64 to secure a/c Jas. Tomkinson, Henry Platt & John Herbert
                                              Alderson, Bankers, Chester
    May 1897 Tomkinson, Platt & Alderson, joint mortgagees, transfer mortgage to Lloyds
                                                                Bank
Folio 139
    Sep. 1898 Lloyds Bank Ltd. b.o.s. Evan Jones, Master Mariner, Portmadoc   64/64
    Feb. 1913 Evan Jones dies: Annie Gregory Jones, Widow   64/64
    Nov. 1913 Annie Jones b.o.s. Falkland Islands Co. Ltd. Gracechurch St. London   64/64
    Nov. 1914 Falkland Islands Co. b.o.s. Mayor, Alderman and Burgesses of the
                                    County Borough of Wallasey   64/64

        Register closed 15.12.1915   Vessel converted into hulk.

[*Note*:—Three generations of the Parry family owned *Glanogwen* in the 43 years between 1855 and 1898, (1) Captain John Parry, (2) his sons Robert Thomas Parry and Thomas Thomas Parry, and his daughter Anne (widow of William Thomas), and (3) her sons, Robert Parry Thomas and John Parry Thomas, the latter continuing in the same occupation at Abercegin as his great-grandfather, Robert Thomas, that of fisherman.

    The changes of ownership during 1883 seem to have been designed to save the vessel for the family from T. T. Parry's impending bankruptcy, which occurred in the following year.]

Beaumaris 1857/17   CITY OF BANGOR   99t.   Sr.
20560 b. Bangor 1857
76.3 x 19.4 x 10.4
Man's bust figurehead.

Meshach Roberts, Druggist	20/64	John Thomas, Master Mariner	12/64
Henry Parry, Slate Dresser	8/64	John Williams, Slate Dresser	8/64
Mary Willoughby, Hotel Keeper	6/64	Owen Morris, Assistant Overseer	4/64
Robert Thomas, Carter	4/64	Hugh Pritchard, Butcher, all of Bangor	2/64

Jun. 1859 John Thomas b.o.s. John Williams, Master Mariner, Portmadoc   12/64
Dec. 1865 John Williams b.o.s. Meshach Roberts, Druggist, Bangor   8/64
Dec. 1868 Owen Morris b.o.s. Meshach Roberts, — — do — —   4/64
1874   Mary Willoughby marries Evan Evans; Evan Evans, Merchant Bangor   6/64

Folio 38
1874 Hugh Pritchard dies; John Pritchard, builder, Elinor and Mary Pritchard
jointly 2/64
May 1874 Elinor Pritchard marries Thomas Pritchard, Smith, Bangor
May 1875 Meshach Roberts b.o.s. Frank Turner, Slate Merchant, Carnarvon   16/64
— — — — do — — — — William Turner, — — — do — — —   16/64
May 1875 Henry Parry b.o.s. Thomas Jones, Slate Agent, Llanllyfni   8/64
May 1875 John, Mary and Thomas Pritchard jointly b.o.s. Thomas Jones,
Slate Agent   2/64
May 1875 Evan Evans b.o.s. Thomas Jones, Slate Agent   6/64
1868   Robert Thomas dies; Ellen Thomas, Widow, Bangor   4/64
= July 1875 Frank Turner 16, William Turner 16, Thomas Jones 16, Ellen Thomas 4
and John Williams 12.

Carnarvon 1875/6   99t.   Sr.
John Williams, Master Mariner, Portmadoc   12/64
Frank Wynne Turner, Slate Merchant, Carnarvon   16/64
William Turner,   — — —   do   — — —   16/64
Thomas Jones, Slate Agent, Llanllyfni   16/64
Ellen Thomas, Widow, Bangor   4/64

Cancelled 17 August 1876.   Vessel transferred to Belfast. Details of registry and ownership unknown.   Re-registered Beaumaris 1878.

Beaumaris 1878/6   79t.   Sr.
Meshach Roberts, Druggist, Bangor   64/64
Dec. 1887 Meshach Roberts dies; William Pritchard Roberts, Merchant,
Bangor and John Roberts, Merchant, Portmadoc   jointly   64/64
Dec. 1887 W. P. & J. Roberts b.o.s. William Parry, Master Mariner, Carnarvon   64/64
Jan. 1891 William Parry b.o.s. Robert Marks, Master Mariner, Llanbedrog   64/64

Vessel run down and sunk off Eddystone, 21 August 1894.

Beaumaris 1858/2   CURLEW   36t.   Sma.
20562 b. Conway 1858
57.8 x 16.5 x 6.4
Arthur Wyatt, Gentleman, Bangor   48/64
John Lloyd, Accountant, Port Penrhyn   16/64

Jan. 1868 Arthur Wyatt b.o.s. John Slater, Chemist, Beaumaris   12/64
Jan. 1868 John Lloyd, b.o.s. John Morland Bennet, Merchant, Manchester   16/64
Jan. 1868 Arthur Wyatt b.o.s. John Lloyd jun. Accountant, Bangor   16/64
Feb. 1868 Arthur Wyatt b.o.s. William Brundrit Dorning, Bootle and
John Dorning, London, Accountants   12/64
Folio 217
Jan. 1868 Arthur Wyatt b.o.s. Edward Jones, Master Mariner, Bangor   8/64
Feb. 1871 Edward Jones b.o.s. John Parry, Master Mariner, Bangor   8/64
Feb. 1871 John Lloyd jun. b.o.s. John Lloyd sen., Gentleman, Bangor   16/64
Sep. 1872 John Parry b.o.s. John Slater, Chemist, Beaumaris   4/64
— — — — do — — — — John Lloyd jun., Bank Cashier, Bangor   4/64
Oct. 1875 John Lloyd jun., b.o.s. William Brundrit Dorning and John Dorning,
Great Crosby, Timber Merchants   4/64

CURLEW — *Continued*

Transaction Register II
Folio 58

Aug. 1880 John Lloyd sen., b.o.s. John Lloyd jun.,   16/64
Aug. 1881 W. B. Dorning and J. Dorning b.o.s. John Lloyd jun.   16/64

Sep. 1882 John Lloyd jun. b.o.s. Thomas Evans, Master Mariner Glan Conway   32/64
— do — John Slater — — — — — —   do — — — — — —   16/64
— do — J. M. Bennet — — — — — —   do — — — — — —   16/64
= Thomas Evans 64.

This vessel was abandoned waterlogged and she afterwards sank 8 miles N.N.E. of the Great Orme's Head on 8th August 1898. Certificate lost with the vessel.

[*Note*:— Vessel bought new from Conwy in 1858 and sold by Wyatt and Lloyd in January 1868, along with *Robert, Penguin, John Parry* and *Alexander,* to John Lloyd junior, John Slater, J. M. Bennett, the Dornings and the master of the vessel, in this case Edward Jones. After his retirement from Port Penrhyn John Lloyd senior bought back his share from his son.]

Aberystwyth 1858/2   SARAH BRIDGET   126t.   Brigantine
b. Bangor 1858, Edward Ellis
86.4 x 22.5 x 11.8
Female figure altered to Knee Head 1864

Owen Owen, Master Mariner	8/64	Daniel Owens, Master Mariner	4/64
John Davies, Master Mariner	2/64	Jacob Thomas, Master Mariner	2/64
Jenkin Phillips, Merchant	4/64	Thomas Davies, Farmer	2/64
David Jones, Blacksmith	2/64	all of New Quay	
Evan Phillips, Master Mariner	4/64	Evan Rees, Master Mariner, both	
Jenkin Owen, Ma. Mariner,			Cardigan 2/64
Llangrannog	2/64	Richard Roberts, Merchant, Aberystwyth	8/64
Margaret Roberts, Spinster	4/64	David Jones, Master Mariner both	
Jas. Thomas, Grocer, Llangwillo	4/64	Aberystwyth	2/64
John Simon, Currier, Bangor	4/64	John Jones, Minister of the Gospel,	
John Edmunds, Schoolmaster,		Newcastle Emlyn	2/64
Bangor	4/64	Robert Roberts, Postmaster, Carnarvon	4/64

'This vessel transferred to Port of Carnarvon 1883'
Carnarvon   1883/3
John Richard Jones, Master Mariner, Carnarvon 64/64
May 1883 J. R. Jones mortg. to James Tomkinson & Henry Platt, Chester
Oct. 1885 J. R. Jones b.o.s. 64/64 to Hugh Thomas, Master Mariner, Bangor subj. to mortgage (Hugh Thomas, Three Salmons Inn, Bangor designated Managing Owner 1885).
Feb. 1889 J. Tomkinson & H. Platt b.o.s. Rbt. Hughes Williams, Port Dinorwic, Ship-owner 64.
Feb. 1889 R. H. Williams mortg. to J. Tomkinson and Hy. Platt Chester.
Nov. 1890 Mortgage discharged.
Nov. 1890 R. H. Williams b.o.s. Robert Thomas, Master Mariner, 103 Gwladys St. Walton 64/64.

Transaction Book 5 Folio 115
Nov. 1890 R. Thomas mortg. to J. Tomkinson and Henry Platt, Chester
Nov. 1890 R. Thomas b.o.s. 16/64 Hugh Thomas, Clerk, Liverpool
— — — — do — — — — 16/64 Robert Thomas, Shipbroker
= Robert Thomas (Master Mariner) 32 Hugh Thomas 16, Robert Thomas (Shipbroker) 16
Mortgage to Lloyd's Bank, Caernarvon to secure current account. 1898. Discharged 1902.

SARAH BRIDGET — *Continued*

Transaction Book 6 Folio 8

Dec. 1902 Hugh Thomas (16) Robert Thomas (Master Mariner, 32) Robert Thomas (Shipbroker, 16) b.o.s. Patrick Curran, Waterford, Harbour Master 64/64

Apr. 1911 Patrick Curran b.o.s. 64/64 Dermot O'Brien, Merchant, Cork.

Apr. 1911 Dermot O'Brien b.o.s. 8/64 Timothy Fitzpatrick, Ship Agent, Cork

July 1912 — — — do — — — 56/64 — — — — — do — — — — —

Folio 73

Oct. 1915 Timothy Fitzpatrick b.o.s. 64/64 Richard Abel and Sons, Steam Barge & Lighter Owners, Liverpool.

Certificate of Registry cancelled and Registry closed 14 February 1936. Ship broken up at Runcorn.

Beaumaris 1860/18   **CAMBRIA**   56t.   Sr.

27730

b. Bangor 1860 (T. T. Parry)

66.5 x 19.3 x 7.7

No figure head

Thomas Thomas Parry, Shipbuilder,	Samuel Roberts, Shipbuilder, Bangor 10/64
Bangor 30/64	William Parry, Brazier, Bangor 8/64
John Jones, Innkeeper, Bangor 16/64	

Oct. 1865 John Jones dies; Jane and Ellen Jones jointly 16/64

1866 Jane Jones marries William Williams, Tal y Foel, Llandegai

1866 Ellen Jones marries William Williams, Garth, Bangor

Folio 15

Apr. 1871 T. T. Parry b.o.s. 18/64 William Roberts, Llanallgo, Mariner

— do — S. Roberts — — 6/64 — — — — — do — — — — —

May 1871 T. T. Parry — — 6/64 Rd. Threlfall Power, Master Mariner, Litherland

May 1871 Wm. Roberts (24/64) mortg. £100 William Williams, Master Mariner, Llanallgo

Oct. 1871 R. T. Power b.o.s. 6/64 Samuel Roberts, Shipbuilder, Bangor

Wm. Parry dies; William David Price, Brazier, Bangor 8/64

Oct. 1871 W. D. Price b.o.s. 8/64 William Roberts, Master Mariner, Moelfre

= 1874 T. T. Parry 6, Samuel Roberts 10, William Williams (Llandegai) 8, William Williams (Garth) 8, William Roberts 8 and 24 (subject to mortgage Wiliam Williams, Llanallgo)

Vessel transferred to Caernarfon — September 1875

Carnarvon 1875/17   56t.   Sr.

b. Bangor 1860, Parry and Co.

Ellen Williams, Widow, Tanymaes, Llanfairisgaer	32/64
John Williams, Mariner, Llanfairisgaer	32/64

1888 Ellen Williams dies intestate; Owen Williams, Joiner, Port Dinorwic 32/64

Jan. 1889 Owen Williams b.o.s. William Williams, Carpenter, Holyhead 5/64

— — — — do — — — — John Williams, Master Mariner Port Dinorwic 17/64

— — — — do — — — — Griffith Williams, Slate Loader, Pt. Dinorwic 5/64

March 1900 John Williams 49, Owen Williams (5), Griffith Williams (5), William Williams (5) b.o.s. Francis Evans, Shipowner, Criccieth 64/64.

Vessel foundered 20 December 1903.   Registry closed.

Beaumaris 1861/12   SARAH JANE   73t.   Sr.
29225
b. Bangor 1861 (?Henry Owens)
70.2 x 19.8 x 9.4   Woman's bust.
    Richard Jones, Master Mariner   10/64   Ellis Roberts, Accountant   10/64
    John Simon, Farmer   20/64   Thomas Byewater, Shipbuilder   4/4
    Robert Roberts, Postmaster   14/64   Henry Owens, Shipbuilder   6/64
                                                             (all of Bangor)
    Oct. 1861 Henry Owens b.o.s. Thomas Jones, Ysgybor Fawr, Master Mariner   6/64
    Mar. 1863 Thos. Byewater b.o.s. Richard Jones, Master Mariner   2/64
    — — — do — — — — John Simon, Farmer   2/64
    Aug. 1868 Ellis Roberts b.o.s. Richard Jones, Master Mariner   4/64
    Jan. 1868 Thomas Jones dies; Ann Jones, Widow, Bangor   6/64

Book 55 Folio 19
    Sep. 1871 Ann Jones   b.o.s. John Simon, Farmer   2/64
    — — — do — — — — Richard Jones, Master Mariner   4/64

    Oct. 1874 John Simon b.o.s. Samuel Radliffe Platt, Mechanical Engineer, Oldham 24/64
    — do — Richard Jones — — — — — — — — do — — — — — — — — — 20/64
    — do — Robert Roberts — — — — — — — — do — — — — — — — — — 14/64
    — do — Ellis Roberts — — — — — — — — do — — — — — — — — 6/64

    Dec. 1876 Samuel Platt b.o.s. William Griffith, Grocer, Runcorn   64/64
    Dec. 1876 William Griffith b.o.s. Richard Abel, Shipowner, Runcorn   32/64
    Dec. 1876 William Griffith (32) mortgage Richard Abel; mortgage discharged June 1877
    Apr. 1877 Richard Abel b.o.s. William Griffith 32/64 (W. Griffith now 64/64)
    Oct. 1877 William Griffith b.o.s. John Heath, Master Mariner, Widnes   22/64
    — — — do — — — — Joseph Palin, Ropemaker, Northwich   21/64
    — — — do — — — — William Postles, Draper, Northwich   21/64

Vessel transferred to Runcorn, November 1877

Beaumaris 1860/7   ALBION   477t.   Barque
1000
b. Jarrow 1854. Reg. transferred from Liverpool.
117.15 x 29.9 x 19.3
Woman's bust figurehead.
    William Pritchard, Slate Merchant, Tanycoed, Bangor   64/64

Certificate of Registry cancelled.   Vessel sold to foreign owners 6 April 1867.

[*Notes*: (1) C.R.O. PQ 65/3 states that in Feb. 1861 she loaded 551t. 5cwt. slate at Port
      Penrhyn for Boston.
    (2) L.R.O. W/DB 14 (Crew Agreement List and Log) records Hugh Owen (19362)
      High St. Poplar as Master, with 1st and 2nd mates, Carpenter, Cook, Steward and
      8 A.B.'s. Sep. 27 1866 loss overboard of Wm. Edwards A.B. born in Anglesey
      etc.]

Beaumaris 1866/1   HELEN   252t.   Barque
53657
b. Souris, Prince Edward Island 1865
114.3 x 24.6 x 14.5
Female bust figurehead.
    William Arthur Darbishire, Gentleman, Bangor   32/64
    Humphrey Williams, Shipowner, Bangor   32/64

HELEN — *Continued*

Dec. 1869 W. A. Darbishire b.o.s. John Richards, Surgeon, Bangor   16/64
Nov. 1872 — — — — — — — do — — — — — — — —   16/64

Vessel foundered. Registry closed July 1873.
[*Note*: L.R.O. W/DB (Crew Agreement List and Log) Dec. 18 1872 cleared at Carnarvon bound for New Orleans. Last seen 31 January 1873. Crew (9) supposed drowned.]

Beaumaris 1867/19   ARGYLE   63t.   Sr.
12079
b. Ulverstone 1802. Trans. from Liverpool
64 x 18.4 x 8.35   Billet Head
    John Thomas Jones, Ship Surveyor, Bangor   64/64

    Nov. 1866 J. T. Jones b.o.s. Morgan Richards, Draper, Bangor   28/64
    — — — — do — — — — — Hannah Ellen Roberts, Spinster, Plas Llwyd, Bangor   4/64
    — — — — do — — — — — David White, Waterworks Manager, Bangor   16/64
    Jan. 1867 David White b.o.s. Morgan Richards, Bangor   16/64
    = John Thomas Jones 16, Morgan Richards 44, Hannah Ellen Roberts 4.

Vessel foundered 7 miles of Skerries April 1872

Beaumaris 1892/3   MARY B. MITCHELL   195t.   Sr. (3 masts)
97575
b. Carrickfergus 1892, Paul Rodgers & Co.
129.75 x 24.45 x 12.35
Frame steel. Clincher built.
Female bust figurehead.
    William Massey Preston, Gentleman, Lleiniog Castle, Beaumaris   32/64
    Samuel Taylor Chadwick, Gentleman, Haulfre, Beaumaris   32/64

    Mar. 1898 W. M. Preston b.o.s. Emilius Alexander Young, Agent, Tanybryn,
                                            Bangor   32/64
    — do — S. T. Chadwick — — — — — — — do — — — — — — — 32/64

    Sep. 1910 E. A. Young dies; L. A. Young, Gentleman, Blackheath, Reg. Young,
        Solicitor, London, M. M. Matthews, Solicitor, London, Eliza Young,
        Widow, Blackheath, jointly   64/64
    May 1911 L. A. Young, R. Young, M. C. Matthews and E. Young b.o.s. Rt. Hon.
                      Edward Sholto, Baron Penrhyn   64/64
Transaction Book II, Folio 173
    June 1919 Rt. Hon. Edward Sholto, Baron Penrhyn b.o.s. Job Tyrrel, Shipowner,
                                        Arklow   64/64

Registry closed 21 Oct 1919 in con.sequence of change in propulsion.

Beaumaris 1919/2   133t.   Sr. (Auxiliary motors-
2 Engines, Paraffin Internal Combustion   twin screw)
4 cyl. 7½" x 10" BHP 100 by Bergins Launch
and Engine Co., Glasgow.
    Job Tyrrell, Shipowner, Arklow   64/64

    Jan. 1921 Job Tyrrell b.o.s. George Kearn, Shipowner, Arklow   10/64
    Jan. 1928 George Kearn b.o.s. George Kearn & Emilie Catherine Kearn jointly   10/64
    = Job Tyrrell 54, George and Emilie Catherine Kearn 10/64.

Registry transferred to Port of Dublin May 1933

[*Note*: Subsequently wrecked in the Solway Firth December 1944.]

Beaumaris 1894/2   BANGOR   119t.   Screw Steamer
101752   Sr. rigged
b. 1894 Scott & Sons, Bowling.
Iron and Steel. Clencher built.
Double bottom. 145 x 24 x 11.9
1 Compound surface condensing,
direct acting by Ross, Glasgow.
20″ & 40″ x 27″ str. 67 NHP, 525 IHP

Sir Richard Henry Williams Bulkely, Bart., Baron Hill	16/64
Samuel Taylor Chadwick, Gentleman, Haulfre, Beaumaris	16/64
William Massey Preston, Gentleman, Lleiniog, Beaumaris	14/64
James Millar, Stock and Share Broker, London	16/64
Owen Thomas Jones, Ship Manager, Erw Fair, Bangor	2/64

March 1898 the above b.o.s. Emilius Alexander Young, Agent, Tanybryn, Bangor   64/64
Sep. 1910 E. A. Young dies; L. A. Young, Gentleman, Blackheath, R. Young, Solicitor,
       London, M. C. Matthews, Solicitor, London, Eliza Young, Widow, Blackheath
       jointly   64/64
May 1911 The above b.o.s. Rt. Hon. Edward Sholto, Baron Penrhyn   64/64

Transaction Book II, Folio 179
       Aug. 1927 Rt. Hon. Edward Sholto, Baron Penrhyn dies; Rt. Hon. Hugh Napier, Baron
              Penrhyn and Claude Douglas Pennant, Barrister at Law jointly   64/64
June 1929 Rt. Hon. Hugh Napier, Baron Penrhyn and Claude Douglas Pennant b.o.s.
              to Rt. Hon. Hugh Napier, Baron Penrhyn   64/64

Apr. 1933 Rt. Hon. Hugh Napier etc. b.o.s. Alexander Johnstone, Master Mariner,
                                       Kilroot, Antrim   64/64
May 1933 Alexander Johnstone b.o.s. Samuel Gray, Shipowner, Stevedore, Belfast 64/64

Certificate cancelled.   Ship totally lost March 1934.

[Notes: (1) Vessel foundered off South Rock Light Vessel, March 1st 1934. Crew saved.
             (2) O. T. Jones managed the ships of the Anglesey Shipping Company from 1892
                until 1920 when he was succeeded by T. J. Humphreys.]